Culture and Class in English
Public Museums, 1850-1914

Historical Urban Studies

Series editors: Richard Rodger and Jean-Luc Pinol

Titles in this series include:

Culture and Class in English Public Museums, 1850-1914

KATE HILL

ASHGATE

Published by
Ashgate Publishing Limited
Gower House
Croft Road
Aldershot
Hampshire GU11 3HR
England

Ashgate Publishing Company
Suite 420
101 Cherry Street
Burlington, VT 05401-4405
USA

Ashgate website: http://www.ashgate.com

British Library Cataloguing in Publication Data
Hill, Kate
Culture and class in public museums, 1850-1914. – (Historical urban studies)
    1. Museums – Great Britain – History – 19th century 2. Museums – Great Britain – History – 20th century 3. Class consciousness – Great Britain – History – 19th century 4. Class consciousness – Great Britain – History – 20th century 5. Social classess – Great Britain – History – 19th century 6. Social classes – Great Britain – History – 20th century 7. Civic improvement – Great Britain /0 Hisoty – 19th century 8. Civic improvement – Great Britain – History – 20th century
    I. Title
    069'.0941'09034

Library of Congress Cataloging-in-Publication Data
Hill, Kate, 1969-
    Culture and class in English public museums, 1850-1914 / Kate Hill.
        p. cm. – (Historical urban studies series)
    Includes bibliographical references (p.) and index.
    ISBN 0-7546-0432-2
    1. Museums – England – History. 2. Social classes – England. 3. Cultural property – Protection – England. 4. Cities and towns – Study and teaching – Great Britain. 5. Great Britain – Cultural policy – History – 19th century. 6. Great Britain – Cultural policy – History – 20th century. 7. Great Britain – History – 19th century. 8. Great Britain – History – 20th century. I. Title. II. Series

    AM42.E54H55 2005
    069'.0941–dc22

2004060766

ISBN 07546 0432 2

Printed and bound in Great Britain by MPG Books Ltd, Bodmin, Cornwall

For David

Contents

List of Figures

Historical Urban Studies
General Editors' Preface

Density and proximity are two of the defining characteristics of the urban dimension. It is these that identify a place as uniquely urban, though the threshold for such pressure points varies from place to place. What is considered an important cluster in one context – may not be considered as urban elsewhere. A third defining characteristic is functionality – the commercial or strategic position of a town or city which conveys an advantage over other places. Over time, these functional advantages may diminish, or the balance of advantage may change within a hierarchy of towns. To understand how the relative importance of towns shifts over time and space is to grasp a set of relationships which is fundamental to the study of urban history.

Towns and cities are products of history, yet have themselves helped to shape history. As the proportion of urban dwellers has increased, so the urban dimension has proved a legitimate unit of analysis through which to understand the spectrum of human experience and to explore the cumulative memory of past generations. Though obscured by layers of economic, social and political change, the study of the urban milieu provides insights into the functioning of human relationships and, if urban historians themselves are not directly concerned with current policy studies, few contemporary concerns can be understood without reference to the historical development of towns and cities.

This longer historical perspective is essential to an understanding of social processes. Crime, housing conditions and property values, health and education, discrimination and deviance, and the formulation of regulations and social policies to deal with them were, and remain, amongst the perennial preoccupations of towns and cities – no historical period has a monopoly of these concerns. They recur in successive generations, albeit in varying mixtures and strengths; the details may differ

The central forces of class, power and authority in the city remain. If this was the case for different periods, so it was for different geographical entities and cultures. Both scientific knowledge and technical information were available across Europe and showed little respect for frontiers. Yet despite common concerns and access to broadly similar knowledge, different solutions to urban problems were proposed and adopted by towns and cities in different parts of Europe. This comparative dimension informs urban historians as to which were systematic factors and which were of a purely local nature: general and particular forces can be distinguished.

These analytical frameworks, considered in a comparative context, inform the books in this series.

Université de Tours   Jean-Luc Pinol
University of Leicester   Richard Rodger

Acknowledgements

This book has been a very long time in gestation, and during that period I have received a lot of help and advice from many people. From museums and museum archives I would particularly like to thank National Museums Liverpool for access to their archive, and Mr le Mare particularly for sharing his knowledge of the material there. I would also like to acknowledge the assistance of the Harris Museum and Art Gallery, Preston, Leicester City Museum, Birmingham Museums and Art Gallery and the Weston Park Museum, Sheffield. Another individual to single out is Mary Hider at Leicester City Museum for her selfless photocopying; and Emma Heslewood, Social History Curator at the Harris Museum, for her help and sharing her enthusiasm for the Harris's history. Chris Rice from Birmingham Museums helped enormously with their floor plans. Staff at Sheffield Archives, Lancashire Archives and Liverpool Local Studies Library also helped with the location of material.

The work has also benefited from the comments of colleagues on drafts; I would like to thank Andrew Walker, Simon Gunn, Susan Pearce, and Sophie Forgan, among others.

An earlier version of chapter 7 appeared as '"Roughs of both sexes": The Working Class in Victorian Museums and Art Galleries', in S. Gunn and R.J. Morris (eds) (2001), *Identities in Space: Contested Terrains in the Western City since 1850*, Ashgate.

I would like to acknowledge the support of the Faculty of Media and Humanities at Lincoln University in the production of this book, through teaching remission and research funding.

Permission to reproduce illustrations has kindly been given by Sheffield Archives, by National Museums Liverpool, by the Harris Museum and Art Gallery, Preston, and by Birmingham Museums and Art Gallery. David Rüder produced the diagrams, for which I am enormously grateful.

CHAPTER ONE

Introduction: Interpreting Museums

In 1888, Thomas Greenwood, a reformer and campaigner for museums and libraries, wrote that museums 'should be considered as absolutely necessary for the welfare of every Municipality throughout the country.' He went on to suggest that 'It is only the rate-supported museums which are doing really useful work.'[1] Such a judgement puts municipal museums at the heart of the Victorian urban fabric and society. Yet it was not at all clear, even to the most committed museum apologist, precisely what function they might fulfil in municipalities. Among the objects that Greenwood listed for such an institution were to provide rational amusement, to facilitate both broad popular education and specialised, advanced studies, and to represent the locality both in terms of its natural features and its commercial concerns. Coming from a very different set of concerns, though, Ruskin argued that museums should aim for education not entertainment, and advanced not elementary education at that.[2] This book, in examining the birth and development of municipal museums up to 1914, attempts to understand why so much in the way of hopes and fears was pinned on these institutions; how they acted on society and how society acted on them. It was not only in the nineteenth century that museums were seen as important if contradictory places; they have increasingly appeared in various studies in history, cultural studies, museology and art history as agencies creating modernity, policing the working class, creating legitimacy for the elite; producing national and imperial discourse and developing new forms of professional and subject-based authority.[3] It has been argued that 'museums were the archetypal institutional form of the modern period.'[4] One gets the impression that these were extremely powerful instruments for the shaping of society, individual consciousness, and knowledge. Municipal museums were popular places, with large numbers of visitors; but they were also quite fragile, chronically and sometimes acutely short of resources, struggling to achieve a professional staff base, and dependent on the whims of a small number of councillors and donors. They were local institutions with local priorities, and need to be seen as part of the machinery for contesting and negotiating class, status and interest claims in the Victorian town.

Despite the quite dramatic growth of interest in museums in general, municipal museums remain rather neglected both by historians and museologists. Yet there is a case for considering municipal museums as particularly worth studying because of the way they can reveal details, weaknesses and inconsistencies that are not present in national and other more prestigious museums. It is worth examining the work of Daniel Sherman in some detail here; it focuses specifically on nineteenth-century municipal museums, in France. As he asserts,

> Paris alone can tell only part of the story. A full understanding of the complexity of the art museum's development in France entails extending the field of investigation beyond the capital and beyond the national museum.[5]

He links the expansion and improvement of municipal museums to the consolidation and access of power of local bourgeois elites, who were assuming, by 1850, roles as councillors; while still indicating the manifold links between centre and provinces, culturally and politically.[6] He then investigates links between the bourgeoisie, the social 'work' they wanted from museums, and the narratives embodied in the museums; and stresses throughout the historical complexity of the 'museum' concept:

> Critiques that neglect the complexity of the museum's construction to focus on its ideological coherence are in effect accepting museums' terms of reference.... A historical approach to art museums entails nothing more nor less than recognising their constituent elements as ... sets of contingencies.[7]

This idea, that one needs to look not at the ways in which museums formed coherent cultural initiatives, but at their historical contingency, is echoed by Marcia Pointon, who has commented, in relation to the expansion of work in museum studies, that

> there is a marked paucity of detailed published research which links the often wide-ranging theoretical concerns of 'museology' with historically specific situations,[8]

although the very source of this quotation goes a considerable way to repairing this deficit. A similar point is made by Prior: 'Theoretically informed empirical studies are particularly needed in moving towards a more robust sociology of museums.'[9] Again, though, although these two books look at a variety of institutions, they do not examine municipal museums.

These quotes also highlight the point that increasing study of museums has brought questions of methodology and theoretical frameworks to the fore. Such questions did not much concern those social historians who considered museums as part of the growth of the civic and leisure provisions of the nineteenth-century town, but they have become a burning issue for those museologists, cultural studies scholars, sociologists and art historians who have joined the debate in the last decade or two; as one commentator has said,

> This body of literature has begun the complex task of widening the scope of analysis in order to subject practices of collecting,

classifying and displaying to conceptual probes drawn from the social sciences and humanities.[10]

Another has contrasted analyses which see museums as 'sites… of architecture, of exhibitions, of national or cultural narratives, or of political and pedagogical projects aimed at different constituencies' with their own which

> focuses on museums as the intricate amalgam of historical structures and narratives, practices and strategies of display, and the concerns and imperatives of various governing ideologies.[11]

This increasing emphasis on a more conceptually complex approach to studying museums has brought to light certain tensions. The first, which has already surfaced, is between theoretical and empirical approaches to museum history. It is unclear, though, how far this distinction does exist, and if it does, why it persists; numerous commentators have bewailed the polarisation, and called for a combination of the two approaches.[12] Yet even the most theoretical of studies marshals a respectable amount of empirical evidence; and equally all but the most antiquarian history of museums utilises a few concepts and theories. It may be the case that there are few studies which try to integrate a close, detailed study of a particular museum or set of museums with a sophisticated set of conceptual and theoretical tools, but that is not the same thing. The second tension that seems to exist is between materialist and discursive interpretations of museums; between those that see museums as produced by a prior social and economic reality, and those which see it as produced by, and producing, discourses which constitute reality. Thus for historians of rational recreation, museums were created by the social processes of urbanisation, industrialisation, and class formation; they can be understood by looking at their context and how it shaped them.[13] For others, though, museums are implicated in the creation of modern urban society themselves, producing modern populations and identities, certain modes of knowledge and authority, practices of consumption, which all constitute a capitalist society.[14] Again, though this may be a creative tension, it does not seem to me that either side can win; this debate is actually giving way to an approach where the material and symbolic realms feed into each other.[15]

Firstly, an overview of the book. The next chapter deals with the urban context for municipal museums, trying to elucidate what if any were the features of nineteenth-century towns that made the creation of municipal museums likely and desirable. The third chapter also deals with context, in looking at changing ideas about whether public money should be spent on arts and culture. It also looks at other important factors which shaped the way municipal museums emerged; their inheritance of the collections and some of the personnel, and sometimes the premises, of scientific societies, and their dependence on donations, not just of objects, but often of money for buildings too. The fourth chapter looks at who was involved in municipal museums; it traces the different groups who had a stake, and argues that rather than a simple middle-class project, such museums were marked by divisions within class lines, and challenges from across society. Chapter five analyses the objects of the museum, trying to unpick in some detail the meanings that were made and circulated through the museum. Although such museums, and particularly their curators, attempted to redefine the museum object as a systematically representative sign standing for knowledge and progress, many of the objects that arrived in museums tended more to signify class or gender belonging, to create legitimacy or status for the donor, or to assert different stories about Britain's empire. Chapter six then examines how the objects were used: the displays they were placed in, and the layout of the building in which the displays were situated. This chapter is crucial for testing many of the arguments developed from national museums, which suggest that museums could act as powerful instruments for shaping the behaviour and consciousness of visitors; in municipal museums, by contrast, this may have been possible but was rarely achieved because of resource constraints, divisions between people in charge, and the nature of the objects. Finally in chapter eight I examine what we know of visitors to municipal museums and their responses to them. This suggests further that they were not necessarily consumed in the way intended, undermining even more the idea that they could function as civilising forces.

The book concludes by arguing that museums were used by bourgeois elites to create distinction and legitimacy for themselves, and even to try and improve or control the working class, but they were not particularly successful in the latter. Rather, as public institutions, museums offered a variety of groups an opportunity to challenge elite ideas and values. Working-class challenges were not always successful, but then the working class seems to have become increasingly unlikely to visit museums; lower middle-class groups may have been more successful, and it could be argued that municipal museums represented a more inclusive version of middle-class-ness by the end of the period.

In the rest of the introduction, I want to pick out some of the themes that concern me most, and try and elucidate what they might mean for museums. Given the expansion in studies of museums and their histories, and the polarities in such studies, it is worth both examining the implications of these studies, and placing myself in relation to them. These are in many ways arbitrary and artificial selections, which overlap in some ways; but I hope they will help to make my assumptions and approach clear.

Museums as Sites of Power

One of the most important of the ways in which museums have been interpreted has been as a means by which power is exercised, or as a creator of power relations. Such analyses unsurprisingly tend to take Foucault's ideas about power as a starting point, and think about how the museum as an institution, and as a producer of knowledge, and as a public building shaping space, constitutes power relationships and exercises power. This includes the use it makes of theoretical disciplines, architecture and the deployment of internal space, and of people and things within that space.[16] The chronology he proposes sees increasing governmentalisation leading to power practices that were at once more dispersed and more effective than those they replaced. Technologies of power were the main weapons developing from the eighteenth to the twentieth century to make power relations both more efficient and more subtle. They can be understood as those practices which release power from dependence on one individual and impersonalise it, so that it either works automatically or can be wielded by anybody in that subject position. They also tended to produce an internalisation of power, whereby people want to do what they are intended to do. This constitutes, in Foucault's terms, a change from juridico-discursive to disciplinary power.[17] The examination of the development of institutions such as prisons, hospitals and lunatic asylums, seen as leading the way in this change, led Foucault to coin the phrase 'carceral archipelago' to describe the tendency for institutions to confine individuals from the eighteenth century; against this commentators have set the 'exhibitionary complex', a contrasting trend to make visible and public that which had been hidden.[18] This was, though, equally a part of the process by which modern populations were shaped. Both Tony Bennett and Eilean Hooper-Greenhill have examined the way modern museums produced a self-improving, disciplined population. Bennett sees the museum as the most notable part of a trend whereby culture was enlisted in the task of governing from the nineteenth century onwards.[19]

The articulation of space is a very important part of this, particularly for Bennett, who argues that the spaces of the nineteenth-century museum formed a new technology of surveillance and regulation, by making visitors visible to one another and eliminating nooks and crannies; and also that the spaces were additionally part of the articulation of knowledge in the museum, as the layout formed part of the narrative. Hooper-Greenhill also considers space to be part of the way modern museums exercised power. She points particularly to the increased specialisation of different areas which could be said to have created and reinforced a distinction between producer and consumer in the museum.

More specific studies have found limits to the way power was exercised in museums. For example, Tony Bennett's article on national public museums and the rational recreation movement argues that while these public institutions were clearly an 'artefact of government',[20] the exercise of power within them was always modified by negotiations among classes and groups. Moreover, this power did not aim at an ideological transformation, that is, at an imposition of ruling-class values on other classes. 'Rather, cultural reformers were often less concerned with questions of consciousness than with the field of habits and manners.'[21] Rational recreation aimed at the realistic goal of mechanistically altering behaviour through the deployment of space and other technologies. There are, thus, some grounds for questioning the switch from juridico-discursive to disciplinary power, and as this study will show, municipal museums were not necessarily as efficient and progressive as some of their rhetoric suggested.

Foucault's interest in the way knowledge and power work together has also been a fruitful way for thinking about museums (although of course the way in which museums produced knowledge and power is a topic that has been looked at by non-Foucauldians as well). Hooper-Greenhill has tried to show that museum displays, and the knowledge they produce, are governed by the epistemological structures identified by Foucault. It is undoubtedly true to say that the museum as an institution implies a certain conception of the world and of ways of knowing; without it, no one would collect, or store and display the collections. Pearce argues that museums reveal the assumptions of Western man (it usually was men) about his ability to know and therefore control the rest of the world, from its physical laws, to the kingdom of Nature, to other cultures and races. A number of simultaneous, interlocking developments show this. Systematic collecting arose at the same time as the natural sciences and museums. All three implied one another. Systematic collecting implies a scheme like the taxonomy of natural history, a two-dimensional pattern of objects which necessitates display, the demonstration of principles, if only to a limited audience. 'Observation and reason' are the important human faculties.[22] This is a version of Hooper-Greenhill's view of museums as participating in the episteme of the time, though Pearce argues that museums, as exhibitions, are the creation and manifestation of the modern episteme particularly.[23]

Museums are sites of power, then, in a variety of ways; they create authoritative discourses, and manipulate space as a disciplinary technology to improve the population. Although authors acknowledge, though, that this exercise of power is probably more fragmented and contested than their studies suggest, there is little attention paid to this aspect. One of my main aims, therefore, is not just to look at how museums exercise power, but to look at the inconsistencies and failures of that power, and at the way it has been contested. And if museums produce certain modes of knowledge, and therefore create certain relationships of power, then a close analysis of their objects and displays is necessary, which requires a consideration of the analytical techniques that might be used.

Museums as Texts

How does one read a museum? Many of the recent works on museums have taken them to be a kind of text, or codification of meaning, which needs to be deciphered. It is not clear, though, how such deciphering should be done. How does one formulate a method for interpreting the evidence; 'reading' museum objects, displays, and exhibitions? They can be considered as having a visual grammar, although there are different views on what this grammar is and how it can best be uncovered. Fyfe and Law, for example, maintain that

> to understand a visualisation is thus to inquire into its provenance and into the social work that it does. It is to note its principles of exclusion and inclusion, to detect the roles that it makes available, to understand the way in which they are distributed and to decode the hierarchies and differences that it naturalises. And it is also to

analyse the ways in which authorship is constructed or concealed and the sense of audience is realised.[24]

One of the most fully developed approaches derives from structural anthropology, especially the work of Lévi-Strauss. It analyses museum objects as representing an underlying structure of thought and categories governing their relationship to each other. Susan Pearce, who has written quite widely on this, recognises its potential but also indicates that structuralist analysis has disadvantages, especially its synchronic nature, and hence an inability to address change.[25] According to a structuralist analysis, relationships between objects are of two types, metonymic and metaphoric.[26] Pearce argues that museum objects are a special type of object with a greater depth of meaning and significance. They operate in the past, their natural context, and in the present, the museum context, simultaneously.

> It is the ability of objects to be simultaneously signs and symbols, to carry a true part of the past into the present, but also to bear perpetual symbolic reinterpretation which is the essence of their peculiar and ambiguous power.[27]

The actual object, therefore, is always metonym and metaphor at the same time.[28] Because of its metaphorical nature its meaning can be manipulated, but because of its metonymic nature - being a 'real' object - it has more power as a symbol than an obvious representation does.

Different meanings and resonances in museum objects are produced by different rationales of collecting, as Pearce points out. For example, the systematic mode, which has always been the museum ideal, chooses objects that illustrate a certain series, such as British birds or eighteenth-century costume, where duplicates, replicas and imperfect items are avoided as far as possible. The fetishistic mode, which reaches the museum through donations of private collections, relies on personal identification with the objects. The collected object is an extension of the collector's personality.[29] The objects chosen in this case are those onto which the individual, or indeed society according to Marx, has projected his or her emotional needs. The souvenir mode, by its nature the most personal and private, rarely appears in a museum without simultaneously being one of the other two. There is, though, a particular form of souvenir, the trophy, which is most typically a head of wild game. Here the collecting is clearly intended to create prestige for the collector, and, as Pearce says, 'ritual hunting establishes the relationship between mankind and the natural world which the trophy on the wall makes manifest.'[30] Sports and regimental trophies carry the same messages.

Trophies may be further seen as fetishes, in the sense that they are objects onto which have been projected the social relations of mastery and domination. In fact, Jordanova has claimed that objects in natural science and medicine displays often expressed that same mastery over nature and the physical world which ethnographic objects did over colonial areas, and were therefore trophies, expressing 'victory, ownership, control and dominion.'[31] Thus the way in which an object is understood to relate to the wider world and wider meanings is important for understanding a display. This may be inferred from what is known of the collector, or from the way the museum treats the object. It may not be knowable; and it is clear, also, that objects may work in different ways simultaneously, or over time.

Various typologies of displays have been constructed, such as the four types of historical display cited by Pearce, those for ethnography developed by Fuerst, or the more general set of variables used by Hall.[32] These include aesthetic, narrative, reconstructive, and taxonomic types of display, among others. However, they are not yet exhaustive or universal, and, I would argue, suggest more the kind of variables to be taken into account than they provide a blueprint for analysis. These include the criteria for the selection of material; the principles dictating the ordering of material; and specific techniques of display, such as lighting; density of objects in the display; the presentation of textual material; the type of case used, if any; the proportion of 'real' objects to other material; the use of 'window-dressing' techniques; and the definition of the route around which the visitor is directed. The route has been seen as one of the key variables in museum display, revealing much about the intentions and presuppositions of the curator. If displays are close together, with few alternative routes around the exhibition and a rigid structure, called low entropy, this implies

> knowledge as if it were the map of well-known terrain where the relationship of each part to another, and all to the whole, is thoroughly understood.

If, on the other hand, the structure is weak, displays are further apart, and many routes could be taken around the exhibition, it indicates 'knowledge as a proposition which may stimulate further, or different, answering propositions.'[33] The extent to which a predetermined route is enforced upon visitors is seen by Bennett as a disciplinary technology: an efficient means of getting visitors to internalise meanings.[34] This can be linked to what Haraway calls 'technologies of enforced meaning'. She sees more realist displays as more positivist, certain that the facts mean only one thing. Thus the development of display practices like dioramas, taxidermy and naturalistic settings restrict the number of interpretations that could be placed on the objects; they are only allowed to tell one story.[35]

To a certain extent, then, museum displays can be seen as a language or text, which can be taken apart and its grammar analysed. I will consider some displays in this way; but not just in this way. For nineteenth-century municipal museums, a number of key issues can be identified. In natural history, the most important division is between classificatory displays and naturalistic displays, while for art objects it is between an educational and an aesthetic approach. The specific implications of these variables are explored in chapter 6. In ethnography, there is a considerable body of work considering the growth and decline of display styles such as typological. It is, however, salutary to remember that the meaning of objects is always the product of an interaction between the intention of the curator and museum context, and the personal conceptual world of the viewer.[36]

Museums and Class

Social historians have been more concerned to consider how museums grew out of and acted on the urban environment of the nineteenth century. This has often meant a focus on class. Class and class relationships were seen as creating a certain set of cultural and leisure activities in new urban settings that were dominated by the ideal of rational recreation; municipal museums took their place as part of the battery of middle-class tactics for reforming the working class. They have been seen as part of the rational recreation movement, a placatory or controlling response to Chartism, as part of the general expansion of the municipal sphere, or as stemming from the increasing Victorian emphasis on popular education.[37] All of these points have some validity, but do not really explain why municipal museums should have been seen as the solution to these problems. The picture of class relationships within the Victorian town that emerges now is of a more unstable and contested terrain, in which conflict and negotiation are more apparent than control.[38] There has also been much more emphasis recently on how class identities are formed, in conjunction with other identities. This has been particularly marked for the middle class, where debates have focussed on the formation of class identity, notably through voluntary activities and the public sphere. It is argued that by 1850, male 'middle class-ness' had come to be defined through various aspects of the urban public sphere, against the female domestic sphere.[39] Work on the middle class after 1850 is a growing field; the concerns which are emerging are the importance of the civic, of gender identities, and of cultural consumption for the assertion of class identities.[40] Bailey has argued that cultural consumption in the modern city after about 1880 was about playing with social identities as older certainties about class and status were eroded.[41] Clearly, municipal museums are implicated in all of these areas, and the question of how middle-class identities were shaped through such institutions must be one of the key ones for this book. The divisions within the middle class are increasingly clear, and attention has focussed on the way in which elites and upper middle-class groups tried to separate themselves out of the rest of the class, and establish themselves as legitimate leaders.

Beyond class, a study of museums' place within Victorian society also raises questions about the growth and nature of the civil society, of different modes of governance, of various ideas about civilisation, and ultimately about capitalism itself. The concept of civil society is a crucial one for understanding museums' role in society.[42] The idea of a realm between the private and the state where public opnion can flourish has been seen as crucial to the working of liberal democracy, and has been associated with nineteenth-century institutions offering for the first time universal access, and developing ideas of citizenship. It is partly about the organisation of consent, but also about creating an ideal rational public, a space for informed debate. Thus, the municipal museum offered universal access and, as an educational, rational, institution, helped to create a population that could be debating citizens. The concept of civil society, though, is not a neutral one, but generally very loaded; in contrast to the idealisation of eighteenth- and nineteenth-century civil society by Habermas, more recent commentators have been concerned to show how this public sphere was very closely bound up with the development of middle-class identities and the consolidation of their power and hegemony in towns. It has also been shown that there were competing public spheres in the nineteenth century, and that some groups were excluded altogether. It is not, therefore, necessarily the ideal, progressive organisation of debate it sometimes appears, but, once more, a historically specific construction, and one that, as Eley shows, may be contradictory.[43]

The concept of governance is of interest to this study in that it is, in the words of one recent work, about 'the organisation and legitimation of authority'; governance encompasses both the state and civil society.[44] The fact that the nineteenth-century town saw an expansion in governance in all forms, and that the legitimacy of such governance rested increasingly on some form of democracy or representativeness of citizens (though not usually full democracy) and openness to public scrutiny can all be seen to contribute to the idea of a municipal museum.[45] Governance was also implicated in the production of meaning; it had a symbolic as well as a purely instrumental function. Governance as a symbolic resource was largely concerned with the naturalisation or contestation of authority, and in this sense could be in some conflict with the idea of openness and representativeness.[46]

Writers on museums have generally been concerned to establish a more schematic relationship between museums and an industrial, capitalist society, rather than looking at the specifics of British urban society in the nineteenth century. The museum has been seen as an institution which 'gathers, stores and provides a sense of social heritage, a fund of social knowledge, a sense of development,' much as myth, poetry, song, dance and ritual may in other cultures.[47] Which particular method a culture uses to deal with social images depends on its social structure and its history of handling such things. A culture which uses museums as a repository of social images, typically also uses literacy for storing and spreading knowledge, and the industrial method to deal with economic goods and services. This whole pattern has been called the 'industrial syntax'.[48] Museums' role within the 'industrial syntax' is to enable capitalism;   not merely by creating hegemony, but by transforming humanity's relationship to the environment. Industrialism requires an assumption of humanity as separate from the environment and able to act on it, to create new originals.[49] This leads to concepts of authorship and ownership, patents and the storage of the original in museums. Similarly, James Clifford has referred to museums as contributing to a specific modern form of Western subjectivity.[50]

Pearce also infers a special relationship of museums with capitalism, as uniquely holders of objects, that is, of materiality. She sites museums within 'characteristic modern meta-narratives', which are all based on a belief in the existence of objective reality, a complex relationship with objects (usually as goods), and the idea of progress.[51] Hence, museums were brought into existence because they could 'hold the real objects, the actual evidence, the true data as we would say, upon which in the last analysis the materialistic meta-narratives depended for their verification.'[52] It seems, therefore, that museums did have a valued place within modern Western states, particularly as they developed, and it is indicated that the two performed supporting and reinforcing roles for each other.

Museums are also argued to have had a role in maintaining the economic value of goods within capitalism. Marx, again, was the first to remark on the transformation effected by capitalism on the value of things when they become commodities. 'It is a definite social relation between men, that assumes, in their eyes, that fantastic form of a relation between things.'[53] The mysterious and illogical way, analogous to religion as he saw it, that the product of men's labour took on different values according to their place within the social relations of capitalism led him to call this process 'fetishism'. In order, then, to maintain the value systems of capitalism, some degree of mystification is needed, and this is where Pearce sees museums as functioning within the social whole. Thus the objects within are imbued with various superior qualities; they are fetishised.[54] A public museum, with official, expert sanction then becomes a storehouse of the spiritual treasures of the nation.[55]

Bourdieu has shown how museums and art galleries take pains to separate themselves from the commodities marketplace, in order to more effectively reinforce market hierarchies of value.[56] They tend, especially the larger and more prestigious museums, to hold items of very considerable economic value, but to represent themselves as exercising purely qualitative judgements as to the non-monetary value of objects. The expertise of their staff enables them to determine aesthetic importance in the arts, significance in human history, and meaning in the natural sciences, and create a body of approved pieces, which then attract monetary value.

> Value accrues to an object according to the place it is given in the classificatory system made legitimate by the institutional signatory.[57]

The museum is therefore a crucial component in the 'interrrelationship of cultural wealth and commodity in the capitalist system.'[58]

It can be seen that, although most commentators agree that museums have been very important in the creation and maintenance of modern western capitalism, there are some important differences as to what it is museums do. The focus on museums' objects place within a total system of objects is not very strongly chronologically elaborated; this is a role they have been fulfilling since capitalism and modernism began, whenever that might be, and will continue to fulfil indefinitely. It thus erodes the differences between different kinds of museum at any point, and in museum practices over time, even quite short periods. It is also quite hard to see the implications of this, or indeed find evidence for it, on any detailed empirical level, although art museums and the art market form something of an exception to this. What is needed, then, is to fill in the broad schema with some chronologically and geographically specific studies.

Museums and the Production and Consumption of Culture

Museums are equally approached from a cultural history or cultural studies perspective. While these are ambiguous terms, and clearly many cultural considerations have already been dealt with, in this section I would like to deal particularly with the production and consumption of culture.

Culture is a flexible concept which has been used in a variety of ways, but has recently been deployed by historians in the sense of a set of practices concerned with the creation of meaning; thus it includes knowledge and values. This leads to questions about how culture is implicated in the social. As Hooper-Greenhill says,

> Culture can transmit dominant values, but can also be seen as a site
> of resistance where dominant shared codes may be disrupted or
> displaced, and where alternative shared codes can be produced.[59]

Increasing emphasis has been laid in nineteenth-century urban history on the ways in which cultural meaning was produced and consumed, and how this affected and constructed social identities. An important model can be drawn on here in the work of Pierre Bourdieu and Paul DiMaggio. Bourdieu's ideas about the role of culture in creating and maintaining social distinctions have become quite influential in museum studies.[60] Although retaining a fundamentally materialist view of power and status, he has developed a very sophisticated analysis of the ways in which manipulation of cultural and symbolic resources worked to produce and maintain power and status. The concept of 'cultural capital' which effectively means an ability to appropriate either cultural goods or cultural meaning, is useful in showing how distinction between social groups, and legitimation of that distinction, comes about. The crucial question is how equally or unequally the ability to appropriate culture is distributed. While Bourdieu sees this ability as a product both of environment or 'habitus', which has been defined as 'total cultural baggage'[61]; and of straightforward material capital, it is something which may be subject to struggle.

> Struggles over the appropriation of economic or cultural goods are,
> simultaneously, symbolic struggles to appropriate distinctive
> signs..., or to conserve or subvert the principles of classification of
> these distinctive properties.[62]

DiMaggio's work gives a clearer sense of how cultural resources could be deployed to create and legitimate status. This is bound up with the organisation of both the production and consumption of cultural goods.[63] The production of culture involves investing in institutions that can differentiate and segregate different cultural forms, thus creating a more or less hierarchical cultural system which allows consumers to place one another and build links or boundaries between each other. Consumption of culture, which could be identified with taste, can serve as a means of constructing social relations, particularly in a dynamic, complex social setting.

DiMaggio has examined this theory through a study of the development of high art institutions in Boston in the nineteenth century; he shows how the formation of a symphony orchestra and the Fine Art Museum created a stable distinction between high and popular culture, which allowed high culture to be used to reinforce the status of those who consumed it. The case is a little more complicated for the Fine Art Museum, though; as DiMaggio shows, it was originally conceived as having an educational function, which is very similar to the idea that museums would civilise the working class. It was, therefore, a public institution. This of course meant that anyone had the possibility of acquiring the cultural capital which could enhance their status, as opposed to the orchestra's concert where ticket prices prevented this. As a result, not that long after its foundation, the museum made a dramatic switch from an educational focus, to a purely aesthetic focus, leaving it, though technically still open to all, increasingly impenetrable to those without prior artistic and art historical education.[64] Although the element of struggle over the appropriation and meaning of culture seems less prominent in DiMaggio's work, it is still there, as he shows clashes between the educationalists and the aesthetes in Boston's Fine Art Museum.[65]

For this study, then, attention to the way production of the municipal museum organises it institutionally, distinguishes it from other cultural forms and polices that distinction, needs to be combined with a focus on the ways in which such museums were consumed, broadly understood, including the sorts of cultural capital they made available, and how that was appropriated and contested. Did museums allow the legitimation of elite status groups or did they create a more complex and variable set of cultural meanings which were appropriated and redeployed by a larger proportion of the population?

Museums as Sites of Inclusivity and Exclusivity

Inclusions and exclusions need to be accounted for. This book looks primarily at municipal museums in England. This is not to devalue the museums in other parts of Britain during this period, particularly in Scotland; however, the rate-supported museum was less common outside England. The British Association for the Advancement of Science found only four rate-supported museums in Scotland, none in Ireland, and two in Wales in 1887. While many smaller towns throughout Britain did not set up municipal museums until around 1900, nevertheless in England in 1887 there were already 50 such institutions.[66] Maybe harder to justify is the decision to concentrate on museums in the north and midlands of England. It can be argued that it was here that the provincial museum was most strongly advocated and supported; some of the earliest municipal museums were founded here, such as Warrington; and the Museums Association was founded in York in 1889 and held most of its meetings in the north in the early years.[67] Yet it is by no means true that municipal museums were solely a northern and midland phenomenon. Places as diverse as Exeter, Folkestone, Ipswich, Maidstone, Northampton, Reading and Winchester all had rate-supported museums in existence by 1880, and some, notably Ipswich and Winchester, had been pioneers. Nevertheless, the outline of development is clear. If museums wholly or partly supported by rates are considered by broad regional divisions, north east, north west, midlands, south east and south west, then there are 36 in the first three regions by 1887, and thirteen in the last two. Conversely, at the same time, there are roughly equal numbers of local society and Mechanics' Institute museums.[68]

I use the term museum in a rather loose sense; primarily I look at municipal museums, including museums of art, and have tended not to examine municipal art galleries. However, differentiating between museums of art and art galleries is a difficult and not always useful task. There is, therefore, some reference to art galleries, though this is patchy; and I have not systematically considered such important Victorian art galleries as the Walker in Liverpool. This is primarily in order to keep the study manageable, both in length, and in issues raised.

This study has the chronological limits 1850 to 1914. These form the natural boundaries of such a study for several reasons. The year 1850 is, more or less, the date of the birth of the municipal museum; the enabling legislation was passed in 1845, and the first such museum itself, Warrington Museum, was founded in 1848.[69] It was in the years after this that municipal museums had to invent themselves, so to speak, and justify their expenditure of rates. In the second half of the nineteenth century and into the twentieth consolidation and expansion were probably the main activity; municipal museums were extremely successful.[70] Gaynor Kavanagh has shown how in the period up to 1914, museums managed to retain a place on liberal agendas, vouching for the 'civic status, scholarship, and civilised' nature of towns and the nation.[71] The First World War brought closure, removal of collections, and restrictions on spending for objects, salaries, and overheads, although it also stimulated new, more effectively communicative exhibitions, which were very popular, on subjects such as health and food preparation.[72] However, in the discussions over commemorating the war, a *national* war museum won out over local war museums, which in itself suggests municipal museums were losing the prominence they had earlier enjoyed.[73] Their decline in comparison with national museums continued in the inter-war years; Kavanagh describes them as 'moribund' at this point. They became seriously underfunded, which led to

> understaffing; very low pay levels; curators still working in their seventies and eighties, being unable to retire without a pension; cramped and dirty buildings; and out of date displays.[74]

Not only this, but as Kavanagh indicates, there was a retreat on the part of curators to the old conception of a museum as a repository of objects; she quotes a letter from the Museums Association to the Ministry of Reconstruction in 1918, thus: 'the primary function of a museum ... is to collect, preserve, and utilize specimens'.[75] In the light of the innovative and educational methods developed up to and during the First World War, this must be seen as a loss of confidence, created by the funding squeeze, the advent of competing media oriented towards mass entertainment, such as cinema, and possibly also to the sense of the end of an era, a new order of things, that the First World War brought about.[76] So the period selected represents that of greatest success, relevance and self-creation for municipal museums.

Museums as Socio-Cultural Formations

In sum, then, this study will concentrate wherever possible on disagreements and negotiation, as revealing contingency and complexity, and the importance of local factors.The municipal museum was an important part of the process of social grouping and hierarchy in the nineteenth century; of class formation, particularly on the part of middle-class elites. Partly this was about internal differentiation, about developing appropriate forms of leisure and authority. However, it was also of course about relationships with other groups and classes, and this process was complex and had to be negotiated with the other social groups.[77] Control of the museum meant control over the displays and knowledge created, which could naturalise and legitimise identities and power relationships through their public status. Municipal museums formed a better arena than private museums for the creation and display of middle-class identities; middle-class elites also saw the municipal museum initially as another means of manipulating social groups and reinforcing their legitimacy in the face of an increasingly complex and democratised urban environment. However, the elites found themselves challenged in their conception of a municipal museum, and in their control of it, as a consequence of its public status. These challenges were not usually particularly dramatic or successful, but they were there. Towards the end of the period museums were exempting themselves from popular challenge by becoming more professionally and academically autonomous, and more socially exclusive. Their relationship with working-class visitors had changed quite substantially by the end of the period, partly because of an overall change in manners, but also because working-class visitors were benefiting more and more from a growing commercial leisure industry and were ceasing to come.

It is the argument of this book that the municipal museum superseded its predecessors because of the number of different roles and functions it could sustain, and the legitimacy its public status gave it. It was an institution, in which a variety of discourses about the world, such as the scientific and the aesthetic, were articulated; and a variety of power structures, including the governmental, the social, and the professional, were articulated. It was also, though, an institution in which such discourses and power structures could be developed, challenged and even ignored. Thus it could simultaneously be viewed as an 'improver' of the working classes; or as adding to the reputation and civic pride of the town. It may be seen as a public story which towns, and primarily the middle classes, told about themselves, although not all museums told the same story, and not necessarily about the same middle class.

It is increasingly clear that social and cultural formations are undoubtedly mutually constitutive in museums. The structure of this book embodies movement from the social to the cultural, or what may be seen as the context to the text. This is of course the 'traditional' social history approach and would seem to imply a causative relationship between that context and text; however, this is not my intention. Rather it reflects the training and habits of approach of a social historian. However, the social context is clearly very important for municipal museums, in explaining their particularity. My argument, therefore, is that discourse and context are linked in a process of perpetual becoming; social groupings and identities are formed by the museum's discourse but in their turn shape the messages and knowledge embodied in it.[78]

Notes

[1]   Thomas Greenwood, *Museums and Art Galleries*, (London 1888), p. viii.

[2]   Greenwood, *Museums*, p. 5.

[3]   These arguments can be found in, inter alia, Tony Bennett, *The Birth of the Museum*, (London 1995); Annie Coombes, *Reinventing Africa, Museums, Material Culture and Popular Imagination*, (New Haven 1994); Duncan and Wallach, 'The Universal Survey Museum', *Art History*, 3, 4, (1980), pp. 448-69; Carol Duncan, *Civilising Rituals: Inside Public Art Museums*, (London 1995); Eilean Hooper-Greenhill, *Museums and the Shaping of Knowledge*, (London 1992); Nick Prior, *Museums and Modernity: Art Galleries and the Making of Modern Culture*, (Oxford 2002).

[4]   Eilean Hooper-Greenhill, *Museums and the Interpretation of Visual Culture*, (London 2000), p. x.

[5]   Daniel J. Sherman, 'The Bourgeoisie, Cultural Appropriation and the Art Museum in Nineteenth-Century France', *Radical History Review* 38, (1987),p. 41.

[6]   *Ibid.*, pp. 44-46.

[7]   *Ibid.*, p. 55.

[8]   M. Pointon (ed), *Art Apart: Museums in North America and Britain since 1800* (Manchester 1994), pp. 2-3. I would also single out as giving a very historically specific analysis of a particular aspect of museums Annie Coombes, *Reinventing Africa*. See also Daniel Sherman 'The Bourgeoisie, Cultural Appropriation and the Art Museum', and *Worthy Monuments: Art Museums and the Politics of Culture in Nineteenth-Century France*, (Cambridge, Massachussets 1989).

[9]   Prior, *Museums and Modernity*, p. 6.

[10]   Prior, *Museums and Modernity*, p. 3.

[11]   Daniel J. Sherman and Irit Rogoff, 'Introduction: Frameworks for Critical Analysis', in Sherman and Rogoff (eds), *Museum Culture: Histories, Discourses, Spectacles*, (London 1994), p. ix.

[12]   Bennett, *The Birth of the Museum*, p. 4.

[13]   See for example Hugh Cunningham, *Leisure in the Industrial Revolution, c. 1780-1880*, (London 1980), chapter 3; and Peter Bailey, *Leisure and Class in Victorian England: Rational Recreation and the Contest for Control*, (London 1978), chapter 2.

[14]   This tendency is particularly marked in Hooper-Greenhill, *Museums and the Shaping of Knowledge*.

[15]   See Prior, *Museums and Modernity*, p. 11; Sherman and Rogoff, 'Introduction'.

[16]   For penal systems, Foucault puts the change from 1770 to 1810. See Foucault, *Discipline and Punish*, (London 1977), p. 7.

[17] Bennett, *Birth of the Museum*, p. 22.

[18] Bennett, *Birth of the Museum*, chapter 2.

[19] Bennett, *Birth of the Museum*; Hooper-Greenhill, *Museums and the Shaping of Knowledge*; see also Tony Bennett, *Culture, A Reformer's Science*, (London 1998), esp. Part II.

[20] Tony Bennett, 'Useful Culture', in *Cultural Studies* 6, 3, (1992), p. 398.

[21] *Ibid.*, p. 399.

[22] Susan Pearce, *Museums, Objects and Collections*, (London 1992), p. 87.

[23] *Ibid.*,pp. 139, 233.

[24] Fyfe and Law (eds), *Picturing Power: Visual Depiction and Social Relations*, (London 1988), p. 1.

[25] Pearce, *Museums, Objects and Collections*, p. 187.

[26] *Ibid.*, pp. 170-171.

[27] *Ibid.*, p. 27.

[28] *Ibid.*, p. 30.

[29] *Ibid.*, p. 81.

[30] *Ibid.*, p. 71.

[31] Ludmilla Jordanova, 'Objects of Knowledge: a historical perspective on museums', in Vergo (ed) *The New Museology*, (London 1989), p. 32.

[32] Pearce, *Museums, Objects and Collections*, pp. 196-207; Hans Joerg Fuerst, 'Material Culture Research and the Curation Process' in Pearce (ed) *Museum Studies in Material Culture*, (London 1989), p. 100; Margaret Hall, *On Display: A Design Grammar for Museum Exhibitions*, (London 1986), pp. 25-9.

[33] Pearce, *Museums, Objects and Collections*, p. 139.

[34] Bennett, *Birth of the Museum*, chapter 7.

[35] Donna Haraway, 'Teddy Bear Patriarchy; Taxidermy in the Garden of Eden, New York City 1908-1936' in *Social Text* 11,(1984), p. 30.

[36] Susan Pearce, 'Objects as meaning; or narrating the past' in Pearce (ed), *Interpreting Objects and Collections*, (London 1994), p. 26.

[37] Cunningham, *Leisure in the Industrial Revolution*, p. 106; Bailey, *Leisure and Class*, pp. 36, 38-9; H. E. Meller, *Leisure and the Changing City 1870-1914*, (London 1976), p. 102.

[38] See for example Geoff Eley, 'Nations, Publics and Political Cultures: Placing Habermas in the Nineteenth Century', in Eley and Ortner (eds) *Culture/Power/History: A Reader in Contemporary Social Theory*, (Princeton, New Jersey 1994); Martin Hewitt, *The Emergence of Stability in the Industrial City: Manchester 1832-1867*, (Aldershot 1996); R. J. Morris, 'Clubs, Societies and Associations', in F. M. L. Thompson (ed), *The Cambridge Social History of Britain 1750-1950*, Vol. 3, (Cambridge 1990); R. J. Morris, 'Civil society and the nature of urbanism: Britain 1750-1850', *Urban History* 25, 3, (1998); James Vernon, *Politics and the People: A Study in English Political Culture, c. 1815-1867*, (Cambridge 1993).

[39] R. J. Morris, *Class, Sect and Party, The Making of the British Middle Class: Leeds 1820-1850*, (Manchester 1990); L. Davidoff & C.Hall, *Family Fortunes*, (London 1994).

[40] See Simon Gunn, *The Public Culture of the Victorian Middle Class, Ritual and Authority and the English Industrial City, 1840-1914*, (Manchester 2000); Alan Kidd and David Nicholls (eds), *Gender, Civic Culture and Consumerism: Middle-Class Identity in Britain 1800-1940*, (Manchester 1999); D. S. Macleod, *Art and the Victorian Middle Class: Money and the Making of Cultural Identity*, (Cambridge 1996); Judith Walkowitz, *City of Dreadful Delight: Narratives of Sexual Danger in Late Victorian London*, (London 1992);

J. Wolff and J. Seed (eds), *The Culture of Capital: Art, Power and the Nineteenth-Century Middle Class*, (Manchester 1988).

[41]   Peter Bailey, 'Adventures in Space: Victorian Railway Erotics, or Taking Alienation for a Ride', *Journal of Victorian Culture* 9, 1, (2004), p. 3.

[42]   Or the public sphere; this term is rather associated with Habermas but the definition is very similar, a realm between the family and the state where public opinion can flourish. Eley, 'Nations, publics and political cultures'; R. J. Morris, 'Civil Society and the Nature of Urbanism: Britain 1750-1850', *Urban History* 25, 3, (1998).

[43]   Eley, 'Nations, publics and political cultures'; see also the articles in *Urban History* 25, 3, (1998) which is a special issue on civil society in Britain.

[44]   Robert J. Morris, 'Governance: two centuries of urban growth' in Morris and Trainor (eds) *Urban Governance: Britain and Beyond since 1750*, (Aldershot 2000), p. 1.

[45]   *Ibid*, pp. 4-6.

[46]   For the symbolic aspects of governance, and the tension between exclusivity and inclusivity in them, see James Vernon, *Politics and the People: A Study in English Political Culture, c. 1815-1867*, (Cambridge 1993), chapter 2; David Cannadine, 'The Transformation of Civic Ritual in Modern Britain: The Colchester Oyster Feast', *Past and Present* 94, (1982); Simon Gunn, 'Ritual and Civic Culture in the English Industrial City, c. 1835-1914', in Morris and Trainor,*Urban Governance*, (Aldershot 2000); Kate Hill, '"Thoroughly Embued with the Spirit of Ancient Greece": Symbolism and Space in Victorian Civic Culture', in Alan Kidd and David Nicholls (eds) *Gender, Civic Culture and Consumerism, Middle-Class Identity in Britain 1800-1940*, (Manchester 1999).

[47]   Edwina Taborsky, 'The Sociostructural Role of Museums', *International Journal of Museum Management and Curatorship* 1 (1982), p. 340.

[48]   *Ibid.*, p. 340.

[49]   *Ibid.*, p. 342.

[50]   James Clifford, 'On Collecting Art and Culture', in Simon During (ed) *The Cultural Studies Reader*, (London 1993), p. 61.

[51]   Pearce, *Museums, Objects and Collections*, p. 3.

[52]   *Ibid.*, p. 4.

[53]   Karl Marx, *Capital*, Student's edition, edited by C.J. Arthur, (London 1992), p. 32.

[54]   Pearce, *Museums, Objects and Collections*, p. 108.

[55]   *Ibid.*, p. 100.

[56]   See P. Bourdieu, *Distinction: A Social Critique of the Judgement of Taste*, trans. R.Nice, (Cambridge, Massachussetts 1984).

[57]   *Ibid.*, p. 236.

[58]   *Ibid.*, p. 237.

[59]   Hooper-Greenhill, *Museums and the Interpretation of Visual Culture*, (London 2000), p. 13.

[60]   Bourdieu has been cited by Bennett, *Birth of the Museum*, and even more centrally, byPrior, *Museums and Modernity*.

[61]   Vera L. Zolberg, ' "An elite experience for everyone": Art Museums, the Public, and Cultural Literacy', in Daniel J. Sherman and Irit Rogoff (eds) *Museum Culture: Histories, Discourses, Spectacles*, (London 1994), p. 56.

[62]   Bourdieu, *Distinction*, p. 249.

[63]   Paul DiMaggio, 'Classification in Art', *American Sociological Review* 52 (1987), p. 443.

[64]   Paul DiMaggio, 'Cultural entrepreneurship in nineteenth-century Boston: the creation of an organizational base for high culture in America', *Media, Culture and Society* 4 (1982), pp. 33-50, and, 'Cultural entrepreneurship in nineteenth-century Boston, part II: the

classification and framing of American art', *Media, Culture and Society* 4 (1982), pp. 303-322.
[65]   See especially DiMaggio, 'Cultural entrepreneurship, part II'.
[66]   'Report upon the provincial museums of the United Kingdom', in *Report of the 57th Meeting of the British Association for the Advancement of Science*, (London 1888), pp. 100-113.
[67]   Geoffrey Lewis, *For Instruction and Recreation: A Centenary History of the Museums Association*, (London 1989), pp. 8-15.
[68]   'Report upon the provincial museums', pp. 100-113.
[69]   *Ibid.*, pp. 100-113.
[70]   G. Kavanagh, *History Curatorship*, (London 1990), p. 14. The number of museums doubled from 90 to 180 between 1860 and 1880; G. Lewis, *For Instruction*, p. 1.
[71]   G. Kavanagh, *Museums and the First World War: A social history*, (London 1994), p. 21.
[72]   *Ibid.*, chapters 3 and 5.
[73]   *Ibid.*, chapters 8 and 9.
[74]   *Ibid.*, p. 163.
[75]   *Ibid.*, p. 163.
[76]   *Ibid.*, p. 164.
[77]   John Garrard has shown the extremely conditional nature of the power exercised by urban elites, compared with that of rural elites. J. Garrard, *Leadership and Power in Victorian Towns 1830-1880*, (Manchester 1983).
[78]   Daniel Miller writes of 'a process of development in which neither social nor cultural form is privileged as prior, but rather seen as mutually constitutive'. D. Miller, *Material Culture and Mass Consumption*, (Oxford 1987), p. 18.

CHAPTER TWO

Negotiating the New Urban Environment

Public museums were urban institutions, but more than that, products of a particular urban environment, which, it may be argued, gave them their shape and purpose. Museums have been so firmly linked with the Victorian town that it is worth examining this link in some detail. They have been seen as part of a battery of tactics by the urban elite to reform and improve the fabric of urban society; others have argued that such cultural initiatives were more about the development and differentiation of that very elite. Both of these arguments have a certain validity, but in addition, municipal museums can be seen as part of a reshaped urban landscape which sought to provide an arena for negotiation between different groups in society, though this was clearly an arena which privileged elite groups. This chapter, then, aims to examine the development of towns in nineteenth-century England, to see both how changing social patterns led to new cultural forms, but also how culture became a central tool in the development of urban social identities and patterns of power.

The nineteenth century as a whole of course saw massive urban growth, though there had been significant growth in the eighteenth century, and the timing of growth varied between different towns and cities. Places such as Liverpool and Manchester grew very fast in the first half of the century, often in the difficult and unstable decades such as the 1830s and 1840s, and overall, urban growth was faster before 1850 than after. [1] However, other towns did not expand significantly until after the arrival of the railways, or even later. [2] Of course, the size of percentage population growth for towns depends on their existing size; thus large towns seem to have slackened in growth as the century progressed, while small towns seem to have grown disproportionately fast; changing boundaries also confuse the issue. [3] Nevertheless, a sometimes short period of extremely rapid growth, followed by a more prolonged period of consolidation, was experienced by many towns at some point during the nineteenth century, although a few, particularly small market towns, actually shrank. For some places, expansion occurred in an urban environment already strengthened by an earlier 'renaissance', where social structures, infrastructure and facilities were in place; [4] in others it occurred in what had been little more than villages; but for all, it produced changes. It would be a mistake to see this expansion as solely due to manufacturing; some of the most spectacular, such as Liverpool and Hull, were due to international trade; and services, to manufacturing but also to agriculture, were also important, even to somewhere as stereotypically 'manufacturing' as Manchester. [5] It is frequently stated that by 1851, just over half the population was living in towns; certainly this point was reached at some point in the nineteenth century, though the exact date depends very much on how a town is defined. For many towns, the rate of population growth slowed after 1850, which may have allowed a more stable, and less conflict-ridden society to emerge.[6]

It is important to stress the diversity in Victorian towns, as a brief survey of the fortunes of different types of town reveals. It is of course risky to categorise towns too simplistically, and to posit a unified development for each type; Briggs has argued that Victorian towns were characterised by their individuality.[7] Yet there were some important social and cultural similarities amongst types of town. Not least, municipal museums were disproportionately founded in the industrial and trading towns and cities of the north and midlands; but not exclusively there. Even among northern towns, there was variation between the 'shock city' of Manchester, and the self-proclaimed genteel port of Liverpool; between towns almost totally based on cotton production, and those which had a background of county administration and agricultural services, onto which industry was grafted. In addition, there were resort towns, some of which established museums as a tourist amenity, and towns which modernised very little during the period. What was it about this varied urban environment which made the creation of municipal museums seem a suitable policy?

The purely industrial town certainly existed; many of the Lancashire cotton towns could merit this description. For example, in 1841 somewhere like Blackburn had over 40 per cent of adult males, and over two-thirds of working adult females, employed in textiles, along with huge employment of teenagers.[8] This was probably the most dominant that textiles ever reached in the nineteenth century; by 1861, the average in cotton and wool towns such as Preston, Bolton, Bradford and Halifax was about 30 per cent for adult males, and 20-30 per cent for adult females, although this varied far more widely.[9] These towns were expanding fast throughout the nineteenth century; one group, including Bury, Oldham and Preston, experienced its fastest period of growth before 1840, though maintaining a sizeable rate of growth thereafter. Others, such as Blackburn and Burnley, had their greatest rate of growth in the middle of the century.[10] The speed of growth of these towns affected their social fabric in different ways; Preston, as a centre of administration and justice, as well as of genteel society, in the eighteenth century, retained a relatively large and diversified middle class, along with a 'season' that attracted gentry and even some aristocratic patronage, although much of this latter disappeared as the town became more visibly industrial.[11] Somewhere like Oldham, on the other hand, was much more clearly a town of cotton masters and cotton workers. The middle classes were relatively few, made up of shopkeepers and cotton masters, with little seasoning of lawyers, doctors, or merchants, such as were to be found elsewhere; masters may not have been all that distinct from their workers.[12]

The bigger towns and cities, such as Leeds, Birmingham, Manchester and Sheffield, were of course also industrial. Textiles and the metal trades formed a large proportion of their occupational make-up, and were also important in driving their expansion, but they had a broader range of manufacturing activity than smaller industrial towns, and tended to specialise in finishing processes. Most of these were, despite their still primitive local government structures and lack of

Parliamentary representation, thriving in the eighteenth century, and acquired the genteel paraphernalia of theatres and assembly rooms during this period.[13] They might be prospering as the centre of a network of outworkers, in textiles, or a town of workshops, in the metal trades; but it was usually their role as a centre of trade and services, as well as their proximity to a pool of skilled labour, that placed them in a good position to take advantage of advances in techniques, as well as the increasing scale of manufacture in the nineteenth century. It was also this factor that gave them a merchant elite demanding a more genteel lifestyle. However, it is important to note that they were far from single-industry towns; rather, their economic profile was characterised by diversification. Correspondingly, they had a larger, more diverse, and probably wealthier middle class than the industrial towns. Their growth was typically very fast in the first part of the nineteenth century, with a gradual slowing, although remaining very high throughout the century.

There was another category of large town, which initially seemed far more dynamic than the industrial town, and that was the port. Liverpool was the pre-eminent example, but others such as Southampton and Hull were equally successful. Liverpool showed faster growth than Leeds, Sheffield and Manchester in the first half of the nineteenth century, and for most of the century was the second largest city in England. In general these ports had benefited from the expansion of overseas trade in the eighteenth century, and by 1800 had complex and established social structures, headed by very wealthy merchants, and tended to stress their sophistication at the expense of the manufacturing towns. However, the port towns were particularly susceptible to social problems, with a large proportion of the working class either transient, or dependent on extremely casual dock work. There tended, also, to be little work for women, which depressed family incomes in comparison with mill towns.[14]

Two other types of town should also be considered: resorts, and county or market towns. Resort towns, at the seaside rather than spa towns as formerly, were a success story of the second half of the nineteenth century. The population of the 48 towns classified as seaside resorts in 1871 had grown 21.5 per cent since 1861, and was to grow another 75 per cent by 1901.[15] These resorts varied enormously, in the extent of their dependence on tourists, as well as in the type of tourist they attracted. Several of the most successful relied on very large quantities of working-class visitor, from the great manufacturing districts: Blackpool, Morecambe and Skegness are examples. Resort towns of course faced problems of seasonal unemployment, the severity of which depended on the extent to which they had maintained other employment such as fishing, or had extended their season. Several of the more middle-class resorts solved this from the 1860s onwards by becoming retirement and rentier towns as well, such as Torquay and Bournemouth; or commuter towns, such as Southport. These towns could therefore have extremely large middle classes, and even the more working-class oriented resorts contained many successful businessmen.

County, or even smaller market towns, have generally received less attention from urban historians; and they are even harder to generalise about than other types of town. They experienced much less dramatic growth than industrial, port or resort towns; some even declined in numbers. However, many saw some manufacturing development, some saw in-migration of retiring middle-class manufacturers and merchants, and all continued to provide services to agriculture. Generally, though not exclusively, any manufacture was on a small scale, based on the workshop, with low levels of unionisation. The other strength of county towns was their historic concentrations of administrative, religious and educational services. Of these, education probably grew, while religion and administration were at least partly relocated to larger new provincial centres. These towns, therefore, had large middle classes, consisting of more traditional occupations such as shopkeepers, dealers, doctors, clergy and lawyers. They have also been argued to be more deferential in attitude towards the landed gentry.[16]

Of course, towns can not strictly be divided into these types; many were a mixture of at least two, or changed in the course of the century. Bradford was in many ways a textile manufacturing town, but also had a large population of merchants, and provided other services to manufacturing, despite its proximity to Leeds. Lincoln was initially a typical cathedral and county town, providing services to agriculture, and with small-scale manufacture of animal feed and beer; however, by the end of the century it was the home of some enormous engineering works, each employing several thousand workers.[17] Yet the broad categories outlined above, as long as they are not seen as precisely pigeonholing every town, do provide an overview of some of the most important variables in the economic and social structures of towns, and of some of the effects these could have.

Class, Conflict and Quiescence

Class was one aspect of the changing social patterns and relationships of the town; new solidarities were formed, as well as new hostilities, and new ways of exercising power and authority (as well as new ways of resisting that power.) While class may no longer be seen as a self-evident, primary socio-economic category, it was nevertheless an important component in organising understanding of urban society, and in forming identities. New municipal elites emerged largely as a result of a growing perception that urban society was a problem, increasingly marked by class tensions; and that town populations, especially the working class, needed to be improved. This perception, however, was informed by all sorts of things, from the new ways of knowing pioneered by Statistical Societies, to new mental geographies brought about by suburbanisation. There is no clear line of causation from urban growth, to class development, to cultural response; any consideration of the way in which people thought and acted in towns is not necessarily secondary to consideration of the physical development of those towns. Rather, the two aspects interacted, in so complex a way that disentangling them is nigh on impossible.

Nineteenth-century towns were much bigger, more complex and more differentiated than those that had preceded them. There were considerable practical problems to be overcome, of public health, pollution and public order. One of the greatest fears, though, of commentators was that these towns intensified class conflict and had lost the traditional ways of dealing with such social problems;

simultaneously, new elites needed to demonstrate authority and win consent from an urban population which was, or could be, more threatening, more fluid and more independent than previously. What was needed was a new machinery for maintaining and justifying the social status quo while allowing for the resolution of differences between groups. The novel problem that was faced was that of a more fluid and unstable class society, where increasingly hierarchies could be challenged, or even unknown. A challenge, therefore, to those who were forming the elite, was to stabilise and police hierarchies while still subscribing to ideals of liberal democracy. Again, though, class relationships varied widely; as we have seen, the proportion of middle class to working class could be different from town to town; and of course, each of these two groupings contained a wide variety of status and income levels.

Urban growth brought social segregation; this was of course a complex process, and the clear 'zoning' which, Engels argued, existed in mid-century Manchester, was not necessarily visible. It is hard to find any historian who would argue that segregation had produced clearly designated areas inhabited by specific status groups, certainly before 1870. Yet the development of middle-class suburbs, especially upper middle-class ones, was a persistent pressure, and could often be observed as a town grew in numbers and wealth, though in a 'protracted and uneven' manner.[18] In some places this process started early; Everton, later a lower middle-class suburb of Liverpool, was a quite exclusive merchants' district at the beginning of the nineteenth century. The desertion of the central area of Manchester by upper middle-class families took place in the 1830s and 40s, even if the process of formation of upper middle-class suburbs took somewhat longer.[19] By the last decades of the century, even county towns such as Lincoln were developing embryonic middle-class areas, though these might only be one street. This of course is crucial: the scale at which one looks for segregation affects the extent to which one finds it; but small areas of exclusivity are not necessarily insignificant.[20] Social segregation was undoubtedly accelerated in those areas where the town centre was becoming increasingly unpleasant to live: manufacturing towns, especially where a lot of pollution was produced, and port towns, where public immorality was a major middle-class fear. An ideology of the domestic undoubtedly helped to popularise the middle-class suburb, but practical concerns were probably uppermost, as the continued residence of the middle class in town centres which remained pleasant indicates. By contrast, there is little evidence to suggest that there was much segregation amongst the broad range of status making up the working class. Instead, they seem to have lived in relatively undifferentiated working-class areas, and to have moved around within these frequently, though there was some segregation by occupation, and by poverty-cycle stage.[21] The lower middle class also seem not to have shown much segregation in choice of housing, certainly before 1900, though London is a notable exception here. The actual social geography of Victorian towns has been described as a 'mosaic', rather than anything more systematised.[22] However, it is clear that there was a widespread contemporary perception that residential segregation by class was unprecedented and growing. Segregation was felt to exacerbate class tensions, and led to a belief that the middle class needed to involve itself more with working-class life, and take a lead in cultural and social initiatives designed to encourage a less divided society.[23]

Social segregation is both an indicator of and a factor in the changes in class relationships evident in Victorian towns. What I want to stress here is the variation in class relationships in different towns. The 'classic' view of urban class relations is based on large manufacturers and their employees; this relationship has been thoroughly investigated, and the various elements of coercion and persuasion in the tactics of both employers and workers have come to light; but even here there is little consensus among historians over the extent of class conflict or collaboration.[24] Moreover, this is not at all representative of the nature of class relationships. Class consciousness did not develop evenly or in similar ways, in different places.[25] Certainly for contemporaries, what mattered for good class relationships was the nature of the relationship between employer and employee, the extent of class segregation, and other ways in which the middle class might demonstrate decent values and ways of life to the working class, such as philanthropy. It has been argued that

> Whether motivated by the duty of wealth, Christianity or liberal principles, the enlightened and locally involved employer was associated with a healthy town in which civic amenities and individual well-being were linked to harmonious social relations and polite civility [26]

It was widely felt that a traditional small employer, who could know his employees individually, and could exercise guidance and supervision over their lives, was ideal, but a large employer could overcome the potential anonymity of his employees by an energetic programme of activities designed to build a relationship between the owner and his workers, as well as encouraging a moral lifestyle among them. It was frequently suggested that the worst situation for class relations was with large but anonymous employers, such as could be found in ports, where hiring was on a casual basis; a Liverpool clergyman in the second half of the nineteenth century drew a contrast between what he saw as the vice-ridden workers of Liverpool, and those of the cotton districts whose employers provided wholesome entertainment in the form of day trips. The absentee employers of Manchester were also criticised.[27]

How far was this the case? Certainly a predominantly casual labour market was associated with poverty, an absence of self-help institutions among the working class, and vices like prostitution and drinking. Whether there was undue class conflict is less clear. After all, unionisation was harder. Similarly, the scale of enterprises does not always seem an important factor, or an easy one to establish absolutely: although there were many similarities between the metal working industries, and their organisation, in Birmingham and Sheffield, they were very different socially and politically.[28] Oldham, which experienced an organised and militant working class in the 1830s, has been seen as both a town with large units of employment and few, aloof employers, and one with relatively small units of employment and higher numbers of masters who were little higher in status and security than their workers.[29] It is, in fact, virtually impossible to generalise about the relationship of class relations with different types of town, or to pin down the variables that determined class relations. Instead, we can restate the point that contemporary observers in the middle class had very clear views about what kind of towns promoted good or bad class relations, and that these views informed their actions as citizens and local leaders.

Certainly, one of the main ways in which people reacted to their changing environment was with fear. Many aspects of the town could be seen as a problem: the pollution, whether industrial or domestic; the overcrowding; the increasing class tensions; the perceived immorality and vice of the working class; the crime; the public health issue. There was a persistent tendency among middle-class commentators to conceptualise all of this as one fundamental problem: the working class. They were immoral, vicious and criminal, and unable to see the merits of the existing social, economic and political order; but they were also overcrowded, subject to pollution and health problems. They needed, therefore, to be improved.[30]

And this problematic urban environment also offered opportunities for the creation of forms of authority and new institutions of power. Historians have recently favoured different concepts when looking at power and authority. The idea of 'governance' has expanded narrow concerns with government to encompass economic and voluntary institutions, as well as culture. New questions are being asked about 'the organisation and legitimisation of authority.'[31] The nineteenth-century town has been seen as the locus of an expanding and changing public sphere, or civil society: that arena of debate and influence that lies between the state and family. This concept has been a favoured one for urban historians in recent years, not least as a means of evaluating how power and authority could be exercised and resisted in urban areas, and in understanding the growth of an ideal of liberal democracy.[32] The nineteenth century saw an enormous expansion in the machinery of local government, the range of charitable organisations, and the number of clubs and societies providing leisure activities. This was matched, of course, by growing numbers of such organisations as trades unions and Friendly Societies. Power and authority in the public sphere were not a matter of a closed elite, but rather were opened up by the growth and increasing complexity of towns. Institutions and organisations were usually, in principle at least, open to all men, and democratic to a certain extent (increasingly so in the case of local government). In addition, expert knowledge, for example of public health, could give a claim to authority, though this was not automatic and had to be fought for in the nineteenth century.[33] Thus the structure of the public sphere was complex and shifting; although it could not be reduced to a simple class structure, class was an important part of it. Class was, in particular, a product of it. Working-class identity could be argued to be most clearly articulated through working-class organisations (though not all of these were formal); and middle-class identity emerged through involvement in voluntary societies and local government. Public sphere organisations also allowed conflict between classes to be managed in some way, and for negotiation to take place. It was as a result of the pressure exercised by working-class and lower middle-class groups that institutions of power and authority had opened up so much more by the end of the nineteenth century.

Voluntary Societies and Civil Society

The voluntary sphere has been identified as a very important part of the nineteenth-century town. It was a means of middle-class formation, a means of promoting a rational, self-reliant citizenship, and a way of attempting to reshape the town in a middle-class vision. It was, moreover, one which had been expanding and changing direction since the end of the eighteenth century. Some towns, of course, had been mere villages in the eighteenth century, and here the Victorian voluntary sphere came from nothing.[34] Voluntary societies were increasingly following the model of the subscriber democracy, and favouring open, transparent proceedings over the more exclusive, even secret patterns of earlier associations.[35] They were also making considerable effort to avoid conflict on party or sectarian lines. Moreover, voluntary activity was diversifying, from the hospital charity and subscription library of the late eighteenth century, to a great profusion of associations, for rational recreation, such as Mechanics' Institutes; campaigning groups, such as anti-slavery societies; missionary societies, welfare organisations, and of course school charities.[36] All of these groups have been described as offering 'a variety of areas of cultural bargaining between classes', along with a variety of styles, from disciplining and coercive, to persuasive and rewarding. Morris argues that the middle-class voluntary sphere could never, therefore, exercise any unified influence over the urban population; however, it did offer an important arena for the negotiation of class relationships, an arena where the parameters were clearly set by the middle class.[37]

The voluntary sphere was more active in some towns than others. To a certain extent, this was a simple function of size; while charity, of varying 'modernity' and organisation, was usually found in some form in most towns, the great scientific and 'improving' organisations were found more frequently, though not exclusively, in large industrial and port towns. In Manchester and Leeds huge ranges of voluntary organisations were set up: scientific, cultural, 'improving', and charitable. However, smaller towns, while not able to cater to such a wide range of interests, could support successful, if not wildly prestigious, scientific societies such as Whitby's Literary and Philosophical Society. The relative size of the middle class in towns was probably an important factor in the extent of the voluntary sphere; Whitby had a large population of retired professionals, whereas places like Middlesbrough, some Black Country towns, and Grimsby, where the middle class was small and quite undifferentiated, had few societies, or at least developed them later.[38]

Of course, the voluntary sphere was not exclusively middle-class, for there were many working-class organisations as well, predominantly of the friendly society type; but they were smaller (though more numerous) and much less wealthy, with premises in pubs rather than imposing building increasingly occupied by the middle-class societies. In the second half of the nineteenth century, though, the working class gained control of a number of middle-class founded organisations, such as temperance, adult education, and working men's clubs.

There is no doubt that many of the middle class felt that many of the functions now undertaken by local government, not only could be done by voluntary effort, but were actually better done that way. Voluntary effort produced independent, self-reliant citizens, whereas relying on local government led to high rates, indolent citizens, and a 'something for nothing' culture. Voluntary effort allowed a remarkably wide range of services and cultural opportunities to be provided, without undue expansion of government, or undermining of the idea of *laissez-faire*. Moreover, in many ways it set the pattern for the later expansion in municipal activity. The salient characteristics of voluntary activity in the first half of the nineteenth century have been clearly established. Societies were transparent and public: anyone could join, upon payment of the subscription – there was a conscious attempt to move away from more exclusive types of membership; and proceedings were publicly reported, accounts were audited, in a display of rectitude. Such societies were also deeply hierarchical, in a way that has been seen as a codification of the urban middle-class pecking order, with local aristocratic figures frequently taking a patron role, and leading figures from the professions, manufacturing and commerce becoming officers of the society. The hierarchical pattern extended through the membership, with the public recording of subscriptions, and the link that was sometimes established between the level of subscription, and privileges such as nominating patients to a hospital.[39] This can be read as a process of middle-class formation whereby values of non-exclusivity, rationalism, and the benefits and responsibilities of wealth were promoted by an elite who exercised considerable influence over the rest by these very acts of social responsibility, and through their contact with the aristocracy. However, the voluntary sphere was undoubtedly also very important in attempting to manage the relationship between the middle classes and the working classes.[40] This, of course, was one of the central aims of many societies, those concerned with charity, medical and educational provision particularly. These frequently distinguished between the deserving and the undeserving, and attempted to instil particular patterns of behaviour and values in the working class. The effectiveness of these very specific campaigns may be doubted; however, it has also been argued that the mere presence of a healthy voluntary sphere, as part of a range of agencies in the new urban environment, acted to decrease   the likelihood of conflict.[41] Again, though, the main effect of voluntary organisations and institutions designed to improve the working class may have been to constitute 'an arena of cultural contest and inter-class bargaining.'[42] In the second half of the nineteenth century, especially in the biggest towns and cities, a new wave of clubs was more concerned with middle-class culture and sociability than with the working class.[43]

The Expansion of Local Government

The development of local government was clearly of crucial significance in the shaping of the urban environment. An important question is how far local government took on the roles of voluntary societies in the areas of mediating class tensions and other social relationships. The Victorian period saw a sizeable revaluation of the role of local government, moving from an ideal of small government, to one of 'municipal socialism'[44] in some places, although a variety of attitudes could be found at any one time. Nevertheless, in all towns local government was playing a much greater role in shaping the urban environment by the early twentieth century, than it had been at the start of Victoria's reign. Certainly, municipal bureaucracies expanded enormously.[45] This expansion of local government had not been uncontested, and it went much further in some places than others; yet overall tackled the worst urban problems and provided the most vital services by 1914. The Municipal Corporation Act of 1835 eradicated closed corporations, allowed Non-conformists to serve, and reformed the franchise for municipal elections, allowing a new municipal elite to emerge. However, incorporation might not happen for some time; among Trainor's Black Country towns it ranged from 1848 for Wolverhampton to 1882 for West Bromwich.[46] In many places the immediate post-reform councils were Liberal, with a significant Non-conformist element, and showed a determination to distance themselves from what they saw as the prodigal, verging on corrupt, high living of the old corporations: selling off their plate, robes, and wine cellars.[47] However, there was little innovative action in new spheres of urban life from these new councils. Growing urban problems of public health, crime and unrest were important as impetus for councils to take on new powers for themselves, through the means of individual acts of Parliament; and in turn, their growing power and resources attracted a broader range of the middle class to seek municipal office. Additionally, while an important trend was to unite powers in the council, a tendency to fragmentation was also obvious and persistent.[48]

    Participation in local government, especially the council where this existed, was an overwhelmingly middle-class affair for the greater part of the nineteenth century, though some working men were starting to appear by 1900. Among the middle class, participation was spread through all groups and status levels.[49] Different middle-class groups participated; in fact, control of the council could be a major point of conflict between these different groups. Overall, lower-middle and middle-middle class groups probably formed the majority of councillors.[50] However, not infrequently, political leaders in towns were the same people who dominated economically, socially and culturally. It has been argued that in such cases, the reinforcing spheres of authority created an urban elite with a similar ability to exercise authority as rural gentry: Garrard's urban squirearchy had an impressive sphere of influence, but nevertheless were constrained by several factors.[51] In Birmingham the social status of councillors increased in the second half of the nineteenth century, and could genuinely be described as an elite group; whereas in Leeds, the social status of councillors fell. This can probably be linked to the prestige and activity of council.[52] Participation in this level of government did not necessarily bring prestige and authority; in Lincoln on occasion it led to death threats – a somewhat extreme example, but defeat by ratepayer lobbies was a distinct possibility. However, the alleged withdrawal of the middle-class elite from local government at the end of the nineteenth century is a hotly disputed point. As Trainor shows, some of the very highest status were living well outside the town boundaries by this point; but equally, many were not.[53] It is also true to say for a town like Lincoln that the wealthiest manufacturers were seeking involvement in national politics at the end of the Victorian period. Nevertheless, this was a far from total withdrawal, even by 1914; and even a small number of high-status councillors could exercise disproportionate authority and leadership.[54]

Birmingham tends to be seen as the clearest example of a new ethos in local government; after a slow start it enthusiastically embraced a number of new roles and responsibilities, and notably espoused a grandiose style for public buildings and rhetoric. It was compared both to medieval Florence, and the city states of medieval Belgium and Germany.[55] It was not the only one, though; Liverpool councillors referred to their city as a modern Tyre, and spoke of the improvements they could make to its fabric. Even Mile End Old Town's vestry hall in east London, built in 1860, had 'more the air of an Italian city state than a nineteenth-century parochial building in the East End of London'.[56] However, there were enormous differences in the wealth, powers, activities and participants in local government across England; for every example of a 'civic gospel', there was a town where even basic sanitation was provided late and grudgingly. In Lincoln, for example, a proper sewerage system was not begun until 1876; there was no borough rate until 1874.[57]

Although the improvement of public health was the most important and expensive task facing councils, the organisation of consent was also crucial, as can be seen by the various expressions of civic pride by local governments.[58] The building of a new town hall was a fairly widespread manifestation of a new conception of local government, whose symbolism has been shown to celebrate local self-government and supposedly ancient traditions.[59] In some cases, especially in the largest towns and cities, the town hall became the centrepiece in a new civic complex, with further improvements focussing on opening up broad avenues through the urban sprawl, and hiding slums behind new facades lining shopping streets.[60] However, many towns did not rebuild their town hall in the nineteenth century; some embarked on elaborate plans, but never brought the project to fruition.

Throughout the period, municipal energy and activity varied; there was a constant tension between a municipal expansion lobby, and a sometimes equally vociferous municipal economy lobby. The balance between these two lobbies was the result of a very complex mix of factors. The size of a town did have some effect; the scale of urban problems could force early action on large towns. Liverpool, the second largest city in England, was the first to appoint a full-time Medical Officer of Health. Income and wealth was another, related, crucial variable. Some towns were very dependent on rates whereas others had other sources of revenue meaning they did not have to burden rate payers; Briggs singles out Bristol and Liverpool, towns with additional revenue from their ports, as particularly wealthy municipalities. The desire for extra revenue could actually drive the expansion of local government, as the municipalisation of gas, water, electricity and trams was often undertaken in order to relieve pressure on the rates.[61] Population rises seem to have strained local government resources without providing concomitant rises in rates revenue. The major provincial industrial towns spent the most per pound of rateable value – and therefore relied most heavily on trading profits and estate income.[62]

Some of the increase in local government was of course a result of central government imposition, but the strong belief in local autonomy and the benefits of voluntary provision meant there was as little of this as possible. Certainly, cultural initiatives by local government were overwhelmingly discretionary.

The improved fabric of the town centre became the setting for more widespread civic ritual. This was a further attempt by elites to draw on symbolic resources to create legitimacy and consent; but such symbolic practices, as Vernon has shown, could be used both 'from above' and 'from below', and in fact became the subject of a contest over the meaning and extent of local government, and even of the town itself.[63] They were aimed at the town's population as a whole, and might actually involve a fairly broad range of social groups, though hierarchies would usually be clearly signalled, indeed actually performed, in, for example, the order in which groups such as friendly societies marched in processions.[64] The 1850s and 60s has been identified as the point where civic ceremonial was increasing fastest, as a result, it is argued, of the changes which had taken place in local government over the preceding twenty or thirty years, and the consequent need for relatively new institutions to legitimate themselves with invented traditions that appropriated the authority of the past.[65] Yet there was not just the invocation of historical, traditional sources of prestige; large industrial cities also portrayed themselves as progressive, scientific and democratic, and stressed their defence of local autonomy against the centralising state.[66]

It is worth paying some attention to the way in which both the new civic spaces and the civic rituals that were intended to legitimate the new institutions of local government were contested. The rhetoric of civic pride set great store by the universal benefits brought to the town by the council; it addressed a constituency of the whole town. This made it hard to dismiss the calls of working men's groups out of hand. Labour groups' participation in processions indicated their presence in, and rights to, public space and public debate.[67] It also detracted from the display of authority in elite rituals.

Finally, it is worth examining the ways in which more informal social relationships, in addition to local government, associational culture, and changing spatial patterns, affected the social and cultural fabric of the Victorian town. In particular, it has been argued that new and distinctive patterns of consumption emerged in major towns and cities in the second half of the nineteenth century. Reconstruction in urban centres was not just to create civic spaces and to cleanse and modernise, but also for new places of consumption. New shopping streets, larger stores including department stores, and arcades, all became features of larger towns, and came to be seen as one of the principal attractions of such towns.[68] Public middle-class leisure was increasingly accessed by cash payment,

> reflecting a shift from a culture predicated on relatively small elites
> and personal acquaintance to the more anonymous pubic world and
> social relationships of the mid-Victorian city.[69]

New forms of commercial and informal leisure encouraged people to display or perform their social identity, and to give and receive confirmation of such identities. This has been observed, both among the bourgeois elite of Manchester, and among the primarily lower middle-class music hall audiences of London. The extent to which the new commercial and leisure spaces of the town also allowed for a respectable, female, public identity has also been investigated.[70] The social uncertainties of the later nineteenth-century urban environment could be resolved, to a certain extent, by an emphasis on stylised, visual ways of affirming collective identities; but this emphasis on the stylised and visual could also be a means to play with social uncertainties. It is clear, however, that public spaces and public consumption of leisure, started to take on a quite different set of meanings around 1880.

In conclusion, then, social, political and cultural relationships changed in the nineteenth-century town along with the physical environment. By 1914, municipal museums, along with parks, art galleries, libraries, baths and schools, were increasingly features of local government provision, overlaying a still important network of voluntary associations, charities, pressure groups and cultural organisations. The extent of change varied dramatically from town to town, though, and it would be overly simplistic to see these organisations and provision as being solely created in order to 'reform' the working class, although many commentators felt that opportunities to broaden the mind, to experience civilised leisure, and to avoid the temptations of the pub were absolutely necessary. Additionally, it seems that elites used such initiatives to try and take control of the popular symbolism of the town to win the support of a broad constituency, as Vernon has indicated. However, it is also the case that much middle-class activity in towns was about themselves as much as about the working class: they were creating an image for themselves, substantially for their own consumption, as responsible, cultured leaders, and contrasting themselves with a working class they needed to believe were uncivilised, ignorant and feckless, though capable of improvement. In addition, in a variety of ways they were using the spaces and institutions of the town to build their collective identity through stylised leisure, the performance of cultural capital, and to show off their persons. Whether they were trying to shape themselves or the working class, though, and of course these two aims are to a certain extent inextricable, they were not acting alone. It is important not just to look at the actions of those in power in transforming the Victorian town, but to see also the ways in which their actions were constrained by conflict with other groups whose access to power and the public sphere may have been less, but who nevertheless could and did oppose the policies of the elite; and who could stage equally convincing displays of their collective identities, or even undermine the whole idea of stable collective identities. It has been said that the public sphere is

> the setting where cultural and ideological contest or negotiation
> among a variety of groups takes place, rather than the spontaneous
> and class-specific achievement of the bourgeoisie.[71]

In this context, municipal museums, along with other organisations such as voluntary societies and municipal buildings, need to be seen not just as the objects of conflict and negotiation, but as part of the mechanics of conflict and negotiation, which was channelled, shaped and made safe by such institutions.

Notes

[1] F. M. L. Thompson, 'Town and City' in F. M. L. Thompson (ed), *The Cambridge Social History of Britain 1750-1950, Vol. 1: Regions and Communities*, (Cambridge 1990), pp. 8-10.

[2] Thompson points out just how small some towns could be, even by 1901: Thompson, 'Town and City', pp. 4-5.

[3] Asa Briggs, *Victorian Cities*, (Harmondsworth 1990), p. 30.

[4] Peter Borsay, *The English Urban Renaissance: Culture and Society in the Provincial Town, 1660-1770*, (Oxford 1989).

[5] Thompson suggests urban growth was indirectly dependent on industrialisation: Thompson, 'Town and City', p. 9.

[6] Thompson, 'Town and City', pp. 2-3; Richard H. Trainor, *Black Country Elites: The Exercise of Authority in an Industrialized Area 1830-1900*, (Oxford 1993), p. 30.

[7] Briggs, *Victorian City*, p. 33.

[8] J. K. Walton, 'The North-West', in F. M. L. Thompson (ed), *The Cambridge Social History of Britain 1750-1950, Vol. 1: Regions and Communities*, (Cambridge 1990), p. 362

[9] Patrick Joyce, *Work, Society and Politics, The Culture of the Factory in Later Victorian England*, (London 1980), p. 108.

[10] *Ibid.*, p.104.

[11] 'Gentility', by about 1800, was largely about cultural comsumption, not birth, and required arenas such as walks, assembly rooms and theatres, to display dress and accoutrements, and promote civilised intercourse. In the eighteenth century there was an 'explosion in the demand for, and provision of publicly available, high-status leisure' in provincial towns such as Preston, with its Avenham Walk. Borsay, *English Urban Renaissance*, pp. 117, 162, 267.

[12] N. Kirk, *The Growth of Working-Class Reformism in Mid-Victorian England*, (London 1985), p. 49.

[13] Thompson, 'Town and City', pp. 29-30; see also Borsay, *English Urban Renaissance*, chapters 5 and 6.

[14] Thompson, 'Town and City', pp. 32, 44.

[15] P. J. Waller, *Town, City and Nation, England 1850-1914*, (Oxford 1983), p. 137

[16] R. J. Morris, 'The Middle Class and British Towns and Cities of the Industrial Revolution, 1780-1870', in D. Fraser and A. Sutcliffe (eds), *The Pursuit of Urban History*, (London 1983), p. 289.

[17] Kate Hill, 'The middle classes in Victorian Lincoln', in Andrew Walker (ed) *Aspects of Lincoln*, (Barnsley 2001).

[18] Simon Gunn, *The Public Culture of the Victorian Middle Class: Ritual and Authority and the English Industrial City*, (Manchester 2000), p. 38.

[19] Simon Gunn, 'The Middle Class, Modernity and the Provincial City: Manchester c. 1840-1880', in A. Kidd and D. Nicholls (eds), *Gender, Civic Culture and Consumerism, Middle-Class Identity in Britain 1800-1940*, (Manchester 1999), pp. 114-5; see also Briggs, *Victorian Cities*, p. 27.

[20] Trainor, *Black Country Elites*, p. 56. For Lincoln, see Hill, 'The Middle Classes in Victorian Lincoln', p. 97; and Dennis Mills and Michael Edgar, 'Social history in Lincoln's Victorian residential streets', *Local Population Studies Society Newsletter* 27 (September 2000), pp. 4-10.

[21] Thompson, 'Town and City', p. 61.

[22] Thompson, 'Town and City', p. 62.

[23] H. E. Meller, *Leisure and the Changing City, 1870-1914*, (London 1976), p. 15; Thompson, 'Town and City', p. 58. See also Donna Loftus, 'Industrial conciliation, class co-operation and the urban landscape in mid-Victorian England' in R. J. Morris and R. H. Trainor (eds), *Urban Governance: Britain and Beyond since 1750*, (Aldershot 2000), p. 186.

[24] A. Howe, *The Cotton Masters 1830-1860*, (Oxford 1984), chapter 5; Joyce, *Work, Society and Politics*; Kirk, *Working-Class Reformism*; H. I. Dutton and J. E. King, 'The Limits of Paternalism: the cotton tyrants of North Lancashire 1836-54', *Social History* 7, 1 (1982).

[25] John Foster, 'Nineteenth-century towns – a class dimension', in H. J. Dyos (ed), *The Study of Urban History*, (London 1968).

[26] Loftus, 'Industrial conciliation', p. 185.

[27] Walton and Wilcox (eds), *Low Life and Moral Improvement in Mid-Victorian England: Liverpool Through the Journalism of Hugh Shimmin*, (London 1991), p. 180; Loftus, 'Industrial conciliation', p. 185.

[28] Briggs, *Victorian Cities*, pp. 36-7; Dennis Smith, *Conflict and Compromise: Class Formation in English Society 1830-1914*, (London 1982).

[29] Foster, 'Nineteenth-century towns'; D. S. Gadian, 'Class consciousness in Oldham and other north-west industrial towns, 1830-50', in R. J. Morris and R. Rodger (eds) *The Victorian City: A Reader in British Urban History 1820-1914*, (London 1993).

[30] But see Trainor, *Black Country Elites*, p. 134, for a reminder that many values, assumptions and traditions were shared by both middle and working classes.

[31] R. J. Morris, 'Governance: two centuries of urban growth', in Morris and Trainor (eds) *Urban Governance*, (Aldershot 2000), p. 1.

[32] See for example R. J. Morris, 'Civil society and the nature of urbanism: Britain, 1750-1850', *Urban History* 25, 3 (1998); this issue as a whole is devoted to the question of civil society.

[33] Morris, 'Governance', p. 9.

[34] Trainor, *Black Country Elites*, p. 93.

[35] R. J. Morris, 'Clubs, societies and associations', in F. M. L. Thompson (ed), *The Cambridge Social History of Britain 1750-1950*, Vol. 3, (Cambridge 1990), p. 406.

[36] *Ibid.*, pp. 409-412.

[37] *Ibid.*, p. 416.

[38] Briggs, *Victorian Cities*, pp. 255-6; P. J. Shinner, 'The Exercise of Power in Nineteenth Century Britain: The Case of Grimsby 1840-1900' (unpublished PhD thesis, University of Lincolnshire and Humberside 2001) p. 9; Trainor, *Black Country Elites*, pp. 312-3. Trainor makes the point that voluntary societies and organised philanthropy appeared in response to social unrest in the 1840s, and a growing sense of civic identity.

[39] R. J. Morris, *Class, Sect and Party, The Making of the British Middle Class: Leeds 1820-1850*, (Manchester 1990), pp. 184-6, 281.

[40] Morris, *Class, Sect and Party*, pp. 232-3, 241.

[41] R. J. Morris, 'Civil society', p. 296.

[42] Martin Hewitt, *The Emergence of Stability in the Industrial City: Manchester, 1832-67*, (Aldershot 1996), p.123; R. J. Morris and R. Rodger, 'An introduction to British urban history, 1820-1914', in Morris and Rodger (eds) *The Victorian City*, (London 1993)p. 30.

[43] Gunn, *Public Culture*, chapter 4.

[44] So-called; as Waller says, this could perhaps be more accurately called municipal capitalism, apart from a few tentative beginnings in social housing. Waller, *Town*, p. 300.

[45] Morris, 'Governance', p. 4; Irene Maver, 'The role and influence of Glasgow's municipal managers, 1890s-1930s', in Trainor and Morris (eds) *Urban Governance,* (Aldershot 2000).

[46] Trainor, *Black Country Elites,* p. 233.

[47] D. Fraser, *Urban Politics in Victorian England: The Structure of Politics in Victorian Cities,* (London 1976), p. 124.

[48] Morris, 'Governance', p. 6; Mike Goldsmith and John Garrard, 'Urban governance: some reflections', in Trainor and Morris (eds) *Urban Governance,* (Aldershot 2000), pp. 16-7.

[49] Trainor, *Black Country Elites,* p. 98.

[50] Thompson, 'Town and City', p. 69.

[51] John Garrard, 'Urban elites 1850-1914: the rule and decline of a new squirearchy', *Albion* 27, 3 (1995), pp. 590-2.

[52] E. P. Hennock, *Fit and Proper Persons: Ideal and Reality in Nineteenth-Century Urban Government,* (London 1973), Book 1 chapter 1, and Book 2 chapter 2.

[53] Trainor, *Black Country Elites,* p. 109, 111; R. H. Trainor, 'The 'decline' of British urban governance since 1850: a reassessment', in Trainor and Morris (eds) *Urban Governance,* (Aldershot 2000), p. 33.

[54] Hill, 'The middle classes in Victorian Lincoln', p. 93; Thompson, 'Town and City', p. 69.

[55] R. Hartnell, 'Art and civic culture in Birmingham in the late nineteenth century', *Urban History* 22:2 (1995), p. 231; Joseph Chamberlain quoted in B. I. Coleman (ed), *The Idea of the City in Nineteenth-Century Britain,* (London 1973), p. 160.

[56] James Vernon, *Politics and the People: A Study in English Political Culture c.1815-1867,* (Cambridge 1993), p. 53.

[57] Hill, 'The middle classes in Victorian Lincoln', p. 93.

[58] Robert Millward, 'Urban government, finance and public health in Victorian Britain', in Trainor and Morris (eds) *Urban Governance,* (Aldershot 2000), p. 50.

[59] Vernon, *Politics and the People,* p. 54.

[60] Gunn, *Public Culture,* pp. 50-2.

[61] Briggs, *Victorian Cities,* p. 39; Millward, 'Urban government', p.55.

[62] Millward, 'Urban government', pp. 48-9; but Briggs argues the opposite: *Victorian Cities,* p. 40. See also Millward p. 61.

[63] Vernon, *Politics and the People,* p. 49; see also Kate Hill, '"Thoroughly Embued with the Spirit of Ancient Greece": symbolism and space in Victorian Civic Culture', in A. Kidd and D. Nicholls (eds) *Gender, Civic Culture and Consumerism, Middle-Class Identity in Britain 1800-1940,* (Manchester 1999), p. 108.

[64] Gunn, 'Ritual and civic culture in the English industrial city, c. 1835-1914', in Trainor and Morris (eds) *Urban Governance,* (Aldershot 2000), pp. 231-2.

[65] Vernon, *Politics and the People,* p. 63.

[66] Gunn, 'Ritual and civic culture', p. 230.

[67] Vernon, *Politics and the People,* p. 77.

[68] Gunn, 'The Middle Class, Modernity, and the Provincial City', p. 117.

[69] Gunn, *Public Culture,* p. 29.

[70] Gunn, *Public Culture,* pp. 75-6.; Judith Walkowitz, *City of Dreadful Delight: Narratives of Sexual Danger in Late Victorian London,* (London 1992), especially chapter 2; Peter Bailey, *Popular Culture and Performance in the Victorian City,* (Cambridge 1998), pp. 8-9.

[71] Geoff Eley, 'Nations, Publics and Political Cultures: Placing Habermas in the nineteenth century', in Dirks, Eley and Ortner (eds) *Culture/Power/History,* (Princeton, New Jersey 1994), p. 310.

CHAPTER THREE

The Public Museum in the Nineteenth Century

In 1888, Thomas Greenwood, admittedly an apologist for rate-supported museums, wrote

> Museums and Picture Galleries belong to the nation, and not to only a portion of it.... For vigour and usefulness there are no museums throughout the entire country which compare at all favourably with those which are the property of the citizens, and under the control of their duly elected representatives.[1]

Although he was undoubtedly making a case for greater financial support and increased scope for municipal museums, he was also describing the existing situation accurately. In the 1880s, a report by the British Association for the Advancement of Science looked at 211 provincial museums in England, Ireland, Scotland and Wales, nearly one hundred of which had been opened in the preceding 16 years. Of the 159 museums in England, 45 were rate-supported. Meanwhile 17 were supported by universities and colleges, 49 by local societies and institutes, and four by central government (this does not include the London museums). 68 offered free admission daily, with the rest either offering some free days in the week, or charging a standard admission fee.[2] The model of the free, rate-supported museum was undoubtedly an extremely, and increasingly, influential one.

Museums became public in the full sense of the word in the nineteenth century: committed to universal access, often free or with low admission charges, increasingly owned and administered by local or national government, and offering at least some opening hours accessible to all. This resulted from a greatly altered view of what a museum was or should be for, what it could offer to society, and who could benefit from it. The change may be attributed to the social and economic developments of the period, some of which were outlined in the last chapter; but the view of culture as determined by society and economy is hard to sustain in the context of historiographical change in the last decade. Culture has been shown to have a much more active, determining role, not just holding a mirror up to society, but with an ability to shape both economic and social activities.

It is my argument that although the new public museum was partly developed, predominantly by the middle class, as a cultural asset for the improvement of the working class, it was equally part of a reorganisation of urban cultural provision which allowed the middle class to demonstrate authority, stamp their own values onto culture, and provide suitable leisure for themselves. It also demonstrates the increasingly complex and sophisticated nature of cultural production in the Victorian city.

Working-class improvement has generally been viewed as the most important motive for the development of public museums, as opposed to their predecessors which were private, exclusive and devoted to displaying the taste and wealth of their owners. Both Eilean Hooper-Greenhill and Tony Bennett interpret public museums, starting with the Louvre, as primarily designed to exercise power over the visitor, who is no longer a specially invited member of the elite, but a member of the general public.[3] Hooper-Greenhill sees the change in aim and outlook of museums, from private to public, and from exclusive to aimed at the population as a whole, as being very abrupt, and precipitated by the French Revolution. Museums swiftly became democratically orientated and committed to public service. They utilised disciplinary technologies to transform visitors, by educating them for 'the collective good of the state rather than for the benefit of individual knowledge.'[4] Staff became more specialised, the way they presented their exhibits became more didactic, and security and surveillance became more prominent to safeguard treasures now exposed to anyone who wished to see them. The birth of the public museum, then, in both these arguments, comes about because of the need that governments of modern populations had to harness a much wider variety of institutions and types of power to the task of governing.

There is undoubtedly much in this argument, though it is usually put forward as a broad, even schematic, overview where many of the details are still unclear. However, there was another motive for the development of public museums, which has been neglected. While the improvement of the working class was a very important justification for the spending of money on public institutions, and public museums could be said to have been conceived as part of the task of producing and governing modern populations; these institutions actually served an important role for the middle class, who by and large had control of them, especially in the provinces. By creating and dominating a new type of culture, they created for themselves an arena for the establishment and consolidation of cultural identity and values, as well as allowing them to develop markers for hierarchy and authority within the class. A process whereby the emergent middle classes gain a toehold in an aspect of culture, then transform it and finally are able to dominate the transformed activity and its institutions, is emerging for science, the art market, and classical music concerts. It seems to have begun first in science, which was more open to the middle-class elites of Manchester and Leeds, from about 1780, although there was a decline in the middle of the nineteenth century.[5] An increasing body of work on middle-class art patrons indicates that initially they were uncertain, and felt they had to follow aristocratic patrons in looking for Old Masters, though they were ridiculed for ending up with rubbish. However, they rapidly gained confidence and developed a taste for innovative art, becoming the major supporters of the British School in the century.[6] This allowed them to become important private and public patrons, and gave them cultural prestige and authority, even fame. Simon Gunn's examination of the Halle orchestra concerts in Manchester in the second half of the nineteenth century suggests that the development of this new institution was used as a tool to demarcate and represent status levels and hierarchies among the middle class.[7] It seems that the higher ranks of the provincial middle class particularly managed to transform, or at least rival older, aristocratic cultural forms and institutions.[8] A worthwhile comparison can be made here with the provincial art museums of France, studied by Daniel Sherman. The origins of such museums lay in the central government's decision to circulate art around the provinces, suggesting that public museums were called into being to help with the task of producing and governing a modern population. However, fairly swiftly these museums came to be dominated by the provincial bourgeois elite, and became exclusive. They increasingly worked to distinguish these elites from the rest of the population, and to legitimise and naturalise their power, partly by associating them with earlier elites.[9]

In this chapter I trace the development of public museums from the beginnings of change early in the nineteenth century to the foundation of several municipal museums after 1850, examining the tension between attempts to improve the working class, to defend older cultural traditions and institutions, and to create a new arena for middle-class cultural authority. There are several themes which will run through this overview. How were allegedly *laissez-faire* governments and councils persuaded to fund museums and art galleries? What were the motives of those who were closely involved in the creation or transformation of museums in the nineteenth century? What did they think a museum should be, and why? Was the changing nature of the museum associated with wider changes in the nature of cultural production?

There were public museums in Britain before the Louvre was transformed in revolutionary France. The Ashmolean opened in 1683, and anyone could visit, for a small fee. It was owned and run by the University of Oxford. The British Museum was created by an Act of Parliament in 1753. Although admission was free, it took considerable persistence to gain entry; prospective visitors had to come back several times for an appointment, and give details of their name, address and condition. Both these museums, although relatively freely open to the public, conformed to the dominant idea of a museum as an elite specialist resource, intended for gentlemen scientists - or at least men from the older professions - and were not designed to cater for the layman or hold large numbers of people. They were very similar to the majority of smaller, privately owned museums in the country, such as the museum of the Spalding Gentlemen's Society, or that of Charles Lennox, Duke of Richmond, or the second Duchess of Portland. Both of these latter could be visited by friends or scholars.[10] They were not the only type of museum to be found around 1800; there were a number of highly successful commercial museums, such as that of William Bullock, who, although quite an eminent naturalist, relied heavily on spectacle and showmanship to draw large numbers to his 'Egyptian Museum', which at various times was based in Liverpool and London.[11] Smaller concerns came and went more rapidly, and overlapped with other spectacles such as panoramas and waxworks. Clearly, this is all a long way removed from the concept of a public, educational museum.

By the late eighteenth and early nineteenth centuries, access to culture was undergoing a structural change. High culture had been an aristocratic preserve, based on patronage; but already in the eighteenth century, the growing size and disposable income of the middle classes was introducing the market into cultural transactions. Nevertheless, access to culture was still policed as far as possible, and tended to be seen as only for those who had an existing level of knowledge, sensibility and refinement. Although the amateur ideal was starting to be undermined in science, in art it still held strong; only a gentleman could be a connoisseur. The important quality for connoisseurs was polite taste, a concept which can be seen as a 'vocabulary of exclusion', in John Barrell's phrase.[12] In the early nineteenth century, Hazlitt was one of the most prominent exponents of this view, although using a Romantic vocabulary of sublime sensibility, arguing that 'The principle of universal suffrage, however applicable to matters of government, …, is by no means applicable to matters of taste, which can only be decided upon by the more refined understandings.'[13] Although commercial and aesthetic awareness could peacefully co-exist by 1800, and the polite audience had been redefined to include the upper middle class, a new tension was introduced with ideas flowing from the political revolutions of the eighteenth century. This suggested that culture was concerned with universal human truths, and that all people were capable of discerning these truths. There was no inherent limit to the ability to benefit from culture, merely limitations imposed by lack of access and education. So while in the mid-eighteenth century, the Earl of Shaftesbury claimed that aesthetic perception could only be achieved in polite culture, and towards the end of that century Adam Smith argued that luxuries like art were good for the economy, in 1800, Wordsworth could write that 'the poet binds together by passion and knowledge the vast empire of human society, as it is spread over the whole earth, and over all time.'[14]

Art and science were claimed to have transcendent qualities at the same time as the middle class was drawing them ever more closely into an industrial economy. By the beginning of the Victorian period, culture was viewed not just as something which offered transcendent possibilities to all mankind, but as a useful, even essential, attribute of a nation, in terms of morals, education, and patriotism. This view was particularly strong among political liberals and radicals of the middle-class. For example, *Douglas Jerrold's Penny Magazine*, with a lower middle-class readership, called in 1847 for the democratisation of fine art, as did others of the 'demotic press'.[15]

The National Gallery was founded in the 1820s, by which time there were already at least two picture galleries open to the public, the Dulwich Picture Gallery and Sir John Fleming Leicester's collection. Other European capitals such as Vienna and Paris had had public art galleries for several decades by this point.[16] When John Julius Angerstein's collection came up for sale, in 1824, the government bought it for £57,000, with more enthusiasm than it had shown for state involvement in culture hitherto. The Chancellor of the Exchequer said, 'It appears to be consistent with the true dignity of a great nation, and with the liberal spirit of a free people, to give a munificent encouragement to the support and promotion of Fine Art', and the Commons was strongly in favour too.[17] This was not necessarily as innovative as it seemed; it was very much in line with the prevailing attitude towards culture and national pride; Britain had to have a national picture collection, just as it had to have the Elgin Marbles, to prove its place in the world. Significantly, this government enthusiasm did not go any further, towards the new ideals of education and moral improvement that were beginning to surface in the Mechanics' Institutes. It has been commented that in the 1820s, the House of Commons 'had no intention of involving itself heavily in an ongoing commitment to foster culture.'[18] The infant National Gallery was neglected, inadequately housed, and effectively ruled by the British Museum into the 1830s, when its situation started to improve. From 1838 it had a large new building in Trafalgar Square, though shared with the Royal Academy and Public Record Office; it gradually developed its own Board of Trustees; and a new attitude towards it, a new expectation of its function, was visible in the government. This is summed up in Sir Robert Peel's statement that '[t]he erection of the edifice [the new National Gallery building] would not only contribute to the cultivation of the arts, but also to the cementing of the bonds of union between the richer and poorer orders of the state.'[19] That this new role for the Gallery was not without its dangers and ambivalences has been demonstrated by Colin Trodd, who shows that at the same time as the National Gallery was re-imagined from the 1830s as a public space for social improvement, the possible consequences of so public a space were causing concern. By around 1850, complaints about the use of the gallery by wet nurses, idlers, and 'the unwashed' were increasing, and ideas about the transformative capability of the gallery were less in evidence.[20] Already, it seems, the high idealism of the 1830s was waning.

Nevertheless, the universality of culture, and the perfectibility of mankind, became a rallying cry for a group of middle-class radicals in the 1830s and 40s. These were men, mostly MPs, such as William Ewart, Benjamin Hawes, James Silk Buckingham and Joseph Brotherton, broadly from an upper-middle-class background, with a bias towards manufacturing and commerce, the north of England, and Dissent. Their decision to support state initiatives in culture, instead of seeing them as a distraction from the urgent needs of the poor for better housing and sanitation, forms a crucial indication of how attitudes to culture were to change. The 1830s and 40s are a critical period for several reasons: the impetus given by the political reforms of the 30s; the growing awareness of superior practice in other countries, especially France; and the acute social tension of the period.[21] This period was one of significant reform initiatives in education, science and culture.[22] However, important as these initiatives were in articulating a new agenda, their actual impact should not be overstated.

In the provinces a change of attitude was also evident, in the so-called 'Rational Recreation' movement. This produced workplace facilities, as well as educational and leisure facilities such as Mechanics' Institutes and Lyceums. However, it is clear that initiatives intended for the benefit of the public as a whole could easily become exclusively middle-class; parks, Mechanics' Institutes, and exhibitions, to take some examples, were either situated in middle-class areas, or imposed *de facto* restriction through dress code or price, or offered events that the working class could not or would not appreciate.[23] One of the greatest hindrances to the success of rational recreation was the reluctance of the majority of the middle class to have anything to do with it. They were disinclined to support such initiatives financially, or to act as superintendents of working-class behaviour.[24]

Not all of this, though, was imposed from above; Mechanics' Institutes in the north became the centre of vigorous natural history activity which seems to have been the result of working-class enthusiasm and work. The Institutes in towns such as Keighley, Bradford and Manchester had museums formed from their members' collecting activity.[25] It has been argued that 'there can be little doubt that these enterprises and the great success of the Mechanics' Institution exhibitions were an important contribution in developing public opinion towards local museums.'[26] These initiatives, then, though often lumped together, in fact represent a mixture of aims and influences; while the rhetoric of Rational Recreation initiatives stressed the overcoming of class divisions, to the benefit of the working class, class groupings were just as prominent in them, if not more so, than in less rational forms of leisure.

A number of Parliamentary committees discussed issues relating to the public provision of culture in the 1830s and 40s. The first of these was the Committee on Drunkenness of 1834, which recommended

> the establishment by the joint aid of the local authorities and residents on the spot, of public walks and gardens, or open spaces for healthy and athletic exercises in the open air, in the immediate vicinity of every town, of an extent and character adapted to its population; and of district and parish libraries, museums and reading rooms, accessible at the lowest rate of charge, so as to admit of one or the other being visited in any weather, and at any time.[27]

This was followed by the Select Committee on Arts and Manufactures, in 1835-6, on which radical and industrial interests were well represented, which produced an equally innovative and wide-ranging set of recommendations for a proper system of state-funded design education oriented towards manufacture and working men; the main proposal, Schools of Design, was realised, with the Central School of Design being set up under the Board of Trade in 1837. Provincial Schools of Design were created in the 1840s, on the principle that Parliament matched local fundraising. They were, however, criticised for focussing on fine art, and being controlled from London.[28]

The Select Committee on Fine Arts of 1841, which led to the Royal Commission on Fine Arts, was appointed to decide how the interior of the new Houses of Parliament should be decorated; but its membership overlapped with that of the 1835-6 Committee, and it was primarily concerned that the programme of decoration contribute to raising national standards of art and design. The Select Committee on National Monuments and Works of Art of 1841 collected evidence concerning the use and popularity of places such as museums, cathedrals and palaces like Hampton Court; its report seemed to offer 'detailed proof that art was increasing its hold on the affections of the British people', and, more importantly, that it was safe to let the lower classes loose among the nation's treasures.[29]

Clearly this period saw a determined campaign by a relatively small group of liberal, reforming MPs, spearheaded by men such as Ewart, Hawes and Brotherton, and lobbyists, such as B. R. Haydon, the painter, for expanded and at least partially state funded cultural initiatives, which should be demonstrably useful. These MPs had shed their hostility to and suspicion of culture as a money-wasting aristocratic pursuit, and had instead come to view it as morally, socially, and even economically beneficial, provided it was universally accessible, had stable funding, and was suitably set out and managed to fulfil an educational purpose. This group were considerably aided by the support of Peel, however lukewarm this sometimes was.[30] It is striking, however, that recommendations to Parliament were generally phrased quite narrowly in terms of cultural provision as a contribution to the economy and manufacturing; Schools of Design, decoration of the Houses of Parliament, and museums were all to improve standards of design and taste in British workers and consumers, and thereby to stimulate the economy, and fend off foreign competition. The improvement in workers which was most eagerly seized on was not in their deportment or leisure, but in the goods they produced.[31]

The first Act which allowed the establishment of municipal museums was not passed until 1845. This Act needs to be seen very much as part of the development of ideas that occurred through the series of Select Committees and Royal Commissions in the 1830s and 40s; and also, importantly, the Act stemmed from the same group of people, including Ewart, Wyse, and Brotherton. The principle that the display of pictures and objects was beneficial for all was one that grew out of the experience of the 1830s and 40s: the lessons of Mechanics' Institutes, the National Gallery and attempts to improve design education. The immense popularity of the exhibition of entries in the competition for the interior decoration of the new Houses of Parliament in 1843 was another important factor, particularly as it was so unexpected. After a fortnight of charging 1s. admission, the exhibition was thrown open for free, and though contemporary estimates of 20,000-30,000 visitors a day may be too high, the crowds were certainly such as to attract attention.[32] Despite the reservations that were soon to appear regarding the National Gallery, in the 1840s the drive and conviction of the Rational Recreationalists was at its height. Though designed to impress, Liverpool's Royal Institute's report on its free exhibition of 1839 suggests something of this conviction: the management's

> faith in the good feeling of the public, and in the aptitude of all minds – even the lowest – to receive refined and elevating impressions, has not disappointed them.... In opening these opportunities to the labouring classes, this institution cannot but feel that it occupies the place of a public benefactor and instructor, awakening in uncultivated minds feelings and ideas calculated to soften the rudeness of manners, and to increase the happiness and virtue of life.[33]

If this was the effect of free public access to museums and galleries, then the argument for state provision was clearly very strong.

Yet it should also be noted that the 1840s were a period where middle-class interest in art and science was becoming much more mainstream, and no longer confined to a specialist group. Art Unions, which acted as subscription clubs helping their members acquire paintings or engravings, were very successful, especially the London Art Union.[34] Engraving of all kinds were very widespread by mid-century; according to W. A. Abram, Lancashire cotton operatives usually had two or three in their homes in the 1840s. Commercial art exhibitions were popular enough to be profitable propositions from the 1820s, and were often tied to the production of an engraving of the exhibited picture.[35] Similarly, in natural history, the practice of collecting was spreading widely, largely as a result of its alleged suitability for education; middle-class children were encouraged to collect specimens and create small museums of their own.[36] It may be argued, therefore, that though public rhetoric was all about the benefits for the working class, those who would most immediately benefit from increased museum provision would be the middle class, who would be able to improve their knowledge of art and have a reference collection for their own natural specimens.

In 1845, then, a group of reforming liberals and radicals, led by William Ewart introduced a Bill to enable town councils to establish museums, levying a rate to do so. Although the beneficial effects of museums and galleries were by and large accepted, the principle of state funding was most emphatically not, and this is where most of the argument and persuasion surrounding the Bill centred. It was acknowledged by the promoters of the Bill that voluntary provision was the ideal for cultural institutions, but, as Wyse, the seconder, said,

> those who were not acquainted with the fact had no idea of the number of contingencies to which voluntary contributions were liable, and how difficult it was to guarantee the existence of institutions which depended on voluntary support.[37]

He stressed the extent to which the proposed Bill would merely supplement voluntary initiatives, by providing an institution to which individuals could donate exhibits, and suggested that it would only need to be invoked in those instances where voluntary support was not forthcoming for a public museum. However, Sir Robert Peel for one, while acknowledging the benefits a museum would bring, was still not convinced that even such limited council support was appropriate, and suggested that councils should raise all the foundation costs of such a museum by subscription, contributing only minimal running costs through local taxation.[38]

Nevertheless, the Act as it was passed allowed for a levy of ½d. in the pound, in towns of over 10,000 inhabitants, for the purposes of housing and running a museum. This ensured that it would not be possible to create a municipal museum without donations of objects, and quite often without some voluntary provision for a building too. The Act was really very limited in scope, even after new Acts in 1850 and 1855 providing for libraries as well, and was taken up by very few councils initially. Only six towns initially took up Ewart's Act of 1845, and ten more municipal museums opened in the 1850s.[39] Although dropping slightly in the 1860s, the number of new municipal museums founded crept up gradually, until in

1900-1910, 72 were created; a number that halved thereafter with the First World War.[40]

Although at a national level, calls for free public museums and cultural opportunities of all kinds were now enjoying considerable support, within local councils there was a much more ambivalent attitude. The principle of using rates for supporting culture was still very contentious, and many councils were committed to public health and sanitation work which was already boosting rates. Ratepayers' and 'economist' lobbies were starting to make their presence felt.[41] Equally, national museums may not have been very encouraging examples, often neglected and overcrowded, and with an alarming ability to absorb all the money sent their way.[42] As a result, in places such as Preston and Sheffield, proposals for a municipal museum introduced in the 1850s were initially defeated, and were only successful when re-introduced in the 1870s.[43] Nevertheless, when adopted, whether immediately after legislation, as in Leicester, or twenty years later, there was generally a very enthusiastic response from sections of the industrial, mercantile, and professional elite. Collections, enthusiasts to arrange and label displays, and in the first years at least, rooms too, were often taken over from Literary and Philosophical Societies, or other learned societies. The clearest case of this is in Leicester, where the Literary and Philosophical Society and the council operated a system of joint control throughout this period, paying the curator's salary between them, and each having members on the Museum Committee. The Society bought many specimens for the museum. Moreover, the Vice-President and the Honorary Secretary of the Lit. and Phil. Society were part of the Museum Committee, and in the 1870s the Chairman of the Museum Committee was from the council of the Lit. and Phil. Society.[44] In Sheffield the collection of the local Literary and Philosophical Society was given over completely to the council once their plans to form a municipal museum were known, and in Preston the Corporation purchased the collection of the Literary and Philosophical Institute, which thereafter ceased to exist, when the Act was adopted.[45] In Liverpool, it was more complicated; for one thing, Liverpool did not adopt the 1845 or 1850 Acts, but instead obtained a special local Act in 1852. Around 1850 the council entered into negotiations with the Liverpool Royal Institution, which had suggested its museum should be managed jointly by the Institution and the council, in what seems to have been intended as a similar arrangement to Leicester. Negotiations proceeded so far that a Bill was brought before Parliament containing the terms of the partnership, rate support, and other details, before discussions broke down, apparently over the issue of divided control, and indeed over the very principle of council funding for a museum. Nevertheless, when Liverpool's municipal museum was created a couple of years later, it had very close links with the other learned societies of the town, especially the Lit. and Phil. One of the most active men in this society, the Rev. H. H. Higgins, who had also put in a lot of work on the Royal Institution's museum, arranged, displayed and labelled the entomological collection for the new museum.[46] In Preston, too, a leading figure from the Lit. and Phil., the Rev. Jonathan Shortt, became the honorary curator of the municipal museum. In many cases, then, the municipalisation of museums failed to prevent 'cliques and coteries' in their management.

Municipal museums were also enthusiastically supported by wealthy elites. In many cases, it was industrial or commercial wealth that was poured in fairly large amounts into new museums and art galleries. William Brown, a merchant, contributed about £35,000 in total for a new museum building in Liverpool, while in Birmingham the Tangye brothers, machine manufacturers, gave £10,000 for purchases to the museum and gallery. In Sheffield, in the 1880s, John Newton Mappin left pictures worth between £70,000 and £80,000 to the municipality, as well as £15,000 towards the cost of extending the building. In Preston, Edmund Harris left a substantial sum of money, around £80,000 of which was used to build a public library, museum and art gallery. Although he was a lawyer, his money came from railway investments and family wealth.[47] Clearly, merchants and manufacturers were not the only people who made spectacular donations and bequests – the core of Liverpool Museum's collection was a large zoological collection bequeathed by Lord Derby.[48] Nevertheless, it is probably true to say that without the very large gifts from manufacturers and merchants, municipal museums could not have been established in the towns of the north and midlands in the second half of the nineteenth century; and where museums were not established, it may have been because of the lack of such a benefactor.

The chief motives behind the establishment of museums seem to have varied. In some cases, such as Birmingham, the need for proper design education for workmen was cited. Civic pride, or more high-mindedly, the so-called 'civic gospel', was also in evidence. In Liverpool, the town was seen as deserving nothing less than an 'intellectual banquet'. By now, the improving, civilising effect of museums on the working class was a commonplace.[49] However, if we examine the effects of the transfer of museums from learned societies to the council, they seem to have less to do with the working class, than with the museum providers themselves. It is clear that issues of control and influence were central to the whole process, as the disagreement between Liverpool council and the Liverpool Royal Institution indicate. Campaigners for municipal museums spoke of the limited influence of proprietary museums.[50] Most of these had offered some public access, but this was usually quite restricted, either by admission fee, the necessity for a letter of introduction from a member, or the short opening hours.[51] In several cases, especially where manufacturing or mercantile donors were concerned, a desire to show that they themselves were not philistines, but as familiar with high art and classical civilisation as any London elite, seems to have been prominent. Richard Newsham, a Preston lawyer who bequeathed a collection of paintings to the Harris Museum and Art Gallery, said in his will,

> If we of this generation were ardent mainly in mercantile pursuits, we also felt, and shared in some degree, the loftier passion for beauty and for knowledge; and set store on those things which embellish life, give present dignity to communities, and furnish their most enduring title to be held in future remembrance and good fame.[52]

So while improvement and reformation of the working man was undoubtedly one motive for the creation of municipal museums, it must also be recognised that the position and relationships of the urban middle class, and their wealthiest and most powerful members in particular, were also at issue. Compared to the museums of learned societies, municipal museums offered a greater sphere of influence, and a clearer form of control. They were more stable; many societies got into financial difficulties or became moribund in the second half of the century, as it became clearer that their support base was too small.[53] For elites, it seemed that supporting municipal museums could effectively boost their authority and legitimacy among their fellow townspeople and in society at large. Similarly for the members of the societies (and as we have seen there was a good deal of overlap between these groups), municipal museums allowed their knowledge and expertise to be displayed beyond the narrow confines of their own circle.

By the time these museums had been set up and were operating properly, the national museums in London had been joined by an important new institution, the South Kensington Museum. This is significant not just because of the innovations it made in the proper subjects and form of museums, but because of the influence it wielded over provincial museums through its system of loans. It was determinedly utilitarian and pedagogic, and saw its role as a supplement to the Schools of Design; Louise Purbrick suggests that it was seen as 'progressive, beneficial, benign', and that, importantly, it was presumed to have an economic function, stimulating the market by acting as a giant promotional centre for good design.[54] However, despite the singular figure of Sir Henry Cole, it may be that the impact of his ideas has been overestimated. Outside London, it was only in places where the relevance of industrial design was strong that museums were seen as raising the standards of working men's taste; Birmingham is the only notable example. Here, the acquisitions policy seemed to follow that of the South Kensington Museum in focussing on applied art.[55] In other places, even where the South Kensington loan scheme was heavily relied on, and art outweighed natural history, like Preston's Harris Museum, the pedagogical function almost disappeared, impressive *objets d'art* and statuary serving merely to signify the classical education and connoisseurship of the middle classes.[56]

How did their new constitution affect the nature of these local museums? Principally, they became more professional, didactic, and authoritative. All municipal museums had salaried curators, where only the biggest learned society museums had; and during the second half of the nineteenth century, a wide range of staff including attendants, taxidermists, and subject specialists came to be employed, with correspondingly fewer voluntary helpers.[57] Where learned societies' museums had been by and for the local scientific community among the middle class, municipal museums were much less collaborative, and producers were clearly separated from consumers. The museums became much bigger, as the core collection was added to by donation and purchase. Many municipal museums outgrew their original quarters quickly: Liverpool Museum was first sited in two rooms in council property, before its very grand new building was funded by Sir William Brown; the museum in Preston followed the same course. In Sheffield, the museum was initially housed in what had been a private house, though a sizeable one, with some alterations; when an art gallery was added, a dramatic alteration and extension program swallowed the house up. In Birmingham, the museum originated as a room in the Library, optimistically called the Corporation Art Gallery; not until 1885 was a separate building opened.[58] These building were not just bigger, they were also grander, classical temples of knowledge.[59] They were explicitly designed to impress, and in most cases were sited near other new, impressive civic buildings.[60] This resulted in the new civic centres to the towns, with large open spaces, new wide streets, and groups of extremely authoritative looking buildings. For the middle-class elite, this was a bid to reclaim the city or town centre, giving themselves a space for rational leisure. The buildings often featured allegorical figures and Latin quotations, making them even more impenetrable for the less educated.[61] Although they technically offered universal free access, it could be argued that they were, practically, still rather inaccessible for the working class, in that none initially offered Sunday opening, and the availability of evening opening was patchy. The rules regarding admission were strict on matters such as dress, and also on occasion forbade the admission of children, even if accompanied, although this affected all classes.[62] Nevertheless, despite the fact that it was still difficult for working people to visit these museums, they were incredibly popular, particularly in the first decade of opening.[63]

All of these institutional developments brought about by municipalisation of the museum worked to enhance its public usefulness, to make it an indispensable cultural provider for the new industrial town. It was educational and rational, with cultural authority; it was open to all, free of charge; and it aimed to produce the self-improving citizen. It was the antithesis of the restricted, specialist museum purveying refined insights to a small social elite, the model which had still prevailed in 1800. However, it was also clearly implicated in the middle class's invention of itself. Clearly, one must acknowledge concern to provide improving culture for the working class as a motive for the development of public museums, stemming from an increasing belief that workers could benefit from exposure to culture, provided it was suitably presented to them. Throughout the first half of the nineteenth century, the drive, by a small group of reformers, was towards improving the usefulness, rationality, and openness of cultural institutions.

However, no sooner was the legislation in place for municipal museums than, in the midlands and north particularly, something different started to happen. Local elites of businessmen and professionals tended to take up the project enthusiastically, pouring their own money and, where possible, public money, into it, while being opposed by groups hostile to rate increases, and indeed government spending of any kind. Local scientific and learned societies, themselves important institutions in the formation of the new provincial middle classes led by the elites, were more than happy to transfer their collections and expertise to the new museums, in a move that often marked the effective end of their existence.[64] Upon foundation, then, the urban elites shifted their cultural capital into the museums in a conclusive way. These institutions could continue some of the functions of the societies,[65] but also offer wider access, much more impressive and well-financed building and collections, and vastly enhanced authority and professionalism. The new museums offered the middle-class elites the opportunity to develop and display new sorts of authority and cultural capital, and, importantly, to communicate them to a much wider group. In addition, they created a, broadly speaking, middle-class space, where middle-class norms of behaviour were protected and, if possible, enforced; middle-class values shaped and strengthened; and middle-class hierarchies displayed. If the working class came to the museum and internalised this, that was an important bonus; but the initial lack of effort to ensure this suggests that the urban elites had primarily created a space for their own class, with the reformation of the working class as a second priority.

By around 1860, the production and consumption of culture had changed fundamentally in Britain. Where in 1800 art and science had been regarded as the products, and therefore the preserve, of cultivated minds, they increasingly came to be seen as a way of creating a civilised and productive population. It was therefore imperative that they be spread to as wide an audience as possible. However, the increasing numbers and wealth of the urban middle classes had accelerated the penetration of the market into culture, leading to two new trends. Art and science were increasingly professionalised, creating new branches of knowledge; and a seemly reconciliation of money and culture was sought. Museums were eminently suitable for middle-class employment and leisure, at a time when the middle class demanded more of both. Indeed, the whole reinvention of the public museum served the interests of the middle class by allowing the reconciliation of the transcendent qualities of art and science with their involvement in the market: public museums allowed culture to stand outside the market, protected from the vulgarity of trading, proclaiming middle-class moral and spiritual values, while at the same time acting as the ultimate guarantor for the monetary value of middle-class possessions.

Notes

[1]   Thomas Greenwood, *Museums and Art Galleries*, (London 1888), p. 106.

[2]   *Report of the 57th Meeting of the British Association for the Advancement of Science*, (1888), pp. 97-130.

[3]   Eilean Hooper-Greenhill, *Museums and the Shaping of Knowledge*, (London 1992); Tony Bennett, *The Birth of the Museum*, (London 1995).

[4]   Hooper-Greenhill, *Museums*, p. 174.

[5]   A. Thackray, 'Natural Knowledge in Cultural Context: the Manchester Model', *American Historical Review* 79 (1974).

[6]   John Seed, ' "Commerce and the Liberal Arts": the political economy of art in Manchester 1775-1860' in Wolff and Seed, ed., *The Culture of Capital: art, power and the nineteenth-century middle class*, (Manchester 1988); Diane Sachko Macleod, *Art and the Victorian Middle Class: Money and the Making of Cultural Identity*, (Cambridge 1996).

[7]   S. Gunn, 'The Sublime and the Vulgar: the Halle concerts and the constitution of high culture in Manchester c.1850-1880', *Journal of Victorian Culture* 2, 2 (1997).

[8]   P. Bourdieu, *Distinction: A Social Critique of the Judgement of Taste*, trans. R. Nice, (London 1984); Paul DiMaggio, 'Cultural Entrepreneurship in Nineteenth-Century Boston: the creation of an organisational base for high culture in America', *Media, Culture, and Society* 4 (1982).

[9]   Daniel Sherman, *Worthy Monuments: Art Museums and the Politics of Culture in Nineteenth-Century France*, (Cambridge, Massachussetts 1989).

[10] Geoffrey D. Lewis, 'Collections, collectors and museums in Britain to 1920' in John Thompson, ed., *The Manual of Curatorship*, (London 1984), pp. 25-6.

[11] He was a Fellow of the Linnaean Society, but also had plans to exhibit Cromwell's head on a spike. E. Alexander, 'William Bullock: Little Remembered Museologist and Showman', *Curator* 28, 2, (1985), pp. 120, 124; R. D. Altick, *The Shows of London*, (London 1978), chapter 18.

[12] J. Barrell, 'Introduction', in John Barrell (ed), *Painting and the Politics of Culture: New essays on British Art 1700-1850*, (Oxford 1992), p. 4.

[13] W. Hazlitt, *Criticisms on Art, and Sketches of the Picture Galleries of England*, (London 1856), p. 235.

[14] R. Williams, *Culture and Society 1780-1950*, (London 1958), p. 41; S. Copley, 'The Fine Arts in Eighteenth-Century Polite Culture', in Barrell (ed), *Painting*, (1992), p. 17.

[15] Bernard Denvir, *The Early Nineteenth Century: Art, Design and Society 1789-1852*, (London 1984), p. 62; Macleod, *Art and the Victorian Middle Class*, pp. 15, 20.

[16] Altick, *Shows of London*, p. 416.

[17] G. Lewis, 'Collections', p. 27; Janet Minihan, *The Nationalisation of Culture: the development of state subsidies to the arts in Great Britain*, (London 1977), pp. 21-2.

[18] Minihan, *Nationalisation*, p. 23.

[19] Quoted in Colin Trodd, 'Culture, class and city: the National Gallery, London, and the spaces of education, 1822-57', in M. Pointon (ed), *Art Apart: Art institutions and ideology across England and North America*, (Manchester 1994), p.33.

[20] *Ibid.*, pp. 42-7.

[21] Minihan, *Nationalisation*, pp. 29-31.

[22] For example, the growth of public parks (Hugh Cunningham, *Leisure in the Industrial Revolution, c. 1780-1880*, (London 1980), chapter 3); the Schools of Design (see below) and the rebuilding and redecoration of the Houses of Parliament (see below).

[23] Peter Bailey, *Leisure and Class in Victorian England: rational recreation and the contest for control 1830-1885*, (London 1978), p. 51.

[24] Bailey, *Leisure*, pp. 172-3.

[25] E. P. Thompson, *The Making of the English Working Class*, (Harmondsworth 1980), p.324; J. Holden, *A Short History of Todmorden*, (Manchester 1912), p. 204.

[26] Lewis, 'Collections', p. 29.

[27] Report of the Committee on Drunkenness, 1834, quoted in Bailey, *Leisure and Class*, p.38.

[28] As Richard Redgrave, one of the men who had set up and first taught at the Central School of Design, said in a letter to Lord John Russell, the Prime Minister, in 1846, 'The School seems liable to merge into a mere Government Drawing School, from which *creative design* [original emphasis] will soon be wholly expelled.' Denvir, *The Early Nineteenth Century*, p. 233. See also Minihan, *Nationalisation*, pp. 44-50.

[29] Parliamentary Papers: Report from Select Committee on Arts and Manufactures, 1835, 1836; Report from Select Committee on National Monuments and Works of Art, 1841; Report from Select Committee on Fine Arts, 1841; Minihan, *Nationalisation*, p. 88.

[30] See the two introductory quotes by Peel at the beginning of Trodd, 'Culture, Class, City', p. 33.

[31] Report from Select Committee on Arts and Manufactures 1836, p. iv: 'It has too frequently ... occurred, that the witnesses consulted by the Committee have felt themselves compelled to draw a comparison more favourable (in the matter of design) to our foreign rivals, and especially to the French, than could have been desired'. Report from Select Committee on Fine Arts, 1841, p. vi: 'As, then, the collection and exhibition of works of Art have not only tended to the moral elevation of the People, but have also given a fresh

stimulus and direction to their industry, so Your Committee is of the opinion that a direct encouragement of the higher branches of Art on this occasion will have a similar effect in a still higher degree'.

[32] Interpretations of what the masses got from the exhibition varied, but it seems the balance of opinion was positive. The reviewer in the *New Monthly Magazine* of August 1844 said 'What if the Exhibition be a mixture of unmitigated trash, *This* is the redeeming, hopeful feature – this patient interest which the people are beginning to take in art, this slow but certain education which they are picking up from every effort that is rightly and honestly directed to the cultivation of a sound national taste.' Denvir, *Early Nineteenth Century*, p. 73.

[33] Minihan, *Nationalisation*, p. 52.

[34] Minihan, *Nationalisation*, p. 78.

[35] Denvir, *Early Nineteenth Century*, p. 67; Altick, *Shows of London*, pp. 410-411.

[36] D. Allen, *The Naturalist in Britain: A Social History*,(Princeton, New Jersey 1976); see also F. O'Gorman, 'Victorian Natural History and the Discourses of Nature in Charles Kingsley's *Glaucus*', *Worldviews: Environment, Culture, Religion*, 2 (1998), pp. 21-2; the Gradgrind children keep natural history museums as part of their utilitarian education: 'a little conchological cabinet, a little metalurgical cabinet, and a little mineralogical cabinet', Charles Dickens, *Hard Times*, (Harmondsworth 1994 [1854]), p. 9.

[37] Hansard's Parliamentary Debates, (3rd series) 78, 1845, p. 382.

[38] *Ibid.*, p. 389.

[39] Lewis, 'Collectors', p. 29; Greenwood, *Museums*, pp. 370-1.

[40] J. Lynne Teather, 'Museology and Its Traditions: The British Experience 1845-1945' (unpublished D.Phil thesis, Leicester University 1983), fig. 12.

[41] E. P. Hennock, *Fit and Proper Persons: Ideal and Reality in Nineteenth-Century Urban Government*, (London 1973), pp. 31-33, and S. Davies, *By the Gains of Industry: Birmingham Museums and Art Gallery 1885-1985*, (Birmingham 1985), p. 10; see also the report of a meeting of ratepayers in the *Preston Chronicle*, 11 March 1854, which resolved 'that any undertaking at the present juncture, calling for increased taxation, will be unwise on the part of the corporate body, and unjust and oppressive to the ratepayers.' It was not long after this that the first attempt to adopt the Free Public Libraries and Museums Act in Preston failed.

[42] The reputation of the natural history collections of the British Museum were so low that it lost out on several significant acquisitions of collections: Edward Miller, *That Noble Cabinet: A History of the British Museum*, (London 1973), pp. 229-232, and W. T. Stearn, *The Natural History Museum at South Kensington*, (London 1981), p. 20. Although a large amount was finally spent on the National Gallery in the 1830s, its new building was delayed by spending restrictions, and was expected to house the Royal Academy and the Public Records Office as well. The Gallery was still cramped, and still poorly catalogued and arranged: Minihan, *Nationalisation*, pp. 54-9.

[43] M. Whittle, 'Philanthropy in Preston: The changing face of charity in a nineteenth-century provincial town', (Unpublished PhD thesis, University of Lancaster 1990), p. 258.

[44] F. B. Lott, *The Centenary Book of the Leicester Literary and Philosophical Society*, (Leicester 1935), pp. 35-50.

[45] E. Howarth, *Notes on the Sheffield Public Museum and Mappin Art Gallery*, (Glasgow 1900), p. 113; S. H. Paviere, *Harris Museum and Art Gallery: Summary Guide*, (Preston 1932), p. 12.

[46] See H. Ormerod, *The Liverpool Royal Institution, A Record and a Retrospect*, (Liverpool 1953), pp. 42-53; Lewis, 'Collections', p. 30.

[47] J. A. Picton, *Notes on the Free Library and Museum of the Borough of Liverpool*, (Liverpool 1857), p. 693; A. Bensley Chamberlain, 'The Corporation Museum and Art

Gallery', in *A Handbook for Birmingham*, British Association for the Advancement of Science, (1913), p. 235; M. Tooby, *'In Perpetuity and Without Charge': The Mappin Art Gallery 1887-1987*, Sheffield Arts Department, (1987), p. 10; Paviere, *Harris Museum and Art Gallery*, pp. 11-12.

[48]   Picton, *Notes*, p. 692.

[49]   On the need for design education, see Sir Richard Tangye, *One and All: An Autobiography*, (London 1889), p. 147; on the civic gospel, E. P. Hennock, *Fit and Proper Persons: Ideal and Reality in Nineteenth-Century Urban Government*, (London 1973), pp. 158, 172, 321; and for motives in Liverpool, both intellectual and for the civilising of the workers, see Rev. A. Hume, *Character of the Liverpool Town Museum, with suggestions for its interior arrangement*, Liverpool, reprinted from the Daily Post (1859), p. 6, and William Brown's speech, in *Ceremonies connected with the Opening of the Building for a Free Public Library and Museum Presented by William Brown, Esq., to the Town of Liverpool*, (Liverpool 1861).

[50]   For example, Picton, *Notes*, p. 691: 'These institutions were proprietary, not public in the proper sense of the term, and their influence, though beneficial so far as they went, was necessarily extremely limited.'

[51]   Greenwood's survey in the 1880s found that of those museums not rate-supported, and not attached to universities or schools, terms of admission varied, but most were either by a substantial annual subscription, restricted to members only, were subject to a charge of up to 6d, or required prior application to trustees. Greenwood, *Museums*, pp. 372-5.

[52]   Quoted in *Preston Corporation Art Gallery Illustrated Catalogue*, (Preston 1907).

[53]   R. J. Morris, 'Voluntary Societies and British Urban Elites 1780-1850: An Analysis', *Historical Journal* 26, 1(1983), p. 117.

[54]   Louise Purbrick, 'South Kensington Museum: the building of the house of Henry Cole', in M. Pointon (ed), *Art Apart*, (Manchester 1994), p. 83.

[55]   Whitworth Wallis, 'The Museum and Art Gallery', in J. H. Muirhead (ed), *Birmingham Institutions*, (Birmingham 1911), p. 486. Chapter 6 below will argue that Birmingham used different principles of display from South Kensington.

[56]   See below, chapter 6.

[57]   'Report on the Provincial Museums of the United Kingdom', in *Report of the 57th Meeting of the British Association for the Advancement of Science, 1887*, (London 1888), p. 118-9.

[58]   For Liverpool, see W. K. Ford, 'Notes on the earlier history of the City of Liverpool Public Museums', *Liverpool Bulletin* vol. 5, (1955); for Preston, J. Hibbert, *A Report to Accompany the Design for the Harris Free Public Library and Museum*, (Preston 1882), p. 6; for Sheffield *Report on the Suggested Extension of Sheffield Public Museum in Connection with the Mappin Art Gallery*, (Sheffield 1900); for Birmingham, S. Davies, 'Birmingham Museum and Art Gallery', *Birmingham Museum and Art Gallery Sheet 9*, (1981).

[59]   Brendan Taylor points out that by the time the Tate Gallery was being designed, buildings such as the National Gallery formed 'museum prototypes' with a weight of authority and prestige associated with them: B. Taylor, 'From Penitentiary to 'Temple of Art': early metaphors of improvement at the Millbank Tate', in M. Pointon (ed), *Art Apart*, p. 14.

[60]   S. Gunn, 'The middle class, modernity and the provincial city: Manchester c.1840-1880' in Kidd and Nicholls (ed), *Gender, Civic Culture and Consumerism*, pp. 115-118.

[61]   The building for the Harris Library and Museum in Preston is a particularly good example of this; see the article on the newly opened building in the *Preston Guardian*, 17 December 1892.

[62]   By the time of the BAAS's Report of 1887 only four offered Sunday opening: 'Report on the Provincial Museums', p. 115. Liverpool Museum had experimented with Monday

evening opening but suspended it because of bad behaviour; Liverpool Museums 56th Annual Report, 1889. The rule preventing the admission of any child under the age of 8 caused some anger in Sheffield; see *Sheffield Telegraph*, 13 August 1887. See also chapter 7 below.

[63]   In 1887 Birmingham Museum and Art Gallery was reporting 22,000 visitors a week; between 1887 and 1893 Sheffield Public Museum had over 7,000 visitors on its busiest day, usually Easter Monday or August Bank Holiday. 'Report on the Provincial Museums', pp. 100-110; Sheffield Museum Annual reports 1885-1895.

[64]   For example, Preston's Lit. and Phil. ceased to exist after selling all its property and possessions to the council for the sum of £150; *Preston Guardian*, 1 May 1880.

[65]   R. J. Morris has identified voluntary societies as essential in the work of producing an elite-led middle class, as they allowed sectarian and political divisions to be overcome, and offered a model for dealings with other classes. Morris, *Class, Sect and Party, The Making of the British Middle Class: Leeds 1820-1850*, (Manchester 1990), especially chapters 7 and 13.

CHAPTER FOUR

The Social Characteristics of Municipal Museums

Municipal museums were the creation of specific groups of people in the second half of the nineteenth century; the museums in turn helped to shape these groups, give them characteristics and status. Little attention has been paid to the exact social composition of museum staff and donors; it is assumed that those in charge of the museum were middle class, part of the new urban elite that reshaped the Victorian city. However this assumption can lead to the simplification that the whole museums project was about the promotion of capitalism and manufacturing, or of 'middle-class values', or of professionalisation; whereas in fact the specific characteristics of museum interest groups in different places can be shown to have produced very different museums. The interests of local government might be at odds with those of commercial donors, or of the nascent curatorial profession. Moreover, there were significant changes between the founding of municipal museums, and 1914; generally, large local benefactors, concerned about civic prestige and philanthropy, and the local amateur scientific community were prominent early on, while later, an increasingly structured curating profession developed. This of course has implications for the way in which museums interacted with society. Museums were used by groups to enhance their own standing or drive forward their own concerns; access to control of the museum was thus an important and desirable asset which was struggled over; negotiation and co-operation among producer groups might be necessary in order to protect and promote the museum.

This chapter, therefore, is an investigation into the characteristics of those who played some part in producing the museum, its displays and its knowledge. This group consists of members of council committees, donors and staff. All of these in some way made the museum what it was, and also, by donating, getting on to the committee, or working for the museum, put themselves in the provider, rather than consumer category. They proclaimed a kind of symbolic ownership. It is for this reason that establishing the characteristics of this provider group is important. Moreover, the question of change over time is significant, indicating whether control, and therefore policy and direction of the museum, altered or was seized by another group

Municipal museums generally fell under the authority of a council committee, frequently the Free Libraries and Museums Committee. Members of these committees were of course already part of the council, and thus involved in local politics. As chapter two has already indicated, councillors were generally middle class, though with varying proportions of an urban elite in different towns. When museums were set up by councils in the second half of the nineteenth century, those councillors who became involved with them were those with the highest social status, and those who had an existing involvement with voluntary scientific societies. Though the specific composition varied according to local politics, generally museums were the preserve of a liberal, cultured elite. One of their aims in creating museums was publicly to position themselves as just such a group; frequently they were concerned to elevate local government from a perceived stagnating or humdrum affair to a high, demanding calling requiring culture, education and devotion to helping the less fortunate, of its members. This aim, and their existing status, enabled them to drive through the creation of a museum often in the teeth of opposition from lower-status groups. However, by the beginning of the twentieth century, serving on the council was generally less attractive to the liberal, cultured elite; accordingly council control of museums was in the hands of a more middling group, who were more concerned with economy and efficiency.

Liverpool is a very clear example of this. The Library, Museum and Arts Committee, the controlling body of the museums, was set up in 1850 to look into the possibility and desirability of setting up a publicly funded museum in Liverpool. The most prominent agitator for this, and one of the first members, was James Picton, an architect. George Holt, merchant, was also important, as was the Reverend A. Hume, who, however, not being a councillor, was not subsequently one of the committee. Other than Picton, the first members of the committee consisted of four merchants and a manufacturer. The number of merchants remained at a high level - between one third and one half of members until 1914. However, the number of members from the professions increased substantially from eight per cent in 1859 to a high point of 54 per cent in 1900. Trades and manufacturing were never represented by more than one member each.[1]

So merchants were an important presence, although outstripped by professions in the first decade of the twentieth century. The large numbers from the professions at this point are partly explained by the co-option of an increasing number of experts, particularly from the new university, to advise the committee. Another indicator of the disproportionate importance of the mercantile interest is that several of the lawyers were the sons of merchants. Moreover, the three civil engineers, counted for these purposes as professionals, worked on ship construction, and the accountants and lawyers will have found most of their work coming from commerce. In addition, if long-serving members and related members are analysed, the strength of commercial interest in the museum is clearer. Out of those serving ten years or more, 60 per cent were merchants or shipowners.

In 1850 at least half the committee were Liberals; in 1859 at least two-thirds were. Until the end of the century the proportion of Liberals stayed between one third and one half. Anglicans and Unitarians were the most common religious affiliations, followed by Congregationalists and Presbyterians, then Catholics. It is also noteworthy that of the group of long-serving members half were Liberal, and half were Nonconformists, most of whom were Unitarians. There are several members of the same family on the committee; three generations of the Holts served, two of the Rathbones, and two Bowrings, skipping one generation. They all had a fairly long average term on the committee as well. These three families were all Unitarian, Liberal, shipowning and merchant dynasties, referred to by a contemporary as 'Our Old Families'. This bloc was also influential in getting the council to create a museum in the first place. Thus, while Liberal Nonconformist merchants were moving out of the council as a whole, for higher status and national and international positions, they maintained an important presence on this committee.[2]

In Preston, the museum was run by the Free Public Library Committee. This body was very different to Liverpool's Library, Museums and Arts Committee. The first committee consisted of seven professionals, two manufacturers, three traders and local merchants, and one manager. From this beginning until 1915, the professions remained an important element on the committee. Tradesmen showed a steady increase throughout the period. The manufacturing element shows a more complex pattern. In the nineteenth century it was a fairly small, but disproportionately important group of large cotton mill owners. By the turn of the century, these were being joined by other manufacturers, especially of machinery, as important new engineering firms opened in Preston from the mid 1890s. Thereafter the numbers decline, and in particular, cotton manufacturers drop out, until the total is only 6 per cent in 1915.[3] In other words, the committee begins as a combination of big cotton manufacturers like E. Birley and M.S. Maynard, and leading professionals such as the proprietor and the editor of the Preston Guardian. In fact, this combination was the standard for charitable undertakings, similar to the Trustees of Preston Hospital, or the large subscribers to the Preston Exhibition. These two elite groups also had marriage links.[4] By the end of this study, though, the committee was formed of leading tradesmen with the professions.[5] Certainly the lower middle classes were a more important force on the council in the later period. Comparison with proportions in the council overall is a complex matter. At this stage, then, both the professions and cotton manufacturers were stronger on the Free Public Library Committee than in the whole council, whereas non-cotton manufacturers and trades and small businesses were considerably under-represented.

Birmingham shows very clearly the involvement of an important bloc within the council (and without) of those who were concerned to develop the role of the municipality, and imbue it with a sacred status as a high, quasi-spiritual form of service. By creating a municipal museum they could develop the idea of the 'Civic Gospel', and constitute themselves as its leaders. The first, unsuccessful demand for the adoption of the Public Libraries Act in 1854 came from ten men, eight of whom were members of the Dissenting Church of the Saviour in Birmingham. John Thackray Bunce and W. C. Aitken were prominent among that ten. Bunce, an Anglican, was at this stage a reporter for the *Midland Counties Herald*; in 1862 he became editor of the Liberal *Daily Post*, continuing there until his death in 1899. He was active in many areas of Birmingham life, such as the Royal Birmingham Society of Artists. He was later involved with the Liberal Association, and characteristically for a Birmingham liberal he was concerned about education. When editor, he used his position to propagate his views on education, and also at that time new ideas about the extent and nature of municipal life and duties. Later on, he was both a donor to the Art Gallery and a Chairman of its Sub-Committee.[6] He also wrote a History of the Corporation of Birmingham (1885) in which certain of his views are expressed. He had a complex view of how various social strata should contribute to the greater municipal good:

> Leading members of the community have aided in sustaining the level of corporate feeling by their co-operation, as, for example, by the generous gifts which Miss Ryland and Mr. Colmore recognised the duties of landowners, and Messrs Tangye and others the duties of the wealthier manufacturers.[7]

He was arguing that the municipality should be the conduit for private philanthropy. Before 1860, when the council was in what has been called its quiescent phase, private philanthropy was the norm, allowing landowners to establish client-patron relationships. W. C. Aitken, Superintendent of brass and glass manufacturers, was known for his essays on the importance of design for the competitiveness of Birmingham goods, and the importance of design education to achieve this.

When the Free Public Libraries Act was adopted in 1860, the impetus in the council came largely from E. C. Osborne, a member of the Church of the Saviour. And on the committee then set up, councillors included Bunce and Aitken, and also Joseph Chamberlain, Jesse Collings and Harris. Collings and Harris were two more members of the Church of the Saviour, Harris a founder member. These two were chairmen of the committee at various points. There was, among the councillors who concerned themselves with the museum and art gallery, clearly a Nonconformist bias. They also seem to have been more professional than manufacturing: Harris an architect and surveyor, Bunce a journalist, Aitken and Chamberlain at one remove from the actual business of manufacturing.[8]

In Leicester, the local science community, in the shape of the Literary and Philosophical Society was as important as the council in setting up and control of the museum; though in fact overlap between the two was significant. Leicester's Museum Committee was actually a joint body, made up of councillors and officials and members of the Lit and Phil, the society which had donated its museum wholesale to the council to become the municipal museum. Up until 1872, the Society had the sole appointment of the Curator and the Honorary Curators (these were almost always members of the Lit and Phil), and paid fifty guineas towards the Curator's annual salary. Thereafter, the council took back the power to appoint the Curator, but Honorary Curators remained the preserve of the Lit and Phil. In any case, this apparent regaining of control by the council was not all it seemed. The reconstituted Museum Committee consisted of ten councillors and six non-councillors, members of the Lit and Phil; but seven of the councillors were also members of the Lit and Phil, two of them on its council. In fact the Chairman of the Museum Committee, a councillor, was on the Lit and Phil's council. The system of honorary curators was scrapped in the 1890s, probably at the insistence of the curator, but the overlap in membership of the council and the Lit and Phil continued, if to a lesser extent.[9]

In Sheffield, non-council members of the committee were also a key feature, but there was no such close collaboration between the council and a voluntary society. The museum was run by the Free Libraries and Museums Committee, which was expanded from the Free Libraries Committee in 1874. At this point the committee consisted of nine councillors and six non-councillors, whose occupations were given as one merchant, one solicitor, a blade forger, a file manager, a mark maker and a designer. It is not clear how these members were selected, but there was a degree of persistence in their membership; three were still members two years later.[10] It is interesting that where other museums showed a strong input from professionals of varying kinds, in Sheffield representatives of the local industry, metalworking, are much more prominent; and not necessarily the leaders of that industry either, but people of much more middling status.

Overall, however, it is fair to say that council committees in charge of museums were made up of a liberal, cultured elite, and that it was often the most elite and cultured of councillors who campaigned for the council to set up a museum in the first place. And of course, these very actions defined them as a cultured elite, uniting, as they saw it, the best of traditions of aristocratic patronage with modern notions of universality, democracy, and education for all. It is also significant to see how many councillors were also members of the local, amateur scientific community, who sought wider exposure for and appreciation of their work.

Donors from outside the council were also instrumental in creating municipal museums. Potential donors were a much larger group than committee members; and correspondingly we see a wide variety of groups and individuals represented among donors to municipal museums. Donation to a museum was an effective way of giving exposure to oneself or one's interests, and was increasingly recognised as such; there was clearly much more conscious use of the museum to promote a specific agenda or just to advertise the taste and discrimination of the donor. This is particularly the case with some of the most important groups of donors: individuals giving very large donations, voluntary societies, and other institutional donors. Those giving very large donations, either of collections or of money, were usually commemorated in the name of the building or museum, or at least their collection would be kept together with their name attached. If they paid for a building, they effectively had a large and impressive monument, not just to their wealth, but to their taste and civic-mindedness.[11] Such a route seems to have attracted particularly industrialists, or those whose money came from industrial sources, and those who were looking for enhancement of their status. The donation was sometimes a bequest, and given the possible other recipients of such a bequest, seems even more clearly intended to preserve and enhance the donor's memory. Donors of very large collections, however, were naturally serious collectors, and as natural history collecting was reasonably spread throughout Victorian society, so were these donors. They were motivated primarily by the need to have their collection cared for after their death; in the second half of the nineteenth century a municipal museum, where available, would be the best and most obvious place for this.

In addition, some of them were motivated by a desire to promote wider access to the collection, and argued that they had always intended it to have an educational purpose; there is some evidence that museums with an avowedly educational stance were more popular with such donors.[12] However, the frequency with which keeping the collection together was stipulated suggests this was the prime aim of such donors.

The Liverpool Museum was effectively created by three major donations: a large natural history collection from Lord Derby, a large money donation to pay for a building from William Brown, and a collection of antiquities from Joseph Mayer. In terms of occupation and status, of course, they were very different. Derby was a peer, William Brown a merchant, and Joseph Mayer a goldsmith. The complete absence of manufacturing in this group confirms that museum donation broadly reflected the local society and economy. This group is, moreover, linked by wealth. Derby was a very wealthy peer, and a major landowner in Liverpool; William Brown was wealthy even by the standards of Liverpool merchants. Joseph Mayer was of course not in this league, but he did possess an extremely valuable collection of *objets d'art* and antiquities, and had opened a private museum in 1852, with only a 'trifling admission charge', that extended to five rooms.[13] Their motives for the donations appear to have differed. Orchard implies that William Brown's contribution was made grudgingly, in the hope of receiving a baronetcy, as indeed he later did. Derby's museum was given as a bequest; he seems to have been concerned mainly to keep it together, by putting it under the ultimate control of a body of trustees in connection with the council. He also mentioned 'the amusement and instruction of his countrymen'. However, the major difference which the donation produced, compared with the collection's previous existence as a private museum at Knowsley, was a greater measure of commemoration for Derby himself, and it is a valid assumption that this was an important motivating factor. Joseph Mayer, by contrast, gave most of his collections to the museum while still alive, and said that he would have done so even earlier, had there been a municipal museum, or even rooms in an institution which would have taken them. In the absence of any of these, he had to take rooms himself, and then charge to cover his costs, though he really wanted a free museum.[14] These donations were very important in establishing the core collections of the museum, but later donations, and more importantly the policies of the committee and curators, were able to alter the character and direction of the museum.

In Birmingham, the largest single donation was that made by Messrs Tangye, totalling £10,000 for purchases. The Tangye brothers were Quakers, originally from Cornwall, who had set up a small factory making hydraulic equipment in Birmingham in the 1850s, which by 1880 was a very large and successful works. Richard Tangye wrote his autobiography in 1889, stressing his belief that educational opportunities were one of the most pressing needs in the country. This governed his actions, first privately in the educational provision at his factory, and then, with greater scope, publicly when in 1878 he became a councillor. In his autobiography he explains the motives that led him to make the donation.

During my frequent visits to the Continent I had been much impressed with the advantages afforded the artisans of almost every manufacturing town by the facilities possessed by them for studying the highest examples of Art in Municipal Museums and other public collections.[15]

The Tangyes wrote to Bunce as editor of the *Daily Post*, to make the offer, saying that

It is all very well for critics to exclaim against Birmingham manufacturers and artisans because of their inferiority to their foreign competitors in the matter of design and manufacture; but what chance have they of improving in these respects? South Kensington is practically as far away as Paris or Munich, while our competitors on the Continent, in almost every manufacturing town, have access to collections embracing the finest examples of Art, furnishing an endless variety of style and design ... If our gift will help in some degree towards the establishment of an Art Gallery worthy of our adopted town, we shall be amply rewarded for any self-denial we may have exercised in making it.[16]

Their commitment to industrial and art education was so strong that they also donated £11,000 to the School of Art. They had a very clear vision of the place of industrial and design education in municipal provision, which would be more comprehensive and far-reaching than anything a private individual could produce, but owing to national government restrictions, could only be set up with private help. Joseph Chamberlain was also a major donor to the Art Gallery and Museum, giving £1,000 towards the purchase of objects of industrial art in 1875, while mayor.[17] A particular commitment to education in the principles of industrial design is thus apparent among donors to Birmingham's Art Gallery and Museum; this echoes much of the thinking behind the South Kensington Museum, but was not, in fact, very common in municipal museums.

In Sheffield there were a number of large donations, the most spectacular associated with the Art Gallery which opened in 1887 as a large and prestigious extension to the Museum. This was as a result of the bequest by J. N. Mappin of paintings and other works of art, valued at around £70,000, as well as £15,000 towards the cost of a building, to the corporation of Sheffield, subject to the construction of a suitable building for them. Sir Frederick Mappin, J. N. Mappin's nephew and a local MP, also donated a substantial collection of paintings. The Mappins were industrialists; J. N. Mappin had been involved in the metal trades before turning to brewing where he made his fortune.[18]

Large donations to the Museum in Sheffield were also made by gentlemen scientists such as Henry Clifton Sorby, who lived on inherited wealth created by his father, who had a metal-working firm and also mined coal on his estate. Sorby was a leader in the scientific community in Sheffield around the middle of the nineteenth century, centrally involved in the Lit. and Phil. Society. He gave a collection of marine invertebrates to the museum, which had apparently been selected for their suitability for educational purposes, and a geological collection.[19]

Large donations, then, were made out of a variety of motives; several donors felt strongly about the educational or research possibilities of municipal museums, or saw them as the safest way to preserve their collections, but overall, large donations were a way of making a mark on the urban fabric, of leaving one's name attached to a grand and imposing civic building that was moreover a storehouse of knowledge. This issue of prestige was much less important for other donors, though they might equally intend to use the museum for specific ends. Literary and Philosophical Societies frequently gave their entire collection to form the nucleus of the municipal museum's collections; this happened in Sheffield, Preston, Leicester, and Hull, as well as, generally later, in smaller places such as Ilkley, Scunthorpe and Keighley.[20] There was, as has already been noted, considerable overlap between the officers of such societies and councillors responsible for museums; if as councillors they were enthusiastic about municipal museums, they were likely to support them in their other capacity too. People who belonged to scientific societies naturally tended to encourage educational and research initiatives. Moreover, giving a society's collections to the municipality solved a number of common problems: primarily space, as even in purpose-built premises, societies did not usually allot much room to the museum which had to compete with library, lecture rooms and so forth, yet often grew alarmingly fast. Other problems included money, the need for more professional curatorship, and how to admit the public relatively freely. In addition, transferring collections to a municipal museum brought increased recognition to the officers of the society, and they tended to be able to use the museum freely for events such as conversaziones; it was therefore a logical and beneficial step for them.[21]

The larger of the municipal museums, and in particular Liverpool Museum, also received donations from other institutions, such as companies, colleges, other museums both in Britain and abroad, diplomatic and colonial sources, and religious missions. It is here that very purposive donations can be found, particularly after about 1890.

Donations from companies to Liverpool Museum nearly all fell between 1896 and 1911. The bulk of manufacturers represented overseas commerce and shipping. Thus between 1896 and 1917, the museum received donations from the Ceylon Cafe Company, the Cotton Association, the Lagos Trading Company, Cunard, and the Chamber of Commerce African Trade section. Early in the twentieth century Liverpool Museum also received a number of donations from colonial officials, mainly from West Africa, such as the Governor of the Gold Coast; the Governor of Senegal; the Governor of Sierra Leone; and the Assistant District Commissioner of Sierra Leone. Others include the Consul at Iquito in 1900 and 1901; and the government of East Bengal and Assam in 1911.[22]

In addition, the museum had made a serious effort to encourage collection and donation from captains and others of the mercantile marine. In 1862, a scheme was launched whereby they could be made Associate Members of the Literary and Philosophical Society if they made donations to the Liverpool Museum. To this end the Mercantile Marine Association was persuaded to sanction, and encourage, the collection of natural history specimens by their captains. By the 1870s such people formed a large proportion of donors.[23] In the 1890s a different pattern emerged; a few ship engineers and surgeons working for the Elder Dempster Line in West Africa contributed huge quantities of natural history and ethnographic objects themselves, and collected and transported donations from missionaries, local chiefs and other residents. Arnold Ridyard, Chief Engineer on the S.S. Niger, donated a total of six thousand objects over twenty years, and acted as intermediary for about fifteen people around West Africa. Mr Lockhead, Chief Engineer on the S.S. Burutu, was not far behind him.[24]

The people who donated from West Africa could all be characterised by a broad motive of wanting to increase knowledge about the colonies; however, their specific motives differed considerably, as the letters attached to many of Ridyard's donations show. For some colonial officials, collecting ethnographic objects may have functioned much like amateur science or antiquarianism in the mid-nineteenth century: a rational hobby that allowed the development of expertise and a peer-group. One donor wrote to Ridyard, enclosing two fetishes, saying

> I have been unable to get much information about them ... [Mr Bennett] is a great student of folklore amongst these natives, and am sure he will be only too pleased to give you reliable information about it. These fetishes are like the Spanish Fleet, i.e. becoming very rare.[25]

Thus, as Coombes has shown, donating to the museum was mutually advantageous, enhancing the donor's standing as an amateur ethnographer, and enhancing the museum's collection.[26]

Missionaries and clergymen, unsurprisingly, seem in their donations, to have been concerned to show the efficacy of their efforts to Christianise and 'civilise' the African. Fetishes and artefacts donated by Archdeacon Crowther were said to have been relinquished by their owners upon their conversion to Christianity. Thus the important group of donors from West Africa represents a variety of motives and agendas.

Professionals and academic institutions became increasingly important to Liverpool Museum over the last years of the nineteenth century. Thus the new university was an important source for the museum, with donations from the Liverpool School of Tropical Medicine in 1901, and donations or loans from several professors. Archaeology professors Newberry and Garstang donated objects such as coffins and textiles from excavations in Egypt between 1911 and 1914. Also important were Liverpool Museum's acquisitions from other museums. These were numerous, especially from 1890 until the start of the First World War, and came from large, international museums. However, despite the specialisation and professionalisation in the production of knowledge which this indicates, the persistence of the older tradition of donations by amateur collectors and voluntary societies can still be seen into the twentieth century. In 1916 the Liverpool Naturalists Field Club gave an entomological collection and herbarium.[27]

Although Liverpool Museum's donors continued to represent a broad range of individuals and institutions, the trend was clearly towards institutions, and towards the interest groups of commerce, empire and academia. Of course, Liverpool was a large and important port, with strong links with West Africa; no other municipal museum displayed such a strong trend towards these institutions. Yet other museums did receive objects from similar institutional donors. Local manufacturers whose products could be classified as 'industrial art' often gave some examples, such as Messrs Elkington, who donated several of their bronzes to Birmingham Museum; there were several donations of Old Sheffield Plate and cutlery by manufacturers to Sheffield Museum, which also benefited from donations of cutlery and tools from consuls in China, Japan and Turkey (these were solicited by the curator, through the Foreign Secretary).[28] Such donations follow the pattern of institutional donation in Liverpool, though on a reduced scale. There were also donations from companies who acquired the objects as a by-product of their main activity: zoos, circuses and excavators. The importance of circuses and travelling menageries as a source of animal specimens for museums such as Sheffield has recently been highlighted. Preston Museum benefited significantly from donations from Blackpool Zoo, and also from archaeological finds unearthed during the Ribble Dock excavation and donated by the Ribble Dock Company.[29]

Municipal museums also exchanged, donated and received objects from other museums; other than in Liverpool, this was on a national level. This process was accelerated by the development of the Museums Association in 1889, one of whose aims was to facilitate the exchange of objects between (mainly municipal) museums. Not strictly donations, the rotating loan exhibits from the South Kensington Museum were extremely important to many municipal museums, such as Preston and Birmingham, and served to diffuse the agenda of that institution more widely.[30]

Finally, what of the staff who were employed at these museums? In certain museums, they underwent a fairly dramatic change in the course of this period, in numbers, training, specialisation and professional standing. The curators of municipal museums were initially subordinate to amateurs from local societies, or themselves came from the local society tradition; but by the end of the period some of them were professionals with authority, qualifications, a sizeable staff under them, a career structure and a peer group. They could act together through the Museums Association, and though they were still severely restricted by the budget set for them by their council, they were in all other respects autonomous. However, this trend should not be overstated; it is clear that in the smaller municipal museums none of this happened. In fact, as late as 1928 Sir Henry Miers found that only 14% of all museums had full-time paid curators; only around a dozen museums had a full-time curator with adequate staff.[31]

One of the most outstanding examples of professionalisation is in Liverpool. The development of the University was important for the character of the staff of the museum. The two most important figures for the museum's first forty years were the Reverend H. H. Higgins and the curator, T. J. Moore. The tradition of voluntary scientific societies was much more important in forming their outlook than was the principle of professional expertise, training, and autonomy. Higgins was a volunteer helper in the museum, who was co-opted onto the Museums Sub-committee, having previously worked on the Royal Institution's museum. He was also a member of the Literary and Philosophical Society, the Liverpool Naturalists Field Club, the Liverpool Microscopical Society, the Lancashire and Cheshire Entomological Society, and the Historic Society of Lancashire and Cheshire, and at various times was President of at least two of these. Clearly he was a leading figure in Liverpool's voluntary societies.[32]

Moore too shows the influence of voluntary intellectual and patronage systems on the museum. His first job was at the Zoological Society in London, where his father had also worked. In 1843, with references from Owen, Gray and Waterhouse, he came to work at the Earl of Derby's menagery, aviary and museum. When this was transferred to Liverpool Corporation on the earl's death, Moore came with it. Not only was his whole career rooted in voluntary societies, he had a similarly wide membership to Higgins'. In Liverpool he belonged to the Literary and Philosophical Society, the Liverpool Naturalists Field Club, and the Geological, Microscopical and Biological Societies. He was a Corresponding Member of the Zoological Society, as well as a member of the Royal Zoological Society of Ireland.[33]

However, after 1890, the University College, later Liverpool University, replaced the voluntary societies as the main source of knowledge and expertise for the museum. Dr H. O. Forbes, who was appointed Director of Museums in 1894, had been educated at the universities of Aberdeen and Edinburgh. During the 1880s he undertook several exploring expeditions in the East Indies, especially New Guinea. Between 1890 and 1893 he was Director of Canterbury Museum, New Zealand. This may be where he developed his ideas for the display of ethnographic material according to racial types. When appointed Director of Liverpool Museums, he was also Reader in Ethnography at Liverpool University College. He does not seem to have taken much part in voluntary societies. Moreover, additional advice and knowledge no longer came from those like Higgins, a product of the voluntary societies. Instead, co-opted members of the Museums Sub-committee were now increasingly professors at the university. Thus co-opted members between 1890 and 1918 included Professor Herdman (Natural History), Professor Bosanquet (Archaeology), and Professor Newberry (Egyptology).[34]

However, in other places the process of professionalisation was very patchy in municipal museums. In several museums in the late Victorian and Edwardian period, curators were in position for a long period, having been appointed young, and were the only curatorial member of staff. Elijah Howarth was curator of Sheffield Museum from 1876 until 1927; Thomas Sheppard was curator of Hull Municipal Museum from 1901 until 1941; Whitworth Wallis was Keeper of Birmingham Museum for over forty years. These men were hugely influential in shaping their own museum, and in developing the profession, through their training of other staff, and involvement in initiatives such as the Museums Association. However, the career paths and educational background of such men did vary. Thomas Sheppard had only an elementary education, and worked as a railway clerk until appointed curator in Hull at the age of twenty-four. This appointment was on the basis of his activities in Hull's scientific societies; he was secretary of the Hull Scientific and Field Naturalists' Club and a member of the Hull Geological Society, and had been elected a Fellow of the Geological Society in 1900. By this time he had published papers and a book on the local geology. The position of curator in Hull was not felt to be an onerous one; Sheppard was told on appointment that he could start at ten and leave when he liked, as long as he didn't spend any money! Howarth had equally little formal education, but his career included what could be called a practical apprenticeship; he was hired by Liverpool Museum at the age of fifteen, five years later becoming assistant curator there. He became curator in Sheffield at the age of twenty-one.[35] Family ties could be very important in stimulating and advancing a curatorial career: Whitworth Wallis at Birmingham was the son of George Wallis, Keeper of the Arts Department at South Kensington, and his brother, George Harry Wallis, became Director of the Nottingham Castle Museum and Art Gallery.[36]

The slow development of curatorial authority is reflected in the fact that curators continued to face conflict with councillors and members of scientific societies. The first curator at Sheffield, Charles Callaway, resigned after an argument with one of the most prominent councillors associated with the municipal museum project. Meanwhile in Leicester, a whole series of curators resigned over the years as a result of their subordination to the Honorary Curators.[37]

The staff of these municipal museums was small, and predominantly devoted to attendant duties; however, it did grow, and become more specialised, over this period. Sheppard started his career in Hull Museum with two attendants and a joiner; by 1906 he had an assistant, a clerk, and two attendants. In 1904 Howarth had two assistants, one superintendent, and four attendants. The assistants were increasingly educated and received training for their role; Charles Bradshaw, assistant from 1876, attended courses of the Science and Art Department in South Kensington, and at the Sheffield Mechanics' Institute, while J. W. Baggaley, an assistant in 1904, had trained at Firth College.[38]

The development of the Museums Association, mentioned above, was an important factor in the professionalisation of curating, although it took considerable time for some of its aims to be achieved, and they lie outside the scope of this study. The Association arose out of a meeting that took place in 1888 of ten curators, including Howarth of Sheffield; its inaugural meeting was held the next year. Although members included Platnauer of the Yorkshire Museum, owned and run by the Yorkshire Philosophical Society, the bulk of the members were from the leading municipal museums. There was also a distinct natural history bias; Birmingham, as a largely art historical museum, did not take part. The aims of the Association included promoting exchanges, and creating a journal for the profession. There was also a good deal of discussion on best practice in areas such as labelling, indexing, lectures to working men, and circulating school collections. The Association also established its interest in seeking support from central government, through means such as legislation, or the extension of the South Kensington Museum's Circulating Department.[39]

In some museums, professionalisation advanced very slowly and idiosyncratically. In Preston, there were few people employed in the museum over this period, and it is difficult to discover anything about them other than the fact of their employment. The first curator was Miss Margaret Barton, the existing librarian of Dr Shepherd's Library. On her death in 1891, Thomas Busfield was appointed. It seems that this position was principally a caretaker one (Teather has referred to the fact that when a curator was also a librarian, they were usually primarily a librarian).[40] Meanwhile in 1882 the Reverend Jonathan Shortt was appointed Honorary Curator. In 1894 his position was converted into a salaried one. In 1899, when he died, Mr W. B. Barton, who since 1895 had held the post of Art Director, was additionally made Curator. Shortt, an amateur naturalist, was vicar of Hoghton, near Preston. W. B. Barton had been born in Bradford-on-Avon in 1849, and was educated at the Royal College of Art.[41] While it is hard to be definitive on the basis of this limited information, it is clear that amateur enthusiasts continued to be important here (Shortt was responsible for the layout of all the objects except Art History in the new Harris building). There were high levels of education among staff, but little sign of a professional museological ethos, or of links with other museums' staff.

The municipal museum began life as a project of the urban elite, who were concerned largely with civic prestige, and with a rhetoric of service and improvement. In alliance with them, and overlapping somewhat in membership, were the amateur science community, who saw in municipal museums an opportunity to safeguard and expand their collections, to increase their audience and thus give legitimacy and prestige to their activities. Over time, this pattern altered, as councillors' social status dropped a little. They were increasingly concerned, in a changing municipal environment, with practical efficiency and providing value for ratepayers' money. Meanwhile donors increasingly, especially in the larger museums, represented special interest groups such as commerce and industry, or academia; and curators' aims, even if these were not fully realised, were to enhance their own professional standing, and they formed a substantial pressure group to this end, especially after the formation of the Museums Association. How did the lines of co-operation and negotiation fall across these groups? The civic elite and the amateur scientists worked together fairly effectively, as a result of the fact that they faced external opposition over the very creation of the museum in the first place. Later on, curators aligned themselves with commercial interests and particularly academia where they could; the first group offered objects, and a clear sense of relevance and practicality; the second offered authority and professional identity. In fact, it has been suggested that the growth in the research orientation of curators in larger museums around 1900 actually hindered the development of a clear curatorial professional identity.[42] The relationship between donors and council committees became more distant in that no longer were there such substantial overlaps between them, and no longer did they share much in the way of ethos; however, there was also no significant conflict between them, unless a donor sought to retain too much control over objects, or imposed conditions that had financial implications. The relationship prone to most conflict was that between curators and their council committees, and by 1914, questions of everyday control had mainly been resolved in the curator's favour, leaving only the issue of money; this was, of course, a major issue.

Curators were not satisfied with the budgets they had to work within, but some, such as Tom Sheppard, took a creative approach to the problem; it was said in 1923 that he had 'filled his museums and store by the laudable exercise of [the] same traits [as Viking raiders], having, like William the Conqueror, an ingrained habit of annexing objects first, and asking, or not asking, permission as seemed expedient afterwards,' or, as a Leeds University professor asked him, 'Well, Sheppard, and how's thieving?'[43]

How did involvement in the municipal museum constitute these groups? For some, such as the curators, this is obvious: they would not have existed without the museum, and the municipal museum in particular gave them an opportunity to create a professional identity, as the dominance of municipal museums in the Museums Association shows. For those councillors involved in the museum, it allowed them to make concrete part of their vision of the prestigious civic arena, to add their creation of the museum to a list of other civic projects, and to try and shape for themselves an identity as town fathers, claiming a heritage of cultural provision as well as a modern, progressive stance. For the amateur science community, it mainly offered a chance to make public a hitherto private identity. For donors, no collective identity developed; rather, it was an important means of highlighting, and stressing the public service ethos of individuals or groups. It was not the only means by which this could be done – there were many outlets for the donation of money and grand buildings – but the combination of the civic with science, art and education was attractive to many potential donors; and for those who sought a public arena for objects, it was ideal.

The question is thus set: what objects did the Victorian municipal museum acquire, and how, and how were these objects used? The following chapters will look at the objects, space and displays of these museums.

Notes

[1]   Liverpool Council Proceedings; biographical information is taken from Hugh Shimmin, *Pen and Ink Sketches of Liverpool Town Councillors*, (Liverpool 1866); B. G. Orchard, *Liverpool's Legion of Honour*, (Birkenhead 1893); W. T. Pike (ed), *Dictionary of Edwardian Biography: Liverpool*, (Edinburgh 1911), and obituary cuttings on microfilm at Liverpool Record Office, ref. Eq330 and Eq429.

[2]   Orchard, *Liverpool's Legion of Honour*, p. 150; Shimmin, *Pen and Ink Sketches*, p. 39; J. K. Walton, *Lancashire: A Social History 1558-1939*, (Manchester 1987), pp. 231-232.

[3]   Committee members are taken from Preston Council Minute Book, in the Lancashire Record Office; biographical information from A. Hewitson, ('Atticus'), *Preston Town Council, or Portraits of Local Legislators*, (Preston 1870), and *Mannex's Directory of Preston*, various years 1870-1914.

[4]   M. Whittle, 'Philanthropy in Preston: the changing face of charity in a nineteenth-century provincial town', (unpublished PhD. thesis, Lancaster University 1990) p. 119; *Catalogue of the Preston Exhibition* (Preston 1875).

[5]   M. Savage, *The Dynamics of Working-Class Politics: The Labour Movement in Preston 1880-1940*, (Cambridge 1987), p. 103.

[6]   E. P. Hennock, *Fit and Proper Persons: Ideal and Reality in Nineteenth-Century Urban Government*, (London 1973), p. 77; Stuart Davies, *By the Gains of Industry, Birmingham Museums and Art Gallery 1885-1985*, (Birmingham 1985), p. 10.

[7]   J. T. Bunce, *History of the Corporation of Birmingham*, vol. 2, (Birmingham 1885), p. xxxv.

[8]   Hennock, *Fit and Proper Persons*, p. 77.

[9]   Cynthia Brown, *Cherished Possessions, A History of New Walk Museum and Leicester City Museums Service*, (Leicester 2002), p. 9; F. B. Lott, *The Centenary Book of the Leicester Literary and Philosophical Society*, (Leicester 1935), pp. 31-32, 48-52.

[10]   Sheffield Council Minutes, 9 December 1874; 13 December 1876.

[11]   For example, the Derby and Mayer Museums which made up Liverpool Museum; the Harris Museum in Preston; the Feeney Art Galleries in Birmingham; and the Mappin Art Gallery in Sheffield.

[12]   Samuel J. M. M. Alberti, 'Field, Lab and Museum: The Practice and Place of Life Science in Yorkshire, 1870-1904' (unpublished PhD thesis, University of Sheffield 2000), p. 86.

[13]   The Derby estate's annual income was £163,273 in 1883 and was the biggest landed income in the nineteenth-century in Liverpool, Belfast, Cardiff, Sheffield, Huddersfield and Birmingham. D. Cannadine, *Lords and Landlords: The Aristocracy and the Towns 1774-1967*, (London 1980), p. 24, 387; H. Perkin, *The Origins of Modern English Society 1780-1880*, (London 1969), p. 19; 'The Egyptian Museum, No. 8 Colquitt Street, Liverpool', *The Liverpool Mercury*, 1 May 1852.

[14]   Orchard, *Liverpool's Legion of Honour*, p. 211; *Ceremonies Connected with the Opening of the Building for a Free Public Library and Museum*, (Liverpool 1861); letter from Earl of Derby to Liverpool Corporation, 1851, National Museums Liverpool (hereafter NML) Archives ref. MM16/1; 'The Egyptian Museum, No. 8 Colquitt Street, Liverpool'.

[15]   R. Tangye, *One and All: An Autobiography*, (London 1889), p. 119.

[16]   Bunce, *History*, p. 241.

[17]   A. Bensley Chamberlain, 'The Corporation Museum and Art Gallery', in British Association for the Advancement of Science, *A Handbook for Birmingham*, (1913), p. 234.

[18]   Michael Tooby, *'In Perpetuity and Without Charge': The Mappin Art Gallery 1887-1987*, (Sheffield 1987), pp. 8-11.

[19]   Alberti, 'Field, Lab and Museum', p. 86; Michael J. Bishop, 'New Biographical Data on Henry Clifton Sorby (1826-1908)', *Earth Sciences History*, 3, (1984), pp. 69-81.

[20]   Brears, P. and Davies, S., *Treasures for the People: The Story of Museums and Galleries in Yorkshire and Humberside*, (Yorkshire and Humberside Museums Council 1989), pp. 33-35.

[21]   Brears and Davies, *Treasures for the People*, pp. 18, 21, 29; Samuel J. M. M. Alberti, 'Conversaziones and the Experience of Science in Victorian England', *Journal of Victorian Culture* 8.2, (2003).

[22]   Minutes of the Museums Sub-Committee, Liverpool Corporation (hereafter Minutes, Liverpool) 1896-1917.

[23]   *Proceedings of the Literary and Philosophical Society of Liverpool* 16 (1861-2).

[24]   Minutes, Liverpool, March 1916.

[25]   Letter dated August 1898 in Ridyard File, NML Archives.

[26]   Annie E. Coombes, *Reinventing Africa: Museums, Material Culture and Popular Imagination in Late Victorian and Edwardian England*, (New Haven 1994), p. 132.

[27]   Minutes, Liverpool for the years 1894, 1896, 1911, 1913, 1914, 1916.

[28]   Davies, *By the Gains of Industry*, p. 35; E. Howarth, *Visitors' Guide to the Sheffield Public Museum, Weston Park*, (Sheffield 1883), p. 256-259; Sheffield Museum Annual Report 1897-8.

[29]   Alberti, 'Field, Lab and Museum', p. 86;, Minutes of the Free Public Library and Museum Committee, Preston Corporation (hereafter FPLC Minutes) 1885, 1886 and 1887.

[30]   Geoffrey Lewis, *For Instruction and Recreation: A Centenary History of the Museums Association*, (London 1989), p. 9 and passim.

[31]   Lynne Teather, 'Museology and Its Traditions, The British Experience 1845-1945', (unpublished PhD. thesis, University of Leicester, 1984), p. 195.

[32]   H. Ormerod, *The Liverpool Royal Institution, a Record and a Retrospect*, (Liverpool 1953), p. 55; 'The Rev. H. H. Higgins MA – A Liverpool Biologist', *Liverpool Bulletin*, vol. 2 (1952-3).

[33]   'Lord Derby's Museum – Reminiscences by Mr T. J. Moore', *Liverpool Review*, 5 November 1892.

[34]   D. Pike (ed.), *Australian Dictionary of Biography*, (Carlton, Vic. 1972), vol. 4; Annual Report Liverpool Museums (hereafter AR Liverpool) 1908; Liverpool Corporation Proceedings between 1890 and 1918.

[35]   T. Schadla-Hall, *Tom Sheppard, Hull's Great Collector*, (Beverley 1989), pp. 1, 32; Alberti, 'Field, Lab and Museum', pp. 78-9.

[36]   Teather, 'Museology', p. 194.

[37]   Alberti, 'Field, Lab and Museum', p. 79; Brown, *Cherished Possessions*, p. 9; Teather, 'Museology', p. 194.

[38]   Schadla-Hall, *Tom Sheppard*, p. 32; Alberti, 'Field, Lab and Museum', pp. 79-80.

[39]   Lewis, *For Instruction*, pp. 8-17; Alberti, 'Field, Lab and Museum', p. 81; Teather, 'Museology', chapter 7.

[40]   Teather, 'Museology', chapter 7.

[41]   J. Convey, *The Harris Free Public Library and Museum, Preston, 1893-1993*, (Preston 1993), p. 71.

[42]   Teather, 'Museology', chapter 7.

[43]   Schadla-Hall, *Tom Sheppard*, p. 9.

CHAPTER FIVE

Reading the Objects

What objects did Victorian museums contain, and how did they get them? This chapter looks at the contents of municipal museums in order to try and understand further the meaning and purpose of such institutions in the period. A museum object can be seen as a special kind of object, through which donors and curators seek to produce and ratify knowledge and power. It has been selected out of the vast possibilities of the material world. In order to understand the principles of selection, we need to think in terms of a system of objects, where some objects are valued more than others, and have different symbolic meanings.[1] This system is constituted by the relationship between people and objects; some people have the power to determine the meaning of objects, but people's possession of different objects can in fact give them power. As Pearce says, objects are 'both active and passive; we make them, and they influence us'.[2] Analysing this interaction between people and objects can help produce a much deeper understanding of the construction of the museum objects, and will help to show both how the middle-class provincial elites in question viewed various aspects of the material world, individually and more important collectively, and what role they expected the museum, as a gathering of objects, to play.

A useful starting point may be the modes of collecting summarised by Susan Pearce. Collecting is seen as a means by which the individual connects with, and acts on, the entire rest of the world:

> The forming of the collection is part of the relation between the subject, conceived as each individual human being, and the object, conceived as the whole world, material and otherwise, which lies outside him or her. The collections, in their acquisition, valuation and organisation, are an important part of our effort to construct the world.[3]

This engagement with the material world can take a number of forms, distinguished by different aims and different rationales of formation. The first distinguished by Pearce is the souvenir. This is an object collected primarily for its association with the collector's life history, whether this collector be an individual or a group such as a family or club. It also includes relics, that is, objects that belonged to famous people that are collected for the glamour-by-association they bring. However, their psychological function is not merely to preserve memories:

> They are an important part of our attempt to make sense of our personal histories, happy or unhappy, to create an essential personal

> and social self centred in its own unique life story, and to impose
> this vision on an alien world. They relate to the construction of a
> romantically integrated personal self, in which the objects are
> subordinated into a secondary role.[4]

Next there is the fetishistic collection where personality construction is led by the objects. The collection becomes an important part of the collector's personality, so that it is often known by the collector's name. Such a collection can be recognised by

> the lack of an intellectual rationale by which the material and its
> acquisition was informed ...: the sets have no rhyme or reason
> outside the covers of the album... The intention is to acquire more
> and more of the same kind of pieces.[5]

The aim of collecting in this way is equally to create personal meaning from the material world:

> The whole accumulation process is a deployment of the possessive
> self, a strategy of desire... . The fetishistic nature lies in the
> relationship between the objects and their collector, in which it is the
> collection which plays the crucial role in defining the personality of
> the collector, who maintains a possessive but worshipful attitude to
> the objects, and it is to the objects that the burden of creating a
> romantic wholeness is transferred.[6]

So both these modes of collecting are bound up with a project of creating intensely personal attributes; they 'attempt to create a satisfactory private universe, and both do this by trying to lift objects away from the web of social relationships.'
   Systematic collecting is different in that it is involved in the creation of a public relationship with objects. It can be defined thus:

> Systematic collection depends upon principles of organisation which
> are perceived to have external reality beyond the specific material
> under consideration, and which are held to derive from general
> principles deduced from the broad mass of kindred material through
> the operation of observation and reason; these general principles
> form part of our ideas about the nature of the physical world and the
> nature of ourselves.[7]

Thus, what is collected are examples, standing for whole sets of objects and concepts. Such a collection is organised by classification and seriality - an abstract context replacing the original one. Thus divisions seem intrinsic, not arbitrary.
   Most important is the aim of systematic collecting:

> Systematics draw a viewer into their frame, they presuppose a two-
> way relationship between the collection, which has something public

(not private) to say, and the audience, who may have something to learn, or something to disagree with.[8]

Thus it is a fundamentally communicative way of engaging with the material world, where the other two modes, on an individual level at least, are private and enclosed, self-referential.

A few caveats should be made about this analysis of collecting. Firstly, collectors do not necessarily follow one mode alone. This point can not be made strongly enough. One would have to say that most collections show characteristics of at least two modes of collecting. A collection might well also go through successive modes as its owner and location change.[9]

Secondly, these modes do not exhaust the rationales in which objects may be accumulated. Particularly relevant here is the idea of the trophy. While it has been considered an extension of either the souvenir or the fetishistic collection, the sense in which it is most useful as a concept for this study is as a form of collecting where the social or power relation it describes is its foremost attribute. It is not disguised by a scientific rationale (although this might accompany it), and the collector does not form a private dialogue with the object. It is rather the celebration, the material expression, of the collector's power over the collected. This interpretation is closer to Jordanova's:

> The trophy simultaneously expresses victory, ownership, control and domination. As such it has three qualities - it presents in material form, however incomplete, sets of practices; it triggers fantasies and memories, and it elicits admiration.[10]

In addition, collecting practices are affected by the category of object they focus on. Thus, natural history collections tend to towards the systematic, with less opportunity for souvenir or fetishistic collecting, notwithstanding the fact that fossil or crystal collecting may be fetishistic; zoology and geology are not generally considered suitable for carrying memories, associations, past experiences, while any expansion of such a collection would tend to follow categories of genera, species and so on, as a universal and easily applicable scheme. Conversely, man-made objects, already resonant, make ideal souvenirs, particularly exotic, foreign ones. Their intrinsic attractiveness also encourages fetishistic collectors, while the degree of specialised knowledge needed to form systematic collections in these areas means that they are less common. Where there is such knowledge, however, as in for example archaeology collections, they will probably be systematic

This is linked to the influence on rationales and methods of collecting that is exercised by institutions and modes of knowledge at any specific time. These act to determine the regulations governing public approval of collections and objects; which collections can receive recognition and which must remain in a scrapbook.

> It is important to analyse how powerful discriminations made at particular moments constitute the general system of objects within which valued artefacts circulate and make sense.[11]

Here a broad chronology of museum development has been developed, where Renaissance and early modern collections were eclectic; rare, exotic, wonder-producing objects were the model, and accorded with ways of knowing; they were also useful for demonstrating the power of individuals. From the seventeenth century, the gradual development of institutional scientific collecting replaced earlier modes. The typical object exemplifying the laws of nature was valued over the rare and exotic. The Repository of the Royal Society, set up in the late seventeenth century, has been identified as an important early example of this trend – a public institution, it was intended to be, eventually, a complete collection, embodying a universal taxonomy, and for 'the most serious and diligent study of the most able Proficient in Natural Philosophy' rather than for 'Divertisement and Wonder and Gazing and like Pictures for children to admire and be pleased with'. However, by the end of the seventeenth century the Repository had failed quite markedly to achieve these aims; the collection was far from complete or exemplary, and was dominated by rare and exotic specimens. One of the main reasons identified for this was the Repository's institutional weakness; it was poorly funded and relied on voluntary support, with an amateur ethos. It relied on donations to build its collection, and these donations, such as a bottle full of stag's tears, did not accord with the aim of completing a universal taxonomy. They were described at the time as 'casual presents, which either strangers or any of their own members bestowed upon them'. Donating had a social cachet, but equally the fledgling Royal Society needed social support and was happy to take anything from an aristocratic source.[12]

Although the Repository of the Royal Society did not achieve a complete change in the nature of the collection and museum object, it is generally felt that it was the beginning of a process which was achieved in the nineteenth century. By the late nineteenth century, the systematic collection had become dominant institutionally and epistemologically, not only in natural history, but in ethnography[13] and increasingly in the history of art and design at the South Kensington Museum. It is also argued that this modernisation of collecting was accompanied by a change in the production and consumption of the collection: Renaissance collections, and even more so the collections of the early scientific societies, were essentially produced and consumed by the same body. Those who built the collection, through donation or other means, were also those who used it. With the nineteenth century, and the birth of the public museum, that connection was lost. The producers of the collection increasingly became the curators, with a professional ethos, and an overall plan for exhibition of the collection. Consumers were now the general public, whose role was to come and be educated and/or entertained, depending on what philosophy prevailed with the curator. The role of donors in this scheme is not clear, but presumably they were to give objects according to the criteria of curators, and not really figure greatly in the production process.[14]

However, it is clear that the process of change from one type of collector and collection to another was much more gradual, and on a local level was never really completed – in municipal museums, individuals could use donation to demonstrate wealth, education and taste, just like a Renaissance prince, or to augment the status of their own collection, or even to claim scientific status for their particular interest. The municipal museum was thus a key site for the negotiation of meaning of good objects and collections. Institutional and epistemological structures affected the range of meanings which any group of donors could make from their objects; yet at the same time their collective donations brought meanings and values which modified the structures curators were trying to implement. This all has a wider significance than just who gave what to museums, in that museums can be seen as one of the institutions underpinning the wider system of objects; the fact that these artefacts are singled out for public display, and removed from the commercial circulation of goods (in fact they cease to be 'goods' at all), highlights the fact that other objects are private, have no scientific or artistic value, or are primarily commercial commodities. The way in which good museum donations are defined, therefore, has implications for all of material culture. Broadly speaking, in the relationship between donors, objects and the museum institution, over time the museum managed to tighten the criteria for what constituted a museum object; it should contribute to producing and disseminating knowledge in certain defined subject areas. This could be to the benefit of donors, who gained scientific authority; but it made donating more difficult as objects had to fit increasingly strict criteria, and their worth to the individual donor was not enough to guarantee their acceptance.

Initially, it is useful to look at the categorisation of objects: we use different categories, such as 'natural history' or 'fine art', to analyse the shape and development of museums, but those categories could be largely created by the museums themselves. In all that follows, therefore, it is important to bear in mind that any category referred to is not an absolute division corresponding to a 'real' group in the material world, but rather an imposition on that world created by structures of knowledge. In fact, individual curators had a large measure of freedom in their categorisation of an object as for example, art or archaeology or ethnography, and municipal museums did not all conform to one standard way of dividing objects up. For example, Liverpool Museum regarded some historical objects as Local History, whereas in Sheffield such artefacts were regarded as either Archaeology or Industrial Art.

It is also the case that in some instances donors could have some influence over the categorisation of objects. In Liverpool after 1900 several new categories of donation emerged, such as local history, local manufactures and economic products, and this was at least partly because of increased donation in these areas. There is no doubt that many commercial donors would have liked to see an economic products room being set up.[15] This is an important reminder that donors could take the initiative in developing the museum, not just curators. However, wider structures of knowledge were probably most important in forming consensus about the nature of the museum object. This was particularly important for validating such new categories of museum object as local history and economic products. The study of local history was emerging with the academic interest in folk culture and British archaeology, while a greater focus on commerce and trade was spreading from, for example, the Imperial Institute and world fairs. A biologist from the Philadelphia Commercial Museum said in the 1890s,

> It is the earnest aim of this department to put the international
> commerce in raw products on a scientific basis, and to most
> successfully aid, with exact data, information and investigation,
> international trade and industry.[16]

Thus, classification is an important tool in the creation of meaning.

Bearing this in mind, we can see that from the beginning of the period until about 1890, natural history, especially zoology, was the dominant category in most municipal museums. In places such as Liverpool, Leicester, Sheffield and Preston, the municipal museum was based on one initial, large donation made up almost exclusively of natural history. In Liverpool, donations and purchases in the years after its foundation also focussed on natural history. Natural history, as Thackray has pointed out, was well established by 1850 as a form of middle-class polite knowledge.[17] After this date it also became caught up with the cult of hunting, bringing new meanings of manliness, social status and often foreign travel. Thus a natural history collection embodied

> the curiosity, classificatory power and destructive capacity of the
> hunter in the service of a scientific knowledge which epitomized
> Western man's command of a global natural world.[18]

Natural history was also the category which would tend to dominate museums at this time because it was the one most linked to a visual display of taxonomies as a means of creating knowledge and understanding. The museum was a vital tool for learning and researching in natural knowledge in 1850, in a way it was not for other subjects.

To some extent, the interest in the man-made was an extension of these meanings to the human world. This is particularly true of Liverpool, where most man-made donations were in ethnography, and fitted into an equally universal classificatory system. If one looks at Elder Dempster staff donations from West Africa, for example, both natural history and ethnography were given with the aim of filling lacunae, achieving complete representation. However, ethnography was not the only classification assigned to man-made objects. Those pertaining to Europe and Egypt were generally treated as existing in a temporal rather than spatial framework; they were put into a system of 'pasts'. Thus these objects were part of the history of the donors and museum, rather than being alien to them. Most of this material was 'great', designed to invoke or demonstrate spiritual qualities, heroism or a high calibre of personal or societal development. Thus coins, ceramics, arms and classical archaeology embodied attributes of civilisation from the past as an integral part of the development of the present.

Man-made artefacts increased massively from 1890. Even before this, though, a shift in emphasis away from an almost purely natural history municipal museum was in evidence. Birmingham Museum was focussed on art, art history and applied art from the start, and did not acquire a natural history section until 1913. In Liverpool, the donation of the Mayer Museum in 1867 brought a large and valuable collection of antiquities and *objets d'art* into the museum, and was the foundation of what would become very important archaeology and ethnography divisions. At the Harris Museum in Preston a fairly heterogeneous collection, dominated by natural history, was swamped by the purchase of reproduction Graeco-Roman and Renaissance statuary towards the end of the nineteenth century. In Sheffield and Leicester, the last quarter of the nineteenth century saw an increase in archaeology, either donated or actively acquired through excavating.[19]

Man-made objects could fall into a variety of categories, such as fine art, industrial art, commercial products, archaeology, antiquities, local history and ethnography. The reason for the expansion of some of these is straightforward; for archaeology, for example, there was much more excavation taking place by 1900, both locally and abroad, and the subject was developing academically. Thus more objects were available, and an increasingly sophisticated taxonomy could be implemented in their display. There were also more professors of archaeology to make a case for archaeology in the museum.[20] For categories such as industrial art and commercial products, expansion was a more complex matter, driven by a belief among donors in the usefulness and educative function of museums, as well as a concern to enhance and celebrate the image of the group providing donors and controllers of the museum.

Where did museum objects come from? This is an important question because of its relevance in competing arguments over what a municipal museum should be. There was a growing body of opinion which suggested that a museum should represent its local area, either because it would be pointless to try and compete with national museums for national and international collections, or for reasons of local pride, or, especially with natural history, so as to form a reference collection for local collectors.[21] However, this was not the only point of view. In natural history, it was also argued that a brief overview of national species, or of principles and processes such as evolution, would also be valuable, and one commentator, the Reverend Higgins, who was responsible for much of the display in Liverpool Museum until the end of the nineteenth century, argued that foreign specimens were better, because often more colourful and exotic, than dull British species, in terms of stimulating and holding the interest of children and non-specialists visitors.[22] Donors certainly gave objects from the locality, Britain generally, and abroad, and while curators seem to have favoured the locality slightly more than donors, they still bought plenty from further afield. It is clear, therefore, that though collections illustrating the locality may have existed in many municipal museums, much of the material illustrated Britain in general, and the wider world. In Preston, the majority of accessions, about 45 per cent, came from Britain, about equally split between the locality and the rest of the country. Europe, Asia and the Americas each accounted for about 15 per cent, with Australasia, Africa and unspecified 'foreign' making up the rest.[23] This rough mix may well have been typical of municipal museums over this period. In Leicester, for example, the second half of the nineteenth century saw acquisitions from New Zealand, Egypt, Canada, India and Italy, along with local Roman archaeology, and locally shot birds. Although Sheffield Museum contained the important largely local Bateman archaeology collection, and objects relating to local industries, it also contained Greek, Etruscan and Egyptian antiquities.[24] In Birmingham, despite the stress on the museum's relationship with local industry, it was felt that any and every example of good design in industrial art was worth displaying, and much of this came from the rest of Europe. The curator himself made collecting trips to Italy. It is significant that purchases here also came from abroad, because in most cases curators focussed more than donors on the locality. In Hull, for example, the extremely active collecting policy of the curator Tom Sheppard often involved his contacting archaeologists and collectors in a wide but broadly local area, and cajoling them into donating to his museum. In this way he acquired important objects from Lincolnshire and all over Yorkshire. However, he was not dogmatic about keeping the collections local, and, for example, acquired a large portion of the exhibits of the Anglo-Japanese Exhibition of 1910.[25]

A detailed analysis of acquisitions at Liverpool Museum allows some understanding of change over time to emerge. However, Liverpool was in many ways not a typical municipal museum, particularly in its access to West African objects. Nevertheless, some suggestive points emerge. While Africa formed an increasingly important source of acquisitions, other foreign areas such as Europe, Asia, and the Americas became much less important in the 1890s and early 1900s. Local objects, by contrast, grew quite dramatically, particularly in natural history. This can partly be explained by curatorial policy; as mentioned earlier, Higgins preferred foreign specimens, while the new Director of Museums, Dr Forbes, appointed in 1894, wanted as a matter of policy to do more to represent the local flora and fauna. It is also clear that Local History as a category was being developed by Liverpool Museum in the early years of the twentieth century.[26]

It seems, therefore, that nineteenth-century municipal museums did not represent their localities to any great extent, both donors, and to a lesser extent curators, seduced by exotic, large, and fascinating objects, both man-made and natural, from all over the world. Around 1900 curators in particular started to try and move towards a systematic representation of the locality, possibly as a field in which they would not be competing with national and international museums, and also as a result of the expansion of British archaeology, and a growing interest in local history.[27]

By looking in more detail at individual donations, we can try and understand the symbolic work they did. In particular, it is valuable to distinguish between systematic collecting, which aims to create a relationship between the viewer and a body of knowledge, and other types of collecting, which aim to create a relationship between the collector and various qualities. For these types of collecting, their symbolic value was to endow the donor with certain qualities, such as prestige, historical depth, civility. For example, most collecting in Preston that found its way into the Harris Museum was an activity pertaining most closely to the personality and ego of the collector, and only secondarily overlaid with a systematic rationale. Souvenirs were numerous, such as the twelve tropical birds, four shells, knife, mask, and axe from the South Sea Islands given in 1882, the objects from New Zealand in 1887, the fragments from eastern temples and mosques in 1890, and the South Sea Islands ornament and arrows in 1890. There were also various example of that type of souvenir which invokes the association of famous people or institutions, such as King William IV's walking stick, given in 1884; medals commemorating the marriage of the Duke and Duchess of York in 1894, and various other commemorative medals; or what is actually described as a 'souvenir of Preston Savings Bank' in 1908.[28]

Fetishistic collections were also frequent, such as the donation of two collections of plaster casts of medallions of famous people in 1903. In these, the collector has defined a category, and then simply accumulated within that category, without attempting to demonstrate principles; they are 'samples...rather than...examples'. This is also true (probably) of the donation of oriental and 'varied' coins in 1896; that of oyster shells in 1900; and antique Japanese jewellery in 1911.[29]

Systematic collections are less common than either of the others, although usually quite important. They include the specimens of minerals and the artificial flints given in 1885; the geological specimens in 1888; specimens of Egyptian textiles in 1895; and thirty-five cases of stuffed and mounted birds in 1905.[30]

Around 1900 one finds another type of collection appearing. This is the trophy, the product of big game hunting. Thus one finds two golden eagles given in 1896; a crocodile skin in 1899; three specimens of sheep and ibex from Central Asia in 1909; and argali sheep head in 1913; and a capercailie and the head of a roe deer in 1916. These are all known to be the results of hunting trips, and their then being donated for the purposes of display is an announcement of their mastery of nature, and of geographical terrain, by the donor base in Preston, which was largely elite and middle class.[31]

Many of these themes, of the souvenir, linked with great people, of the fetishistic accumulation of objects, of the demonstration of domination and superiority, and of the systematic demonstration of principles about the world, are present in two of the largest donations made to the Harris Museum over this period. Although bigger, and in Jacson's case more valuable, than 'typical' collections, they are not strikingly different in terms of content from many other donations. They are worth looking at so that the interlinking of these themes can be examined. The Jacson Collection and the Foster Collection were both given in 1894. The Jacson Collection was given by Mrs Jacson in memory of her recently deceased husband, C.R. Jacson, who had been one of the most important people in Preston. He was a millowner and member of the Masters' Association. He was active in local government, being Mayor of Preston in 1865, a JP, and Deputy Lieutenant of the County. He was also a Trustee of or on the council of the Hospital, the Harris Orphanage and the Preston Exhibition of 1875, as well as donating to the new parish church. He had, moreover, a Rugby education and a country house and estate. He was clearly one of the leading elite figures in Preston.[32] His collection consisted of:

Plaster casts of Parthenon friezes and medallions
Casts of Phigaleian marbles
A miniature of Napoleon I
Coins

Medals
Chinese, Japanese and Algerian curiosities
Microscope and lenses[33]

Here there are several elements. The systematic mode can be seen in the casts, which seem to be a systematic representation of the principles of classical statuary, and of the principle that classical statuary is one of the great categories of art history. This collecting gains importance from the art historical value of the subject matter: it is a 'good' collection. And it is valuable for the collector also, because it shows a familiarity with high, classical art and art history; it demonstrates cultural capital. The miniature of Napoleon I creates a direct association between the historical depth, and in this case historical figure represented, and the possessor of the object. The Chinese, Japanese and Algerian curiosities are more complex. The description 'curiosities' suggests an older type of museum object, where the strange and exotic are displayed with emphasis on each individual object, rather than the links between them. At the same time, these ethnographic objects are quite easily transformable into a systematic representation of comparative ethnography, or of the cultural categories of a particular society. The subject matter is not the same as the historically loaded objects in the rest of the collection; here it is a representation of other cultures, seen as less significant but more 'curious' than the Western tradition of civilisation. They do not bring the associations of greatness, of being an important actor in the historical process. Instead they allow the owner or museum visitor to satisfy curiosity, to develop knowledge about these cultures. If the earlier objects represent a beneficial relationship between the possessor and the great figures of Western history, the latter objects represent a relationship of power and exploitation between the possessor or viewer, and the people of the country of origin.

The Foster Collection was somewhat more systematic, and had been on loan to the museum for some time. It was given to the museum on the occasion of its owner moving to Australia, on the conditions that it was publicly and suitably displayed, and known as the Foster Collection.[34] It consisted of:

Clothing showing needlework of India, China and Japan
Pictures
Ornaments
Charms
Pottery from India and Japan
Japanese swords and curved sticks
South Sea Island shells
New Zealand ferns[35]

Here again one sees a combination of the ethnographic and the European and historic. In addition, this collection contains natural history. These specimens here have the attributes of exoticness, of appropriation from another place and people, as well as those of polite science. Thus by association their possessors gain not only culture and scientific knowledge, but knowledge specifically of foreign areas, and therefore a position of superiority in relation to those areas and their people. In addition there is a range of rationales for collecting represented. The group of clothing showing needlework from India, China and Japan incorporates the elements of demonstration, the fundamental function of education that defines the systematic mode. However, the general focus of the ethnographic part of the collection is on the visually attractive and unusual; it is in many ways a more developed version of a collection of curios. Though groups have internal systematicity, the variety of objects collected is not systematic. There are strong elements of the fetishistic accumulation of objects within a collector-defined category. One may also speculate that the focus on India and Japan reflects an acquaintance with these areas, from travel or work, and that these collections may have originated as souvenirs. So this collection may show at least traces of all modes, in a progression from souvenir, to fetish, to systematic group.

What one sees in these two collections, then, is a combination of types of object and ways of collecting, deployed by the collector in order to gather a variety of attributes, or qualities-by-association, around themselves. The collection thus formed, when donated to the museum, is actually the gift of a series of statements about the (now collective) owner, the town of Preston, or its middle-class elite. These statements can be summarised thus.

- The owner is knowledgeable about the canon of Western European art. He or she knows not only good art from bad art, but historically significant art.
- The owner shares qualities with the great men of Western history, as well as being knowledgeable about history in general. He has historical depth.
- The owner is thus the inheritor of the entire symbolic legacy of the Western historic and artistic tradition. He is superlatively civilised.
- The owner is intrinsically superior to other cultures and societies, by virtue of his ability to represent that culture through its objects; the constitution of that culture as the *object* of Western collecting and exhibition.
- The owner has appropriate middle-class interests, using natural history collecting to demonstrate polite knowledge and facilitate social contact and solidarity.
- The owner also has a symbolic mastery of nature, and is thus entitled, in fact obliged, to act as its custodian, worldwide.

As a result, Preston as a town was endowed with attributes of historical depth, and associated with famous people. Its civic history was celebrated.[36] The fact that in Preston systematic collecting was less frequent than either fetishistic or souvenir collecting means that very few of the donations carried the impulse of demonstrating a principle, or any educative or informative imperative. They were mainly directed towards the end of defining, representing and augmenting the personality of the collector, and hence the analysis of their qualities above is central to understanding the museum. The weakness of systematic collecting in Preston undoubtedly relates to its very local and unspecialised donor base.

In Liverpool, by contrast, donations were formed with a much more educative, systematic rationale. Very little fetishistic collecting appeared, even allowing for under-representation of this particular mode in the sources. Souvenirs were nearly as infrequent, but in 1891 there was a donation of two skulls from a battle, a coral plaque from an East African mosque, and a coco de mer, from Surgeon Weightman, RN.[37] This is a very clear example of the souvenir collection: the documentation and preservation of a life in objects. Yet this is also the commemoration of a power relationship: a trophy. The skulls particularly are trophies in a basic and visceral way; the physical remains of the enemy. The plaque as well would seem to be plunder of a straightforward kind. The qualities of the trophy collect around many of Liverpool's donations: there is also the donation of two gorilla skeletons by a resident of Gabon in 1862, or one donation (among many) by Mr St George Littledale in 1902 of a Himalayan ibex, wild camel, and Saira sheep.[38] He was a big game hunter in Central Asia who regularly donated to the Liverpool Museum. In general, then, it seems that power relations over nature could be expressed more nakedly and in a more celebratory fashion than power relations over other cultures and societies. Where other cultures were involved, attention to the educative and informative aspects of the collection, to the principles it demonstrates, overlay and justified the power relation. Thus in 1904 there was a donation of a large group of fetish figures and head ornaments 'obtained during punitive expeditions in the Ijoh country, South Nigeria', which was held to demonstrate African religious beliefs and ornamentation principles. These of course are Western categories, with Western interpretations of the principles and beliefs as primitive and inferior. Thus the collection demonstrated the moral and intellectual inferiority of African cultures. This is the source of the particular symbolic importance of these objects, which may be called trophy-systematics; at the same time as they celebrate and materially demonstrate an unequal power relation, they explain and naturalize the reason for it, as a matter of inherent, scientifically determined superiority and inferiority. Other examples are the brass weights and boxes from Ashanti, from the Governor of the Gold Coast in 1905, and the group of 600-800 Maori artefacts in 1911. The trophy-systematics, which are connected with other cultures rather than nature, cluster in the colonially active 1900-1910 period.[39]

There are also a lot of what appear to be straightforwardly systematic donations to Liverpool Museum. Their extreme numerical dominance may well result from their being thought more worthy of being recorded in full than less scientifically rigorous donations, but nevertheless this is clearly the most important mode of collecting. Thus in 1879 one finds the Phillips Collection of minerals being donated, comprising, according to the Annual Report, 'a typical collection of great value to students of mineralogy'. In 1887 the Taylor Collection of humming birds was given, and in 1896 a portion of the Tristram Collection of Birds was donated (the rest was sold). This was reported to be:

almost the last of the great undispersed private collections which
were amassed by wealthy cultivators of this science in England
during the past half-century,

the significance of this being the emphasis on collecting as a science.[40] There were
systematic collections in human history too, mainly after 1900. In 1890 the 15th
Earl of Derby gave a collection of over 300 prehistoric implements. In 1892 a
systematic collection of the industrial manufactures of the Chinese was given, in
1913 a large collection of Pre-Columbian antiquities from Honduras, and in 1914
Professor Newberry donated the basis of a systematic collection of ethnographic
textiles, comprising a Nubian wedding dress, a Chinese army uniform, a lady's
costume from Lima, and a headdress from Admiralty Island.[41] As someone who
taught and researched in this kind of field, he can be expected to have focused on
the demonstration of theories and principles in his donating.

The largest group of donations between around 1890 and the First World War
were those given by regular donors in West Africa, mainly through Arnold
Ridyard, who was also the largest donor, and transported by Elder Dempster. As
they collected specifically according to the needs of the Liverpool Museum, they
were not souvenirs or fetishes; they were not collected either to preserve life
experiences or to bear and extend the collector's personality. The donors' names
were associated with the objects nowhere except within the pages of the Minutes
and Annual Report, until after Ridyard's retirement when a plaque commemorating
his contribution to the museum was placed there. In other words, despite their
somewhat haphazard appearance, these are systematic collections. The difference
is that the principles they demonstrate are those determined by the museum. The
donors are acting more or less as outworkers, filling gaps in the museum's stocks.
This means that the collection follows the rationale of the museum rather than that
of the donors. A typical donation through Ridyard would be this from 1898:

Ethnographic objects, gazelle, monkey, gorilla from Ridyard himself
Monkey and fish
Four animals
Photographs of natives and scenery, from various associates[42]

It seems possible that these donations were trophies of Britain's commercial
and political dominance of this area, yet they came from native rulers in more or
less the same numbers as they did from British commercial and political officials.
This indicates that there was a consensus that these objects demonstrated scientific
knowledge about West African nature and societies, rather than celebrating the
naked exercise of power. This kind of donation continued, indeed flourished after
1910, when trophy donations were becoming less common. It appears that as
museum objects, trophies were becoming less acceptable, and a systematic,
particularly educational or informative orientation, more or less compulsory. This
parallels the increasing specialisation and development of expertise among staff
and donors.

In addition, commercially-driven systematic donations formed a steady contribution to the museum. For example, in 1879, one finds the gift of

> a complete collection of samples of cotton of every known growth, made up according to Liverpool classification and named and arranged in case, presented by Messrs Hornby, Hemelryk & Co.,

and in 1911, a collection of tiles, stamps and plates 'illustrating modern methods of tile manufacture' from Pilkington's Tile and Pottery Works.[43] As with the systematic ethnographic collections from colonial areas, the demonstration of knowledge gained justified the control exercised by the commercial or colonial body; in this case over areas, products, workforces and to a certain extent consumers.

Thus the dominant mode of collecting and donating in Liverpool was systematic, and it was usually found in collecting of the Other; of geographically distant flora, fauna, and human cultures. This means that in contrast to Preston, it overtly focussed on informing and educating. Donations were made with the primary aim of demonstrating abstract ideas about the world, rather than as a means of deploying associated qualities about the collective body of the donors.

As a corollary, the principles to be illustrated were different to the qualities collected in Preston. There, domination was only a minor theme; the attributes of civilisation, art and high culture were far more important. In Liverpool, a major port, there was a significant emphasis on superiority and domination. Donors gave objects which conformed to a scientifically ratified type of collection, objects which illustrated apparently naturally occurring divisions and hierarchies, particularly in the natural world, and in non-European cultures and societies. Such donations not only demonstrated the inevitability of hierarchies of power, they demonstrated the actual fact of this power; were in fact an important part of the exercise of power, in that they demonstrated the Europeans' ability to appropriate, to interpret and to know the culture or nature they controlled.[44] That knowledge was the end product of this appropriation was its most important justification.

These two museums probably represent two extremes of donation patterns; for most municipal museums, donation fell somewhere between the two, though closer to the Preston than the Liverpool model in most cases. However, the extent to which the aims and values of the donor were retained after the object entered the museum depended on the curator, and as we shall see, curators had a significantly different outlook. Their main goal was to enhance their professional authority and expertise, by amassing systematic collections which were complete and illustrated modern theories and knowledge; they were also very keen to eliminate anything that seemed to be a curiosity, resembling an earlier type of museum object by being strange and rare. Donors' ability to dictate the meaning and use of their gifts declined during this period. Early in the period, large, prestigious donors had a considerable amount of say in the use of their objects. They often stipulated conditions such as that the label should read 'Donated by ...', or that it should be, for example, used to demonstrate industrial processes. In Liverpool in the 1860s, a few individuals, not even donors but lending objects, were allowed to put their fully formed displays in the museum: one case of educational geology displays, and one series of models of engineering works. By the end of the century, not only were donors less able to stipulate conditions, but increasingly curators rejected donations which did not meet their criteria. From the 1890s Liverpool Museum was rejecting quite a number of donations on the grounds of lack of space, keeping only the best. Curators developed embryonic acquisitions policies by giving guidelines for donors. As early as 1862, Liverpool Museum launched a scheme to encourage donations from the mercantile marine, and produced a pamphlet instructing sailors how to go about collecting specimens. In a rather less systematic manner, in 1882 Leicester Museum's chairman wrote to the press asking 'sporting friends' to donate animals they might shoot to the museum; he added a list of the specimens most wanted. A few museums, notably Liverpool, mounted their own collecting expeditions in order to have maximum control over the nature of their collection.[45]

Although such a thing as an acquisitions policy for purchases seems to have been unknown, most museums favoured one or the other, or both, of two approaches to building collections in natural history. The first was to build a complete collection of the flora, fauna, and geology of the locality. This approach was recommended by commentators on municipal museums, such as Thomas Greenwood and William Flower. It coincided very closely with many local collectors' aims, and indeed, one of the arguments for museums focussing on local specimens was that they should act as a reference service for collectors from the town. The second approach was to form a so-called index collection illustrating the main divisions in the animal and plant kingdoms, and, as such theories developed, key concepts like habitats, natural selection, protective colouring.[46] Generally speaking, donations could be used for this, and purchases were only necessary to fill the odd gap. Thus Howarth, the curator at Sheffield, spoke of 'judicious expenditure from time to time, of comparatively small sums in the purchase of specimens to fill the gaps'. However, all curators had less money than they would have liked for purchasing objects, and relied additionally on exchanging with other museums. This was particularly useful for natural history collections, where duplicates could be exchanged, and were sometimes accepted for this very purpose.[47]

In other areas such as industrial art, archaeology and anthropology, objects might be much more expensive, and potential sources of such objects were not so plentiful as for natural history. While Birmingham's Whitworth Wallis went on purchasing expeditions to Italy, he was an exception. Birmingham's museum had received significant donations of money rather than objects, which of course allowed the curator to purchase what he wanted, and one sees a lot of expensive acquisitions in fine and applied art there.[48] However, in the 1890s both Liverpool and Preston did spend quite large amounts of money on prestigious items in art and anthropology. Preston is the most dramatic example: around £3,000 was spent on reproduction Graeco-Roman and Renaissance statuary; this sum was matched by grant-in-aid from the Department of Science and Art, the source of the reproductions. Liverpool's most obvious purchase in these years was of objects from Benin City, from various military officers who took part in the Punitive Expedition there in 1897.[49]

In sum, then, purchases formed a much smaller proportion of acquisitions than donations, but did follow a somewhat different rationale. Curators were concerned to fill gaps in their collection, to follow a scientific plan, and to acquire objects that might be useful for display, such as models, that donors were less interested in. However, they also bought some prestigious, expensive items, particularly art objects.

How far are the class and gender divisions of Victorian society apparent in the museum's objects? This is not a straightforward issue; it has been pointed out that Lancashire handloom weavers and the Earl of Derby were both engaged in natural history collecting in the first half of the nineteenth century.[50] Yet it is equally clear that status is involved here: Lord Derby and the weavers were certainly not collecting together, for example, or on the same scale, and only Derby's collection went on to become the foundation of one of the largest municipal museums in the country. The weavers' collections often became part of so-called 'inn-parlour' museums, and though these might eventually become part of municipal museums, they tended to be the late-developing, smaller museums, and the names of the collectors would not be preserved.[51] However, collecting and donating could act to enhance social status; this is borne out in the donation of the Hodgkinson collection of British birds to the Harris Museum, Preston, in 1881, by Mr J. B. Hodgkinson, yarn agent and amateur naturalist. This appears to have been an impeccably scientific and rational collection. The 500 specimens were all mounted, cased and arranged by Mr Hodgkinson, and some of them were stuffed by him. Hodgkinson's knowledge of natural history was extensive; he contributed articles to *The Entomologist* and *The Zoologist*, and was described by a local newspaper as 'one of the most accomplished of unprofessional investigators of the present day'. His bird collection had previously been lent to the Preston Exhibition of 1875, to which he had also lent some invertebrates. For this exhibition he had chaired the Natural History and Scientific Sub-Committee.[52] All of this suggests a social benefit bestowed by the collection; in Thackray's formula, it was polite knowledge for marginal men, and Hodgkinson was certainly marginal.[53] A former cotton mill hand, his collection allowed him to develop expertise, demonstrate his rational use of his leisure, and to take a sizeable role in events like the Exhibition. However, we can, I think, go further, and argue that his collection constructed Hodgkinson as a self-made man, that most mythical of Victorians. As a local newspaper put it,

> Mr Hodgkinson has risen from a very humble rank in life to a position of respect and independence... He owes all his achievements to his patience and steadfastness in research.[54]

Needless to say, women as well as men were involved in collecting; yet the archetypal Victorian collector was always a man. Davidoff and Hall argue that for women in the nineteenth century, the joys of possessing, classifying and arranging were limited to the domestic: linen, clothing, plants in their garden. In other words, their collections, like themselves, were restricted to the private sphere, and thus by definition would not form part of a museum. It has sometimes been assumed that men collect, and that this is a serious, creative activity, whereas women merely consume, which is a frivolous and ultimately meaningless activity.[55] The question of gender identities is, therefore, interestingly illuminated by the examination of women's collections in the public sphere after 1850; the terms on which such collections appear change over time, allowing women more scope for public self-definition yet also limiting their roles.

Gender is implicated in collecting in two ways here. Firstly, as I have indicated, gendered qualities cluster around the activity of collecting, seen as aggressive and competitive, and creating mastery of the world. Secondly, the objects collected may be gendered, such as dolls or guns.[56] Initially, women whose own collections eventually went to museums were exceptional, and those collections were very much the same as the kind of collection being donated by men. An example of this can be found in the ethnographic objects donated by members of the Tinne family to Liverpool Museum. Alexine Tinne was the daughter of a Liverpool merchant, and on inheriting a fortune from him, set off to explore Africa. In 1862 and 1863 she undertook expeditions in North Africa accompanied by her mother and aunt, who both died on the return journey. In 1870 she set out on another expedition to cross the Sahara, but was killed during the course of it.[57] Her collection can thus be seen in terms of the male paradigm of collecting; it was about exploring, mastering, dominating the world through collecting, classifying and displaying it. It was a serious, creative act, as opposed to the supposedly passive and useless act of domestic consumption. The very exceptional nature of such female collectors, though Alexine Tinne was not the only one, meant that they did not disrupt either the gendered nature of objects, or the gendered relationship with objects: public collection versus private consumption.

However, from about 1900, changes start to emerge in women's collections, particularly those given to museums and thus given public validation. This trend really becomes visible during the First World War. Certainly from about 1910, women donors to museums become much more numerous, but more interesting are the contents of the collections they give.

Between 1900 and 1918, donations made by women to the Harris Museum include a tortoiseshell fan, some Brazilian pillow lace and a handkerchief; antique jewellery; a North American pillowcase, embroidery reputed to be by the Empress Josephine, and some Brussels lace (donor's own work).[58] These seem to be gendered, 'female' objects; the crucial point is that they have left the domestic setting and entered the public sphere, on more or less equal terms with 'male' objects, high art and science. For the earlier Victorians, the idea of such collection being donated to and displayed in a museum would have been incomprehensible; there was little one could learn through looking at them about the natural world or the development of civilisation. Nor did they really conform to the previous paradigm of the museum object as curious and remarkable.[59] Around this time, the Arts and Crafts movement was suggesting that traditional domestic crafts were worthy of study and consideration, and embodied taste and moral excellence as much as did traditional high art. Although it has been shown that within the Arts and Crafts movement women's roles were 'circumscribed by contemporary stereotypes of women', the encouragement and revival of traditional crafts such as lace-making at least provided a new philanthropic outlet for women. In the 1890s, for example, lace associations such as the Midlands Lace Association were set up, and Anthea Callen has commented, 'many public-spirited ladies involved themselves in the lace revival, trying to assist workers to improve their lace-making'.[60] The donation of such objects to the Harris Museum is clearly a reflection of the new emphasis on these crafts initiated by the Arts and Crafts movement; and importantly offered new roles for women, as donors, as well as new objects. Thus the re-evaluation of women's objects allows the re-evaluation of their social positions, though but slight. And it certainly refutes, if refuting it needs, the idea that women interact with objects only as passive consumers; they, as much as men, were involved in a creative act of self-representation when they collected and donated objects.

In conclusion, then, the objects in municipal museums were an important resource for creating meanings, values, and knowledge in Victorian England. Most donors and curators were in agreement about what should be shown and why, but there were some important differences, based on status, gender, location and most of all interest group. Curators attempted to act as gatekeepers and impose their idea of the ideal museum object on donations, but their weak position, and particularly their lack of funds to make purchases, meant that there was room for negotiation and change in the nature of municipal museums' collections in the course of the period. Any chronology of the museum collection which sees it as having achieved a systematic, scientific and institutional basis by the nineteenth century needs to be modified, at least for the municipal museum; collecting at this level showed characteristics of the Renaissance collection, and especially of the Royal Society collection, throughout this period.[61]

Notes

[1]   S. Pearce (ed), *Interpreting Objects and Collections*, (London 1994); D. Miller, *Material Culture and Mass Consumption*, (Oxford 1993); S. Stewart, *On Longing: Narratives of the Miniature, the Gigantic, the Souvenir, the Collection*, (Durham 1993).

[2]   S. Pearce, 'Collecting as medium and message', in E. Hooper-Greenhill (ed), *Museum, Media, Message*, (London 1995), p. 15.

[3]   S. Pearce, 'Collecting Reconsidered' in S. Pearce (ed), *Interpreting Objects and Collections*, (London 1994), p. 194.

[4]   *Ibid.*, p. 196.

[5]   *Ibid.*, p. 197.

[6]   *Ibid.*, p. 200.

[7]   *Ibid.*, p. 201.

[8]   *Ibid.*, p. 202.

[9]   *Ibid.*, p. 203.

[10]   L. Jordanova, 'Objects of Knowledge – A Historical Perspective on Museums' in Vergo (ed), *The New Museology*, (London 1989), p. 32. See also John M. MacKenzie, *The Empire*

of Nature: Hunting, Conservation and British Imperialism, (Manchester 1988), p. 41 and Susan Pearce, *Museums, Objects and Collections: A Cultural Study*, (London 1992), p. 69.

[11]   J. Clifford, 'Collecting Ourselves', in S. Pearce, *Interpreting Objects*, p.261.

[12]   Eilean Hooper-Greenhill, *Museums and the Shaping of Knowledge*, (London 1992), chapter 6.

[13]   Pitt-Rivers' museum is an example of this; see W. R. Chapman, 'Arranging Ethnology: AHLF Pitt-Rivers and the Typological Tradition' in Stocking (ed), *Objects and Others: Essays on Museums and Material Culture*, (Madison 1985); and David K. van Keuren, 'Museums and Ideology: Augustus Pitt-Rivers, Anthropological Museums and Social Change in later Victorian Britain', *Victorian Studies* 28 (1984).

[14]   *Ibid.*, p. 190.

[15]   *General Guide to the Collections contained in the Free Public Museums (William Brown Street) Liverpool*, (Liverpool 1906); AR Liverpool 1901; Minutes, Liverpool 16 November 1917.

[16]   Robert W. Rydell, *World of Fairs: The Century of Progress Expositions*, (Chicago 1993), p. 33; see also M. Worboys, 'The Imperial Institute: The state and the development of the natural resources of the Colonial Empire 1887-1923' in MacKenzie (ed), *Imperialism and the Natural World*, (Manchester 1990). For local history and folk culture see Gaynor Kavanagh, *History Curatorship*, (London 1990), pp. 15-16.

[17]   A. Thackray, "Natural Knowledge in Cultural Context: The Manchester Model', *American History Review* 79, (1974).

[18]   MacKenzie, *Empire of Nature*, p. 36.

[19]   Stuart Davies, *By the Gains of Industry, Birmingham Museums and Art Gallery 1885-1985*, (Birmingham 1985), p. 49; Curator's Report on Mayer Museum, 1884, NML Archives; FPLC Minutes, 15 February 1894; 'Sheffield Museum and the Bateman Collection', *Sheffield Telegraph* 18 December 1891.

[20]   The career of A. H. L. F. Pitt-Rivers illustrates the increasing prominence of British archaeology; his museum at Farnham displayed artefacts found during excavations he had organised, and arranged according to his principles of typology: Chapman, 'Arranging Ethnology', p. 38. In 1904 the new Liverpool University created an Institute of Archaeology, with four Chairs by 1908: T, Kelly, *For the Advancement of Learning: The University of Liverpool 1881-1981*, (Liverpool 1981), p. 149.

[21]   For example, W. A. Herdman, 'An Ideal Natural History Museum' in *Proceedings of the Literary and Philosophical Society of Liverpool* 41, (1887), argued that museums should have a local collection 'for the local naturalist'; see also W. H. Flower, *Essays on Museums*, (London 1898), p. 21, and Thomas Greenwood, *Museums and Art Galleries*, (London 1888), p. 390.

[22]   H. H. Higgins (1883), "Museums of Natural History', *Proceedings of the Literary and Philosophical Society of Liverpool*, 38, (1887), p. 195.

[23]   FPLC Minutes, 1881-1913.

[24]   Cynthia Brown, *Cherished Possessions, A History of New Walk Museum and Leicester City Museums Service*, (Leicester 2002), pp. 6-7; E. Howarth, *Visitors' Guide to the Sheffield Public Museum, Weston Park*, (Sheffield 1883), pp. 257, 300.

[25]   Davies, *By the Gains of Industry*, p. 38; Tim Schadla-Hall, *Tom Sheppard, Hull's Great Collector*, (Beverley 1989), pp. 10-14.

[26]   'Report of the Director, 1901', in Minutes, Liverpool 1901; K. Hill, 'Municipal Museums in the North-West, 1850-1914', (unpublished PhD thesis, Lancaster University 1996) pp. 185, 189.

[27]   Sheets-Pyenson, S., *Cathedrals of Science: The Development of Colonial Natural History Museums During the Late Nineteenth Century*, (Kingston and Montreal 1988),

pp. 3-23; but see Alberti, S. 'Field, Lab and Museum: The Practice and Place of Life Science in Yorkshire, 1870-1904' (unpublished PhD thesis, Sheffield University 2000) p76 for the argument that both aims co-existed throughout the period.

28 FPLC Minutes, February 1882; August 1884; July 1890 December 1894; April 1908.
29 FPLC Minutes October 1896; April 1903; February 1911; Pearce, 'Collecting reconsidered', p. 200.
30 FPLC Minutes October 1885; July 1888;July 1895; July 1905.
31 FPLC Minutes December 1896; February 1899; June 1909; April 1913; September 1916.
32 FPLC Minutes February 1894; Henry Fishwick, *The History of the Parish of Preston in Amounderness in the County of Lancaster*, (London 1900), p. 81; M. Whittle, 'Philanthropy in Preston: the changing face of charity in a nineteenth-century provincial town' (unpublished PhD thesis, Lancaster University 1990), pp. 119, 181, 395; *Catalogue of the Preston Exhibition* (Preston 1875); A Hewitson ('Atticus'), *Preston Town Council, or Portraits of Local Legislators*, (Preston 1870), p. 49.
33 FPLC Minutes, 16 March 1894.
34 FPLC Minutes, May 1894.
35 FPLC Minutes 24 May 1894.
36 Cf. A. J. Vickery, 'Town histories and Victorian plaudits: some examples from Preston', *Urban History Yearbook*, (1988), for other celebrations of civic history.
37 AR Liverpool 1868; Minutes, Liverpool January 1891.
38 AR Liverpool 1862, 1902.
39 AR Liverpool 1904; Minutes, Liverpool March 1905, February 1911.
40 AR Liverpool 1879, 1896; Minutes, Liverpool March 1887.
41 Minutes, Liverpool July 1890, March 1892, November 1914; AR Liverpool 1913.
42 Liverpool Museum Minutes 9 August 1898.
43 AR Liverpool 1879; Minutes, Liverpool February 1911.
44 D. Haraway, 'Teddy Bear Patriarchy: Taxidermy in the Garden of Eden, New York City 1908-1936', *Social Text* 11 (1984-5), p. 25; Jordanova, "Objects of knowledge', p. 32.
45 *Proceedings of the Literary and Philosophical Society of Liverpool*, 16, 1861-2; Brown, *Cherished Possessions*, p 6.
46 See note 27; also Greenwood, Thomas, *Museums and Art Galleries*, (London 1888); Flower W. H., *Essays on Museums*, (London 1898); H. H. Higgins 'Museums of Natural History', *Proceedings of the Literary and Philosophical Society of Liverpool*, 38 (1883-4), p. 195; Herdman, W. A., 'An Ideal Natural History Museum', *Proceedings of the Literary and Philosophical Society of Liverpool*, 41 (1886-7), p. 69.
47 Alberti, 'Field, Lab and Museum', pp. 87-88.
48 Between 1885 and 1899 the Art Gallery Purchase Committee spent nearly £10,000 on objects of industrial and decorative art: Davies, *By the Gains of Industry*, pp. 37-38.
49 FPLC Minutes 1896; Minutes, Liverpool 1897.
50 Susan Pearce, *On Collecting: An Investigation into Collecting in the European Tradition,* (London 1995), p. 368.
51 S. Davies, 'The making of a municipal museum: Huddersfield and the naturalists' in E. A. Hilary Haigh (ed) *Huddersfield, A Most Handsome Town: Aspects of the History and Culture of a West Yorkshire Town*, (Huddersfield 1992), p. 682; Anne Secord, 'Science in the Pub: Artisan Botanists in Early Nineteenth Century Lancashire', *History of Science* 32 (1994), pp. 269-315; Mosley, Charles, 'Inn-Parlour Museums', *Museums Journal* 27 (1927), 280-281.
52 *Preston Guardian* 26 November 1881; *Catalogue of the Preston Exhibition*, Preston 1875.

[53] Thackray, 'Natural Knowledge in Cultural Context', p. 682.

[54] *Preston Guardian*, 26 November 1881.

[55] L. Davidoff and C. Hall, *Family Fortunes: Men and Women of the English Middle Class, 1780-1850*, (London 1994), p. 443; R. W. Belk and M. Wallendorf, 'Of mice and men: gender identity in collecting' in Pearce (ed), *Interpreting Objects and Collections*, (1994), p. 241.

[56] *Ibid.*, pp. 241-245.

[57] 'Africana from the Liverpool Museum', *Liverpool and Africa: Exhibition Guide*, Liverpool University (1974).

[58] FPLC Minutes 1908; 1911; 1915.

[59] Pearce, *On Collecting*, (1995), chapters 5 and 6.

[60] Anthea Callen, *Angel in the Studio: Women in the Arts and Crafts Movement 1870-1914*, (London 1979), pp. 221, 142.

[61] See note 12 above.

CHAPTER SIX

Decoding the Displays and Layout

The way in which the museum displayed its objects and organised its space was the major tool it had for shaping visitors' interaction with those objects; it was the museum's most significant method of creating meaning. The nineteenth century saw a whole series of technical advances in building and in display techniques, and a significant amount of debate over these questions.[1] For the purposes of this chapter, two aspects of the display space have been distinguished and studied separately, the layout and architecture of the museum as a whole, and the individual displays in which the objects themselves were exhibited. Of course, in practice it is less easy to find a clear division between these two aspects; layout and display techniques are intimately connected with each other, and mutually reinforcing. However, for investigation, it is useful to separate the two.

While it could be argued that historians have always had an interest in space and the configuration of buildings, this interest has certainly become more prominent and more theorised in the last fifty years, and a lot of this interest can be attributed to the writings of Foucault. Foucault's distinctive contribution was to point out how the configuration of space was implicated in the exercise of power. He argued that in the architecture of broadly defined state institutions such as prisons and hospitals, a change was visible from the eighteenth century, as a modern, liberal/progressive state emerged. In his own terms, the nature of power changed from juridico-discursive, to governmental. Juridico-discursive power was all about glorifying the monarch, while governmental power aimed to be more efficient, more continuous, and to serve a variety of ends, not just to reinforce the monarch's rule. So the main characteristics of the new configuration of space was that it acted directly to reform inmates, or to encourage self-improvement, by individuating, making visible.[2] The most famous and widely know example of this is the Panopticon, the model prison designed by Jeremy Bentham, which guaranteed the good behaviour of prisoners by making them always visible to a warder, without them being able to tell whether anyone was in fact watching them. Such architecture was described by Foucault as a disciplinary apparatus, in which power is exercised on populations, but not by anyone in particular.

In recent years, Foucauldian ideas have been applied to the museum, and it has been argued particularly that the configuration of space in museums, from the late eighteenth century onwards, constituted a disciplinary apparatus in some way. This analysis has been most fully developed by Tony Bennett, who argues that public museums from the nineteenth century 'exemplified the development of a new governmental relation to culture in which works of high culture were treated as instruments that could be enlisted ... for new tasks of social management.'[3] Museums were therefore part of the same shift to modern techniques of government and self-government, but faced a more acute problem in that they were not dealing with incarcerated inmates but with a general population which was freely admitted by right. In order to function in this way, their use of space was crucial. He sees the classic nineteenth-century museum as a machine, which through its layout policed the behaviour, indeed improved the behaviour, of the visitor, and also produced knowledge which the visitor internalised through the process of walking round the museum. In support of this analysis, Bennett cites changes in museum architecture: the increasing use of large halls with galleries, making visitors visible to each other, and to attendants, as opposed to the small, cluttered rooms of earlier museums; and the development of linear, chronological schemes of interpretation, which necessitated a pre-ordained route to follow around the museum, that visitors were constrained, by the layout, to follow. He points to:

> the clearing of exhibits to the sides and centres of display areas, thus allowing clear passageways for the transit of the public, and breaking that public up from a disaggregated mass into an orderly flow.[4]

He stresses the development of streamlined and defined visitor routes, 'one-way systems which do not allow visitors to retrace their steps'. Bennett proposes that another general principle embodied in museum architecture from around the middle of the nineteenth century is:

> the provision of elevated vantage points in the form of galleries which, in allowing the public to watch over itself, incorporated a principle of self-surveillance and hence self-regulation into museum architecture.[5]

Everyone could see, but everyone could also be seen. He says:

> Relations of space and vision are organized not merely to allow a clear inspection of the objects exhibited but also to allow for the visitors to be the objects of each other's inspection – scenes in which, if not a citizenry, then certainly a public displayed itself to itself in an affirmative celebration of its own orderliness in architectural contexts which simultaneously guaranteed and produced that orderliness.[6]

Bennett's is a persuasive argument, based on trends in the architecture of museums, and a description of the feel of different spaces. Thomas Markus uses a more quantifiable and comparable methodology, but also tends to suggest an increase in the coercive nature of institutional space from around the end of the eighteenth century, or the beginning of modernity. The broad argument here is that spaces became more clearly delineated between producer and consumer (or jailer and prisoner, teacher and pupil), with the producer having the power to control and survey all spaces, while the consumer is kept to certain spaces and given limited choices for movement. Markus also refers to the syntax of space, an idea which echoes Bennett's analysis of interpretive schemes mapped onto the space of the museum. The overall direction of this analysis, then, is very much the same as Bennett's.[7] But these are big claims, and this chapter will investigate whether this pattern of development can be found in municipal museums in England.

One major problem in various analyses of space is that taken alone, there is only so much they can reveal. The spaces of a building change over time, and they are modified by people's use of them. As Forgan says, buildings

> are constantly subject to reuse, adaptation, and reinterpretation, both during their lifetime and by historians today. A Foucauldian analysis may be appropriate at the moment of planning or initial construction. But buildings are rarely constructed exactly as planned, and there is a multitude of intangible ways in which perceptions about particular places are modified, not only through use, but by the fabric of the building itself, its texture and durability, its decoration, the passage of time, as well as the varied careers and reputations of people associated with them. They carry multiple meanings and can mean quite different things to people at the same time. Buildings may remain in the same place, but they rarely stand still in terms of function, representation or in the ways that they are interpreted by historians.[8]

Thus, although this chapter will analyse the spaces and displays in a fairly isolated way, such an analysis also needs to be seen in terms of the factors examined in other chapters.

Certainly there was intent to impose control and produce knowledge on the part of curators and museum managers, as previous chapters have shown. Councillors were frequently keen to suggest the beneficial effect that visiting a museum would have on particularly working-class behaviour, and this was, implicitly, related to its spatial arrangements: the opportunity to observe good behaviour in others, while curbing opportunities for bad behaviour.[9] To a lesser extent, it was argued, mainly by curators, that the spatial arrangement of exhibits could disseminate theories and narratives. The museum would educate, rather than simply forming a collection of objects. There are some impressive examples of this, such as Pitt-Rivers' museum plan of concentric circles, where movement inwards and outwards represents movement through time, and each segment of the circle represents a different geographical area.[10] However, a significant point about this museum is that it was never built. There were increasing precedents for purpose-built museums; significant ones that Yanni looks at from the early and mid-nineteenth century include the Hunterian Museum of the Royal College of Surgeons (1837), and the Museum of Practical Geology (1851).[11] However, many municipal museums did not get a new building at all during this period, especially the library-museums Brears and Davies identify, where the museum remained a room in the library; or had to make do with adapted buildings, like Sheffield and Leicester.[12] Certainly in municipal museums, curators tended not to have the clout to get space- and resource-intensive interpretive schemes adopted. In practice, I would argue, such schemes were undermined by resources issues, which necessitated the use of existing buildings; by conflicts over the use of space by local groups; and by the desire for prestige on the part of museum founders, donors and curators, which could clash with the needs of scientific exposition and rational layout.

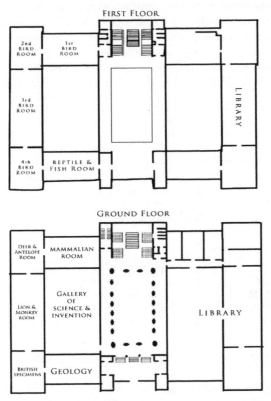

Figure 6.1 Ground Plan of Liverpool Museum in 1869
Source: Adapted from *Descriptive Guide to the Liverpool Free Public Museum* (1869)

Firstly, the actual layouts of various municipal museums will be examined, to see how far they matched the picture of a disciplinary apparatus. Rather than just an impressionistic analysis of such layouts, the focus will be on how rooms connect with each other, to give a clearer basis for comparison, based on the methodology used by Markus, and by Hillier and Hanson. Buildings can be represented in diagrams with each room a dot, and routes between rooms as lines.

This may produce diagrams that are 'ringy' or 'tree-y', shallow or deep. Thus rooms are either relatively isolated from each other, or integrated.[13] These configurations produce different possibilities of social interaction; for example, in prisons, prisoners are typically kept in deep sections of the building, far – in terms of rooms – from the entrance, and in rooms isolated from each other but integrated with the warders. Buildings that the public enter typically have very shallow areas for the public, and deeper areas for the staff, which nevertheless permit surveillance. Thus they are about control of the public.[14] A disciplinary museum, therefore, could be expected to have shallow spaces for visitors, with opportunities for surveillance, and any deep isolated spaces would be reserved for staff. In addition, in order to educate in the way Bennett suggests, museums would also need exhibition areas to be arranged in big rings, producing one-way routes round the exhibits, thus allowing a greater degree of control over the way visitors interpret the displays. What do the layouts of nineteenth-century museums show?

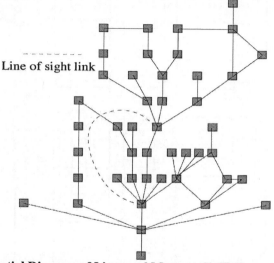

Line of sight link

Figure 6.2 Spatial Diagram of Liverpool Museum in 1869

Liverpool is the largest museum, and as such, its building is the most complex to analyse. The museum opened to the public in a temporary location in 1853. The permanent building on William Brown Street opened in 1860, and was significantly extended around the end of the nineteenth century, with the new galleries opening in 1906.[15] The 1860 building was very imposing, and double-height, galleried halls allowed for surveillance of visitors in some places. Figures 6.1 and 6.2 show the museum as it was in 1869. The main hall was the most integrated room in the museum, and also had a line of sight link with the first floor, making it a very controlling space. The diagram of this museum indicates that the main museum rooms were arranged in classic large rings. There was, in fact, a one-way route around the museum. A look at the subject matter of the rooms, though, shows that this was not necessary for the interpretation of the displays. The layout of the museum contained no message about any subject's relationship with any other; in particular, there was no evolutionary message. The one-way route could be followed in either direction. So at this point, the overall spatial arrangements seem more designed to discipline behaviour and regulate the visitor, while the dissemination of knowledge was on a room-by-room basis.

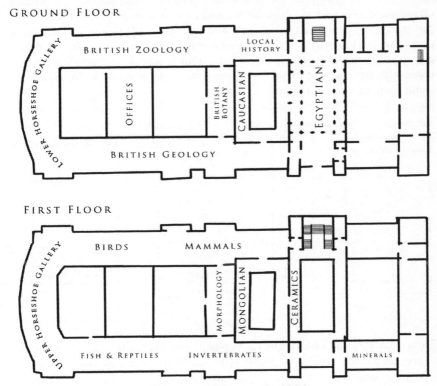

Figure 6.3 Ground Plan of Liverpool Museum in 1906
Source: Adapted from *General Guide to the Collections Contained in the Free Public Museums (William Brown Street) Liverpool* (1906)

After the extension, the configuration of the building was significantly changed (see Figure 6.3). The Horseshoe Galleries were impressive spaces, long and curved, giving good possibilities for surveillance. However, they disrupted the simple one-way routes of the earlier building. This is very clear from the diagram, which does not contain the large rings, but is a much more complex affair. In addition, the basement was now extensively used, and the previous Gallery of Science and Invention had become a hall with two storeys of galleries; increasing the visibility of members of the public, but further complicating the layout. The fact that it is now harder to get visitors automatically to follow a certain route is more surprising as there is now a definite narrative to the displays. Moving away from the entrance, one starts with geology and botany; moves through invertebrates; birds, reptiles and fish, mammals; and then on to human history.

Among human history, Caucasian ethnography is in the impressive main hall, Melanian is in the basement, and Mongolian on the predominantly natural history first floor. So the relationship of different subject areas to each other, spatially, suggests a certain developmental sequence, or relative importance. Yet in order to follow this conceptual plan one would have to retrace one's steps and rely heavily on the guidebook. Overall, then, the layout of the museum has become less rational and regulatory, as a result of infilling and adding on galleries. This indicates the constraints that working with the existing building created. It also suggests a change in emphasis by this point; the behaviour of visitors was no longer such an issue; whereas the production of ideas about the natural world and human civilisation was now a priority.

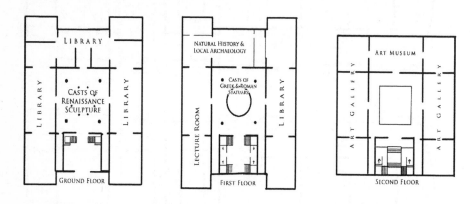

Figure 6.4 Ground Plan of Harris Museum and Art Gallery, Preston, 1932
Source: Adapted from S. Paviere (1932), *Harris Museum and Art Gallery: Summary Guide*, Preston

The Harris Free Public Library and Museum building in Preston opened in 1893, replacing a two-roomed museum, and was extremely ambitious. It was neo-classical, with much attention paid to the statuary and inscriptions on the façade. The interior was similarly lavish with friezes and lots of marble.[16] The focus of the interior was the central area, surrounded by a ring of rooms (see figures 6.4 and 6.5). It could be argued that this central area was a disciplinary space: each storey is visible from the one above, and the staircases give elevated vantage points for the entrance hall. These massive and echoing spaces exert a disciplinary effect, it may be argued, through the awe they inspire, with large areas of floor that need to be crossed, and a sense of being observed from afar. A diagram of the Harris is very 'tree-y', and the deepest rooms are not open to the public. The entrance hall, and the three levels of the central atrium, are clearly the areas that control access to other areas, and given that they have a line of sight link with each other, these are very controlling spaces. This analysis tends, therefore, to reinforce the idea that the Harris was a disciplinary institution. However, the rationale of the layout of the museum rooms is less clear. There are small rings, but they cannot produce a one-way route, so any kind of overall interpretive scheme is very hard to create, and in fact there was none. Objects were pretty much placed in any room that was free. The curator attempted in planning the natural history displays to follow some kind of interpretive scheme, with an index collection in the centre room, and rooms on geographical distribution and local collections on either side, but this had to be modified in practice.[17] So the Harris acted to some extent as a disciplinary space, but in terms of producing knowledge was much less didactic.

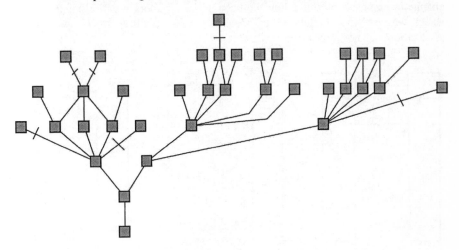

Figure 6.5 Spatial Diagram of Harris Museum and Art Gallery, Preston

The art museum in Birmingham is a very different case, resulting, I would argue, from the constraints of building on a limited budget, and the persistence of an older mode of arranging space, particularly for art. The corporation in Birmingham was not very swift to develop a museum and art gallery, even after adopting the Public Libraries and Museums Act. From 1867, a room in the library contained paintings and *objets d'art*, but it was not until 1880, when Richard Tangye, an engineering manufacturer, offered £10,000 for the purchase of exhibits if the council would build a Museum and Art Gallery, that anything more substantial was attempted. However, the only way it was thought financially feasible to achieve a permanent location was to make it part of another construction. Thus the Gas Committee undertook to erect a building with their offices on the ground floor and the Museum and Art Gallery on the first floor.[18] However, the new building was not at all a utilitarian office block, but an extremely ornate and impressive structure. This emphasis was continued within, where the entrance stairway was large and almost entirely marble. The floor plan of the galleries themselves is very simple, the most simple of any we will examine. It was basically a line of rooms, with a few offices tucked away; but there were no alternative routes, and no rings. This 'en filade' arrangement of rooms is the most straightforward museum plan; but in most cases it is made more complex by

Figure 6.6 The Industrial Gallery, Birmingham Museum and Art Gallery
Source: Birmingham Museums and Art Gallery

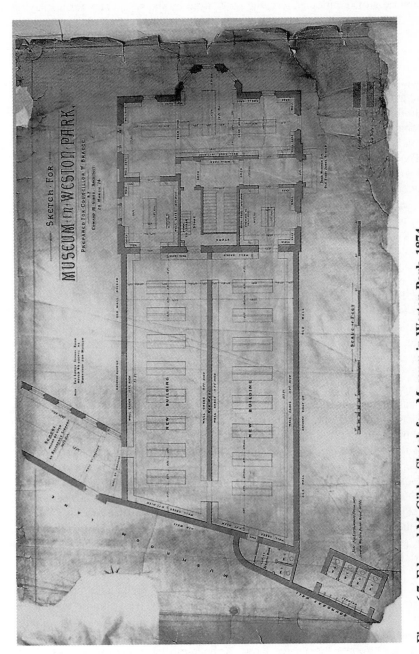

Figure 6.7 Edward M. Gibbs, Sketch for Museum in Weston Park, 1874

Source: Sheffield Archives, AP207/1

having the entrance in the middle, giving two branches. As it is in Birmingham, it is reminiscent of the long gallery, the space used by the aristocracy for displaying art; by the nineteenth century, most art galleries were creating circular or even more complex routes for visitors.[19] The floor plan in Birmingham created deep and very isolated spaces, without any very privileged spaces for staff. If this floor plan is taken together with the style of the building, it seems possible that the aim was to emulate a private, aristocratic art collection, rather than to create the best space for the public exhibition of art. However, there were some modern features. The Industrial Hall in particular was top lit, and used a gallery and the layout of cases to arrange the space rationally (see Figure 6.6), forming a classic self-policing space in Bennett's terms.

The Museum and Art Gallery was not extended until 1912, so I do not want to spend too much time on it. It should be said, however, that the extension followed the pattern of the original building; council offices formed the ground floor, and the museum the first floor. This determined the basic ground plan; and though it was more complex than the original, it could now be said to be too complex for a clear and rational layout. The extension connected with the original galleries via a bridge, and formed a ring, though with several rooms coming off it. These rooms were very deep, spatially speaking, and it seems that the museum employed a large number of warders to compensate for the irrational nature of its layout.[20]

In Sheffield, the municipal museum was housed from 1875 in a converted private house, in grounds which the council had also acquired and turned into a park. It is not clear how much alteration was made to the house, except that some partition walls were removed to give one large room, along with two smaller ones; and the stable yard was converted into two long galleries covered with a glass roof. An 1883 Guide to the museum mentions six rooms, two galleries (those in the yard), and one passage.[21] Three of these rooms would have been on the first floor of the main house, but no floor plans have been found of this. The ground floor and extension, somewhat surprisingly given that the building was not new, formed a simple but quite definite ring (see Figure 6.7). The new galleries were large and light, with low table cases, and formed a rational, fairly disciplinary space. While the older part of the building could not reach these standards, as far as possible nooks and crannies were eliminated, and the building opened up. Just wall cases and table cases were used, so displays would not hide people. However, the Sheffield Museum also relied quite heavily on attendants to police the visitors. The rooms themselves seem to have followed no particular logic in terms of subjects, as the guidebook mentions the Industrial Products room, the Natural History gallery, British Antiquities, Egyptian Antiquities, armour, pottery, cutlery and coins.[22] There does not seem to be any overarching narrative being developed here. In 1887, the Mappin Art Gallery was opened, attached to the museum in Sheffield, and here there was a different approach. The Gallery was purpose-built from scratch.[23] The floor plan (see Figures 6.8 and 6.9) shows a quite simple arrangement, centring on a lobby and main gallery, which contained the main bequest; other rooms surrounded these. A diagram of this plan shows two basic rings, with staff space and cloakrooms leading off them. The lobby is clearly a key area; and indeed even today has an attendant in it. The main gallery was very large and imposing; but, as I will argue in the next chapter, the rationality of the space of the Mappin Art Gallery was overwhelmed by the number of visitors.[24] The lobby, in particular, was not very big, and in order to keep some control, a turnstile was introduced so that people could only enter singly. In the main gallery people had to circulate in one direction, and barriers were placed in front of the pictures; these barriers had to be moved further out to ensure the safety of the pictures.[25] So even where the space was reasonably rational and disciplinary, it could not, by itself, control visitor behaviour.

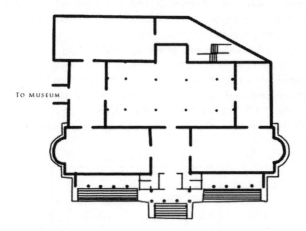

Figure 6.8 Ground Plan of Mappin Art Gallery, Sheffield, 1887
Source: Adapted from M. Tooby (1987), *'In Perpetuity and Without Charge': The Mappin Art Gallery 1887-1987*, Sheffield Arts Department, Sheffield

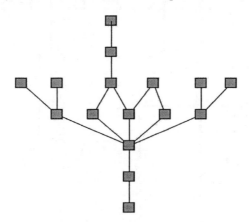

Figure 6.9 Spatial Diagram of Mappin Art Gallery, Sheffield

The museum in Leicester formally came into being in 1849. The council bought a school to house the collections, and spent £1000 on alterations and fittings for the museum.[26] The original layout of the building covered two storeys, with predominantly natural history exhibits. School buildings, by the nineteenth century, had their own disciplinary use of space, but it was not the same as museums; it was about privileging teachers and curtailing the movement of pupils.[27] Museums, by contrast, wanted visitors to move, but in a predetermined way, whilst inhibiting undesirable behaviour. In particular, Leicester Museum was unable to produce any kind of sophisticated route around its exhibits, with little more than a simple 'en filade' arrangement. However, the rooms were very large and reasonably light, and the building was certainly imposing, with a portico of Doric columns. The building was extended, and by the early twentieth century incorporated a large number of other functions, including a suite of rooms for the mayor. If these are discounted, the extended museum did employ a more sophisticated and rational use of space, with rings and less isolated spaces, although there was still little in the way of an overarching interpretation governing the layout of various areas within the museum (see Figure 6.10).

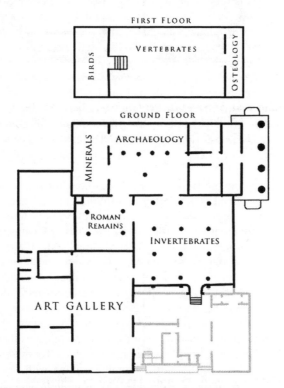

Figure 6.10 Ground Plan of Leicester Museum, 1904
Source: Adapted from Leicester Council Proceedings, 1903/4

There was, therefore, a wide range of strategies, resources and outcomes in municipal museums in the second half of the nineteenth century. Where all museums probably wanted their visitors to behave well, only some created buildings that helped to enforce such behaviour; others either could not do so, or put other aspects of the building first. It is probably more striking how much other methods of policing behaviour were used, such as police, attendants, and regulations stipulating that all umbrellas, bags and so forth should be left in cloakrooms.[28] Creating a pedagogic narrative in the museum seems to have been an even lower priority, with most municipal museums having too incomplete and idiosyncratic a collection to create any overarching coherence. The one place where it is obvious is Liverpool, which had the largest and most academic staff, as well as huge collections and reasonable resources. One clear aspect of the building and space that was clearly important to many municipal museum founders was that it be imposing and prestigious. In nearly all cases museums had some large, marble-filled space, and plenty of effort was lavished on the exterior. This aspect, which can be labelled civic pride, had no particularly rational or disciplinary agenda but was more about validating the wealth, public spiritedness and culture of the civic fathers. This is reinforced by a comparison with France, where Sherman shows the construction of provincial art museums in the second half of the nineteenth century foregrounded monumentality. 'Specific stylistic precedents mattered less than the symbolic power of style itself' in legitimating new urban elites.[29] In fact, this equates more to Foucault's juridico-discursive power, rather than his disciplinary power – it is more about demonstrating power for its own sake, than about using power efficiently and productively. Finally, in some cases, municipal museums could not command the resources to rebuild from scratch, usually just remodelling the existing building somewhat. Expenditure of rates on new museum buildings was always hard to achieve, and museums were thus often dependent on donations of money and exhibits, which exacerbated the tendency to glorify local leaders.[30]

So, to return to the prevailing idea of Victorian museums as disciplinary institutions which produced self-policing, improving citizens, and also produced knowledge which was embedded in the very routes visitors took around those museums, it has to be modified, particularly in the case of municipal museums, though the same is true of national museums, to a lesser extent. Museums acted in a much more conditional and fragmented way. The main reason for this is because their resources were controlled by a very small number of people. One of the effects of this was that hostility to publicly funded cultural institutions played an important role in constraining plans for museums. As chapter 3 showed, there was considerable resistance to the spending of rates on museums, throughout the period. It was cheaper, if less rational, to employ more attendants than to rearrange the building. Even where hostility was not a major problem for museums, the small number of councillors on the Museums Committee, along with any major donor, inevitably exercised the most control over the institution, and could overrule curators. It was frequently their concerns which were reflected in the museum, and these were more to do with prestige, and instantly recognisable signs of high culture, than with scientific theories or the improvement of the people. Victorian museums were not disciplinary spaces, they were relatively unplanned, underdetermined spaces which responded to local conditions.

Less work has been done on nineteenth-century techniques of display, and certainly there has been less attempt to interpret them as part of a project of Foucauldian modernisation in museums, although lighting, display cases themselves, and taxidermy have all been mentioned as showing advances in the Victorian period, and taking up a great deal of curators' time.[31] Display is essentially a matter of combining objects with textual and other interpretive material to create and communicate meaning. How the Victorians thought about meaning, the epistemological basis of their displays, is thus important. Hooper-Greenhill, drawing on Foucault, argues that in this modern period, display was intended to make visible hidden relationships between objects, through analogy and succession; this may be true, but does not help much with detailed analysis.[32] Bennett on the other hand argues that Victorian displays tended towards becoming a spatial narrative, where visitors started at the beginning, and walking through the museum, followed the story to the end.[33] Forgan looks at more subtle processes of meaning creation, such as juxtaposition. She argues that merely placing objects next to each other to create a relationship was as important as labels and guidebooks; she gives the example of the juxtaposition of raw materials and finished products.[34] This is demonstrated most fully in the Museum of Practical Geology, opened in 1851, which focussed on the economic uses of geology. Here, the idea of showing movement from raw material to finished product was highly developed. In addition, the two galleries were used to show the stratigraphy and geography of British geology; a kind of map, in essence.[35] By the end of the nineteenth century, though, Forgan shows that many of the museum's exhibits were no longer seen as illustrative of manufacture, and the idea of a museum as a map was falling out of favour. Ideas about the creation of meaning through the display of objects were, it seems, developing quite fast in the second half of the nineteenth century, and affected by (and affecting) subject development, local priorities, and other popular techniques of display.

Among curators, there was, certainly in the early days of municipal museums, a widespread feeling that a modern, public museum should be distinguished from less noble, commercial ventures such as fairs and exhibitions, and museums like Bullock's Egyptian Museum. These were disorderly and sensational, not scientific, rational and improving, and a distinction in display techniques was essential to differentiate, and thus justify the expenditure of public money.[36] Strict taxonomy dominated the mid-century: Yanni argues that, to the nineteenth century, knowledge was about rows of specimens.[37] However, as Bennett shows, museums learned about techniques of presentation from more popular forms of display during the nineteenth century. Many curators started to move away from 'old-fashioned' display methods, in natural history at least, where taxonomy was the main guiding principle, producing rows and rows of related species.[38] Displays could be used to tell stories, as Bennett suggests, but the ways in which this could be done, and the stories which were told, were more diverse than he implies. There was, thus, a fine line to tread between the overly dry and dull, and the overtly entertaining.

There was a huge range evident in municipal museums before 1914 in the sophistication, aims, and pedagogical effectiveness of display techniques. Liverpool was, in display as in layout and staffing, a particularly advanced example, much more developed than most municipal museums in the thought, research and resources put into display. Education was a particular priority, and Liverpool can be argued to have played a leading role in developing techniques to enhance the educational value of an exhibit. However, it was far from typical, with most municipal museums either not interested in education, unwilling to put popular education before specialist science, or unable to develop more sophisticated display because of staffing, collections and resource restrictions. It is also clear that displays drawing on popular culture, such as dioramas were liked by the public, and curators were far from immune from a desire to attract visitors.

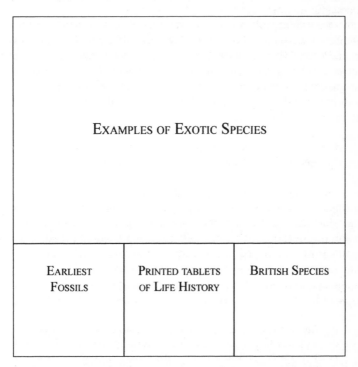

Figure 6.11 Diagram of a Display Case, Liverpool Museum, 1873
Source: Adapted from Rev. H. H. Higgins (1873), 'Synopsis of an Arrangement of Invertebrate Animals in the Free Public Museum of Liverpool with Introduction' in *Proceedings of the Literary and Philosophical Society of Liverpool* 28 (Appendix)

If we first examine display techniques in science, especially natural history, we can see curators grappling with the issue of what sort of audience the displays should be targeted at: general visitor or specialist student? Should displays entertain or act as reference books? Liverpool Museum started thinking seriously about its displays fairly early on; it is instructive to look at the re-arrangement of the invertebrates carried out by the Rev. H. H. Higgins when the museum moved to the William Brown building. This is described fully by Higgins in 'Synopsis of an Arrangement of Invertebrate Animals in the Free Public Museum of Liverpool' in the *Proceedings of the Literary and Philosophical Society of Liverpool* for 1873, which gives a very detailed account of the display, and the principles underlying it. It serves to show that as soon as the museum was able to plan its displays, there was considerable and innovative emphasis on planned, systematic, purposive and educational display. There is evidence to show that the invertebrate displays were very carefully planned; Higgins indicated that the display scheme was drawn up first, and then specimens were acquired or chosen to fill the gaps. He wrote 'The importance of a suitable ground plan for cases in museums seems to be much under-rated.'[39]

A main consideration was rationality; this tended to mean the representation of taxonomy, in particular, how to represent the different classes of invertebrates. Higgins maintained the best way to show relationships was to have cases arranged to resemble a tree formation from a bird's eye view; but the provision of cases in a linear arrangement was limited by space. As a result their proper positions relative to each other could not be shown.[40] Order was put before financial worth in display:

> It is far better to forgo the possession even of a valuable series of specimens, than to sacrifice order for their sake.[41]

However, education, and specifically education for the general visitor, was the greatest imperative in creating the display. Higgins himself made this clear when rejecting what he regarded as 'the only thoroughly scientific mode' of giving information on lifeforms: 'This method seems more suited for students than for a mixed company.' He stressed the need for 'an instructive arrangement.'[42]

In the end each table case – ten feet long; twenty to a room – was divided into a series of trays, each with an upright section behind it. The trays were divided into sections, and the upright section carried material related to the specimen, such as:

> drawings, plates and photographs of structure and anatomy, economic products, silk in various stages, marine and freshwater pearls, cameos, polished shells, sections showing the interiors of shells, eggs, and egg cases, preserved larvae and pupae, preparations in spirit[43]

amongst others. The main tray carried the specimen itself, an exotic species, along with related fossils, a life history, and related British examples (see Figure 6.11). There are various significant points about this. Firstly evolutionary theories were very succinctly demonstrated. A display such as Liverpool's did not allow any interpretation other than that a species was descended from a fossil form. The inclusion of examples of British species essentially created a reference or local collection of the kind that was often urged on provincial museums, without necessitating a separate section.[44] The most notable features, though, are the large sections given over to exotic specimens, and to interpretation and additional information, including economic products. Higgins stated that for pedagogical reasons the most spectacular and colourful specimens possible should be used in displays, rather than the small dull ones typical of British species.[45] He wanted to catch the attention of people who would not be immediately interested by the intricacies of British invertebrates. The text of the species' life history contained some complex biological information, but also anecdotal elements.[46] Overall, this display is very unusual for such a thorough attempt to engage the ordinary visitor at such an early date. The museum was engaged in transforming scientific knowledge into popular knowledge, and the main aspect of the scientific knowledge that it transmitted was evolutionism.

These two elements of Higgins' displays, their didactic and pedagogic nature, and their emphasis on an evolutionary paradigm, stressing scientific authority, remained central and developed further over time. In addition, and supporting this, Liverpool Museum was one of the first in the country to set up habitat groups with its zoological specimens. This was first mentioned for the bird collections in the 1865 *Annual Report*, where it was stated that some species were being arranged in family groups showing male, female, eggs, nest and young. This adds a third dimension, that of realism, to display in Liverpool. There was an increasing emphasis on contextualising the object, indeed on presenting it as still part of its original context, and as being 'real' rather than a representation. This 'reality effect' is taken further as museum techniques develop. In 1888 it was reported that there was an accelerating programme of 'the mounting of stuffed specimens, so as to show, where possible, the male, female, and young, with natural surroundings, and artistically displayed'; and by 1903 'over 70 rock-work, sylvan or water scenes have been planned and constructed.'[47] It is significant that these displays are now described as *artistically* displayed, and as 'scenes'. This indicates that the realistic display actually exercises complex and diverse forms of power. It works on an aesthetic and imaginative level; it does not merely give scientific facts, but elicits fantasies, memories and admiration.[48] Realistic display thus creates a message of both 'truth' and 'beauty', which is an extremely powerful combination. It is, according to Haraway, experienced as a magical revelation.[49] It is this, rather than Bennett's 'backwalking', that may be the most significant innovation in municipal museums' displays. Of course, realistic displays were not new; some of the most famous of Bullock's displays were dramatic tableaux of stuffed animals, elaborately staged for maximum sensory and emotional impact.[50] Yet initially, municipal museums shunned such methods in favour of the strictly taxonomic.[51] Only from about 1870, as they strove to engage with a popular audience, did they return to realistic displays, now redefined as scientific and rational.

At the same time, the didactic exposition of evolutionary themes was developing. By the 1890s, mankind was being included in the zoological displays, as the highest, most evolved animal form. The vertebrates were rearranged from 1895 to this end, culminating in:

> an entirely new series ... exemplifying the various races of mankind,
> by crania, casts, and drawings, or enlarged photographs

and 'illustrated by comparative preparations of their osteology and internal anatomy.'

Figure 6.12 shows a good example of the various elements present in natural history display at Liverpool Museum by the twentieth century. Many of the cases are naturalistic, as if containing the living animal in its natural environment. Most of the monkeys and apes appear to be arranged in habitat groups. This is combined, however, with a heavy emphasis on didactic demonstration of the scientific principle of evolution, as revealed by the case containing ape and human skeletons arranged so as to show a sequence of development. In order to reinforce the scientific authority of this theory, non-realistic techniques such as drawings, extensive labelling, and the display of skeletons and whole animals next to each other are used. This is the typical form of natural history display in the Liverpool Museum; using both the creation of illusion and the invocation of scientific authority to convey a message, of increasingly strident evolutionism. Natural history display was the first really to take shape at Liverpool, and the principles developed here are important precedents for the way display develops among the ethnography and antiquities sections.

However, there was an exception to this type of display, and that was the horns and antlers of big game shown running around the top of the Wild Animals gallery in Figure 6.12. These were not displayed for strictly scientific reasons, but rather as being 'of special interest to sportsmen.'[52] Although many of these specimens were collected earlier, mainly in the nineteenth century, it is only around 1914 that this form of display as trophy seems to be adopted. John MacKenzie has argued that the hunting of big game was increasingly bound up with the extension of empire; it embodied the 'curiosity, classificatory power and destructive capacity' of imperial domination.[53] A display such as Liverpool's horns was thus about much more than just scientific enquiry. It demonstrated imperial power, and suggested the wide range of exotic fauna, and the glamour and adventure of colonial life. Its emergence in the twentieth century would fit in with the chronology of imperialism, the turn of the century seeing both more competition from other European nations, and harder 'selling' of Empire to the British public.[54]

Thus at Liverpool, there was a considerable advance in display techniques; objects were well-kept, clearly labelled and generally well-lit, but also used to demonstrate scientific theories, in as popular a way as possible. It managed, in its own terms, to tread a fine line between popular appeal and sensationalism. A brief survey of other municipal museums at the time will show just how unusual an achievement this was.

Leicester Museum, largely natural history like Liverpool, did adopt similar display practices, and in particular developed quite a high level of realism in some displays, from the late 1870s. The first 'habitat group' was created in 1877, and under the new curator, Montagu Browne, from 1880, this trend was continued. Birds were displayed in 'realistic settings', and, most famously, Browne created a

Figure 6.12 Natural History Displays at Liverpool Museum, c. 1906
Source: National Museums Liverpool

display of two tigers fighting over the body of an elephant. He was a skilled taxidermist himself, and benefited from the three animals all dying in the same week at a local circus. Although realistic, this display verged on the sensational,and in fact recalls the most famous exhibit at Bullock's Museum, the tiger fighting the snake. In addition, there were series of skulls of different animals with the various bones coloured, so as to facilitate comparison; another attempt to increase the educational potential of the museum. It was argued in a local newspaper that Montagu Browne had increased the general popularity of the museum. However, it is also noticeable that Browne had to put considerable effort into the basics of display upon taking up his position; he noted that many specimens were mouldy, and spent a considerable amount of his budget on new windows and new display cases.[55]

Similar tensions between ambition and practical constraint, as well as between scientific ideas and the desire to attract visitors, can be seen at museums such as Sheffield and Hull. By 1904 Howarth at Sheffield aimed for displays that would:

> enable the general public to comprehend the main principles and
> laws governing the life of various animals [...] which have an
> attractive and instructive interest far beyond anything that pertains to
> the crowding of individual specimens on stands in cases.[56]

He clearly wanted to signal his difference from older approaches to display, both in terms of the science to be demonstrated and the emphasis on popular education; however, he maintained a commitment to offering a specialist reference service by using display cases with drawers beneath in which something like a full range of species, an index collection, could be available for advanced students.[57] The types of cases used were the same throughout the museum, limiting the possibilities of realistic display, and for distinguishing between natural history and man-made displays.

Alberti argues that in Yorkshire museums, society-owned and university as well as municipal, an evolutionary approach to display did not develop until the 1870s and 1880s, at which point there was a 'subtle revolution' in display methods. These museums followed Liverpool Museum in displaying fossil and skeletal specimens with stuffed ones, and by 1904 Hull Museum was showing human skeletons alongside other primates, as Liverpool did. Habitat groups were being constructed in Yorkshire museums from the 1880s up to the early years of the twentieth century.[58] As Alberti points out, all museums suffered from a lack of space for what were usually extensive collections in natural history (and sometimes the exhibits themselves were big, such as the 40 foot Sibald's Rorqual whale at Hull), and curators tended to favour the discipline with which they were most familiar.[59]

In Preston, the desire to engage the visitor at a popular level, and to educate through entertainment, seems to be almost completely absent, unlike not only many municipal museums, but other museums such as the Horniman, and exhibitions in the nineteenth and twentieth centuries.[60] While the museum was in a rather makeshift state in the rooms in Cross Street, although being described as 'in very nice order', it was also said to consist of 'some cases of birds and miscellaneous curiosities.'[61] No mention was made of any labels, photographs, or any other interpretative material. However, the classification of material was referred to, and the birds were described by donated collection. So it can be inferred that the bulk of the natural history room consisted of birds, divided by donor, and then sub-divided by order, genus, species and so on, all plainly stuffed and mounted. What was primarily being presented to the public, then, was the collections *in terms of* their donors. The rest of the material in this room was rather a miscellany; there were only a few specimens of each, so the overall effect would have been cluttered. Interestingly, along with the birds, skulls, shells, and fossils, were 'weapons of savages.'[62] In other words, the principle division created in the material universe was between European civilisation and everything else, rather than between the man-made and the natural.

When the museum was transferred to the Harris building, this began to change, although not uniformly. Rev. Jonathan Shortt, the honorary curator, made plans to create natural history displays that would meet the criteria of both science and popular education, unusually aiming to follow the ideas of A.R. Wallace.[63] Wallace had advocated a combination of attractive, well-mounted specimens, and information on geographical distribution, as well as anatomical models, and any economic products derived from them, as well as special sections devoted to comparative anatomy and geographical distribution.[64] These techniques of display are similar to those used at Liverpool. It showed increasing complexity and progress in life forms, up to the culmination in man, but did not insist on sequential development.

What is interesting, though, is how little of Wallace's vision was achieved in the Harris museum. In 1896, shortly after the building was opened to the public, an article in the *Preston Guardian* described one room containing mainly skulls and casts of extinct animals as a 'Chamber of Horrors' and compared it to Madame Tussaud's.[65] However, the article acknowledged the provisional nature of the arrangement, and overall praised the displays, although more, it would appear, for their extent than for their quality. A photograph of part of the natural history section (Figure 6.13) gives a clearer idea of the display. The most striking aspect is the pyramid of skulls and antlers, visible through the doorway. This is the collection of prehistoric remains discovered in the Ribble Dock excavation, and the display that caused most revulsion to the *Preston Guardian*. Shortt describes them as 'the distinctive feature of the museum,'[66] and displayed them accordingly. It is an extraordinary display, with a monumental ziggurat shape, creating an effect of size and distance, and drawing the eye up to the pinnacle. It has nothing to say about the skulls and antlers as evidence of prehistoric life forms within an evolutionary paradigm, or about the context from which these objects came. Instead it creates an aesthetic spectacle from them; in effect, a self-conscious display of trophies.[67] They may be seen as representing domination and power over the past, and the earth itself; they show the triumph of modern engineering, adding to human knowledge. Most of all, it is an emotionally charged display, and provoked a corresponding reaction in at least one visitor, the author of the *Preston Guardian* article.

Figure 6.13 Natural History Displays at the Harris Museum and Art Gallery, 1896
Source: Courtesy of the Harris Museum and Art Gallery, Preston

By contrast, the rest of the natural history displays are neutral to the point of dullness. The mineral cases visible in the foreground of the picture appear to have a minimal amount of labelling, and no other explanatory material at all. The walls are completely bare, unlike those of the Liverpool Museum. Any didactic aim is lost. The use of cases is inefficient, with table cases against the walls rather than proper wall cases which would allow more display space. There is no attempt to create any realism in the displays. The objects are not overcrowded, but in most other respects this is a very old-fashioned natural history display. The impression conveyed by the purchasing policy is that as the Harris developed, natural history became a neglected discipline, with the money and prestige going to art history,[68] and this is clearly reflected in these exhibits, with very low-key display techniques. The widespread nature of attempts in other museums both to illustrate more up-to-date scientific ideas, and to be more accessible to the general visitor, makes Preston's lack of interest all the more notable; it may well be attributable to the lack of a professional curator with a scientific background there. For the art, historical, and ethnographic objects held by museums, display methods were even more eclectic. Curators were similarly driven by a need to differentiate themselves from the sensational, and to stress their educative function, but how to do so was much less obvious than with natural history. For art galleries, the practice of hanging in chronological order of schools was now seen as the correct pedagogical strategy, but for archaeological and, especially, ethnographic objects, there was little precedent,[69] and it was not entirely clear how objects designed to illustrate the principles of design should be displayed. In addition, as objects which signified so much about the taste, culture and background of the owner, as well as their intrinsic prestige and cost, there was a strong impulse to focus attention on them as objects to inspire awe, rather than as illustrations of various principles. As a result, markedly different strategies of display can be found.

In Liverpool, ethnography dominated the man-made artefacts, and a clear contrast between European and, especially, African objects was constructed. Initially, after the Mayer donation, and the appointment of Thomas Gatty in 1871 as curator of the Mayer Museum, work was directed primarily to the classification and recording of objects in a methodical manner.[70] By the time of a Report on the Mayer Museum in the Minutes for 1884, there were still many basic problems with display. All the cases in the basement were described as rather dark, crowded and badly labelled. The emphasis on popular accessibility that was already present in some of the natural history displays was conspicuously absent here. Some cases had no labels at all, and some had near illegible hand-written ones. The Report found there was an urgent need for 'large labels, in few words, for popular information.'[71] There was, similarly, little to be learnt from the internal logic of each case; overcrowding meant that like could not always be grouped with like. For example, the west wall cases contained ethnographic specimens and Greek vases, and the east balustrade cases contained, *inter alia*, 'instruments of social discipline' and Mexican and Peruvian gold. Overall there was a rough distinction between Ancient and Classical objects; European antiquities; and ceramics, but this was implicit. As a result of the overcrowding, the non-European objects, designated as ethnography, were on temporary display in the Walker Art Gallery in

1881 and 1882; in a temporary annex behind the Gallery from 1882 to 1885, and were not displayed at all between 1886 and 1890.[72] After this date some small temporary exhibitions were mounted in table cases in the Main Hall. It was not, in fact, until after the appointment of Forbes, himself an anthropologist, as Director of Museums in 1894 that any kind of deliberate display techniques were used for ethnography, and that any development occurred among antiquities. He almost immediately produced some ethnography displays, in 1895, and after the Horseshoe extension created more space in the museum, he implemented his idea of integrating the ethnography with the antiquities and art history, by classifying all man-made objects by the race of their maker, Melanian, Mongolian or Caucasian.[73] So now all the man-made objects could be used to carry a message about racial characteristics, and accordingly display techniques became more didactic.

These three races were defined partly through differentiated display techniques. The clearest division was between Melanian and Caucasian, which together formed the bulk of the Mayer material before the First World War. Although there are no photographs of the African displays at this time, it is clear that methods emphasised the body of the African in a way that could be compared to the natural history displays. There was a group of life-sized casts of Africans, a Mankoja man, and a Bechuana woman and child.[74] This corresponds exactly to the composition of habitat group displays in zoology. Annie Coombes has shown how, in the period 1890 to 1914, throughout museum ethnography but particularly in Liverpool, the *body* of the African became central to display, with the techniques of anthropometry being borrowed from eugenics.[75] In Liverpool, the group of casts was supplemented by photographs. By 1899, the 'Races of Mankind' series of photographs consisted of 128 photographs, twenty-five casts, and five maps.[76] Again a comparison with the natural history displays can be drawn, in the emphasis on contextualisation and interpretation through additional graphic material. On the other hand, the African Hall aimed to represent 'the Arts, Crafts and Industries of the African tribes', and displayed such objects as looms and specimens of cloth together.[77] This interest in the process of production and manufacture might appear to counteract the link between natural history and African ethnography; but Coombes makes clear that by around 1900 African artefacts were increasingly being presented as 'art', and a re-evaluation of African manufactures was taking place.[78] It was suggested that African art showed evidence both of degeneration, for example in the Benin bronzes, once a native origin was established for them from about 1900; and of primitive stages in the development of art long since left behind by Europe,[79] and Liverpool's displays appear to have demonstrated both of these appraisals. So a comparison with the natural history displays can undoubtedly be drawn; the African ethnographic displays are similarly based on an evolutionary paradigm, and utilise realistic and pedagogical methods, which both naturalise and give scientific authority to the message.

Within the Caucasian section, though, it was quite different. Although by the twentieth century it was incorporated into Ethnography, there was no evolutionary paradigm. The objects were there more to be admired than to be interpreted;

display emphasised the inherent qualities of the object rather than contextualising it, or using it to illustrate a principle.

Of course, there was some attention paid to chronology, with an implicit message of progress, but this was removed from the discourses of genetic inferiority that informed the African displays. Thus the Egyptian Hall contained displays arranged according to the chronology of Dynasties.[80] Photographs of the Egyptian Hall (Figure 6.14) reveal a quite high number of statues and busts, arranged so as to maximise their monumental and aesthetic impact; all facing the entrance, arranged symmetrically, so they almost look like decorative features of the room. In contrast there are also very small and delicate objects displayed so as to set off their complexity. Sarcophagi and coffins are given cases to themselves. There appears to be very little interpretative material: only labels, no maps or photographs. There are no attempts at realistic display, at reconstructing a context for the objects. Their context is just the other objects, arranged in a sequence which is purely self-referential. The invitation is to view this display in terms of form and aesthetic qualities, rather than, as in the case of the African displays,as a direct reflection of the physical, social, and moral qualities of the manufacturers.

The distinction is even clearer when the Old Liverpool Room is examined. Significantly, where African ethnography made extensive use of photographs, in the Old Liverpool Room there is an almost equal emphasis on water-colour sketches and engravings.[81] Thus the African ethnography invokes science, objective authority and detached inquiry, the Old Liverpool Room relies on explicitly artistic, imaginative work, invoking nostalgia and reminiscence, a much more subjective, anecdotal order of truth. It is also an intensely *historical* display, whereas the African ethnography is ahistorical; the scenes and objects represented in the Old Liverpool Room are ones that have since disappeared, often relatively recently; for example, Liverpool Delft ware and its potteries, street scenes in seventeenth-century Liverpool, and a model of Liverpool in 1650.[82] In fact, it could be said that if the display of African ethnography is dominated by an evolutionary paradigm, Caucasian sections are characterised by a historical paradigm; human actors creating change in their environment rather than being subject to forces of nature such as evolution. This of course reflects the widespread view that Africans were 'prehistoric', although there were voices, mainly from Africa, arguing for the historicity of Africans, in the last quarter of the nineteenth century, even if rarely heard. The Benin bronzes brought a more widespread, though still limited, acceptance of Africa's historical dimension by the end of the century.[83] An arrangement by dynasty, such as was used in the Egyptian Hall, stresses individual human agency; whereas the Africans were grouped communally, as 'tribes'. Caucasian displays also invited a more subjective, personal response to exhibits, rather than acting to popularise scientific, objective ideas.

No other municipal museum had such extensive ethnographic collections as Liverpool, and its archaeological, art historical and local history collections were also larger than most. However, under the pervasive influence of the South Kensington Museum, there were serious attempts by municipal museums to use

Figure 6.14 The Egyptian Hall, Liverpool, c. 1906
Source: National Museums Liverpool

the display of man-made objects to teach aesthetic and design principles; it is actually noteworthy that Liverpool seems not to have attempted this. Birmingham Museum provides the clearest example of this intent. In Birmingham there was clearly an aesthetic approach to display. Nevertheless, the aim was not solely to provide opportunity to experience and commune with art, but also to educate taste, and improve standards of design. How to do this, of course, was a challenge with which many in the nineteenth century wrestled. It is clear that Whitworth Wallis, despite coming from the South Kensington Museum, differed from the rather reductive ideas of Henry Cole, who favoured a very didactic approach based on the display of clearly labelled examples of good and bad practice.[84] Wallis, by contrast, seems to have created very little in the way of didactic display, and to have stuck to displaying as many examples of good design from different periods and cultures as possible in a way that emphasised their intrinsic aesthetic qualities, while leaving it to the visitor to draw out ideas about what precisely constituted good design. It is significant that the South Kensington Museum and its empire placed great importance on casts, while Whitworth Wallis tended to acquire only originals. He quoted Ruskin's ideas on museums, and Ruskin was a noted opponent of Cole's.[85] Objects were linked only by a very loose connection with the industries of Birmingham. There was no desire to illustrate any particular theme, or to create a strictly chronological display, or to cover particular geographical areas, although there was an Italian Room. A photograph of the Industrial Gallery (Figure 6.6) shows a minimal display technique, with similar objects grouped in cases, but no other interpretative material at all, though it is recorded that there were descriptive labels, and cheap guidebooks are also mentioned. Wallis laid great stress on the fact that the museum was for ordinary people, not just artists and connoisseurs, and referred to the descriptive labels, which were intended to prevent people 'wondering what on earth all these things mean', but he also referred to 'cultivating ... powers of observation', 'teaching people to think for themselves', and of providing inspiration.[86] There was thus a very different conception of how a museum could aid popular education here, than at Liverpool.

Preston again forms a completely different example of display of man-made objects. It always had loan exhibits from the South Kensington, at some points forming a large percentage of its displays, which one may assume demonstrated a certain degree of educational intent, careful labelling and demonstration of decorative principles.[87] Ethnography, art and local history were initially secondary to natural history and displayed in a fairly amateurish way. When the museum moved into the Harris building, however, there was a marked change in the techniques and aims of display, which came very much to emphasise aesthetic and monumental qualities, while also attempting to show a developmental sequence of art. The loan collections from South Kensington continued, and there were various *objets d'art*, medallions, coins, scale models of Renaissance palace interiors, and a small quantity of local history and ethnographic objects.[88] There is little information on how this was displayed, either as to the intended or actual effect. For the large sculpture casts, however, there is both. The plan given for their arrangement in the FPLC Minutes aims to illustrate

distinct periods in the history of the Art, co-ordinated so as to
harmonise with the Architecture of the Central Hall, and to form a
symmetrical and artistic composition. In respect of the chronological
order and the ascription therewith implied of schools and dates,
recourse has been had to eminent authorities, including the most
recent German archaeologists, Waldstein and Furtwangler.[89]

This plan embodies three main effects to be achieved through display: a pedagogic
effect, to create knowledge of the history of art; an aesthetic effect, to make a
visually attractive display; and an authoritative effect, to fix the meaning of the
display and to link it to authorities of greater stature; all to be mutually reinforcing
and to reinforce the prestige of the providers of the museum.

Looking at figure 6.15, showing some of the Roman and Greek casts, it can be
seen how far these aims were achieved in practice. The most striking effect is the
aesthetic. The statues are artistically and symmetrically arranged, on fairly tall
plinths, which increases their monumental effect. They do not, however, have very
much to say about art history, although a chronology is established from the top
floor with the oldest sculpture down to the most recent. This is hardly spelt out,
however. The lack of interpretation and textual or graphic information, giving
background to the statues, means attention is focused on the inherent qualities of
the object, which tends to encourage an aesthetic and subjective, rather than a
historical and objective, appreciation.[90] Because there is so little labelling, the
authority for classifying and forming the chronology is not made known to the
public. The statues do not have the status of 'truth' that natural history objects
might assume from being part of a discourse of objective, scientific knowledge;
they act in a more subjective, evocative way. Within the neo-Grecian setting of the
Harris building, they may be seen to stand for all that is beautiful and true,
civilised, progressive, and European, and to invest the museum itself, by inference,
with these qualities.

So, in summary, it can be said that display at Preston does not so much work
to transmit ideas about the material world illustrated by the objects, but, by
encouraging a personal communion with them, to invoke a set of qualities,
primarily beauty, monumentality, ownership and power; and to associate these
with the museum setting, and with those who provide it. The visitor may partake of
these qualities, if they have sufficient knowledge to interpret the objects correctly;
helping the visitor to understand is not part of the function of display here.

It can be seen that manipulation of the display space of a museum is its
principal means of communicating and interacting with its visitors, and three main
aspects of this developed in the course of the period between 1850 and 1914.
Firstly, certain ideals and patterns of behaviour were to be communicated to, and
indeed as far as possible imposed upon visitors; secondly classification and
articulation of objects, the links and divisions between branches of knowledge, or
races, or periods of history, were portrayed; and thirdly, emotional responses from
visitors to objects were sought. The techniques available to shape the museums'
communication became more effective; but they mainly came from outside the
environment of these museums. Thus many of the architectural changes were

Figure 6.15 Classical Casts at the Harris Museum and Art Gallery, 1896
Source: Courtesy of the Harris Museum and Art Gallery, Preston

pioneered in department stores and exhibitions, filtering later into museum buildings.[91] The classification and sequencing of museum objects was undertaken by curators according to the theories of others, increasingly after about 1890 of professional academics attached to a university; in Liverpool this was particularly true of archaeology,[92] and the Harris Museum relied on authorities in art history. Before this, gentlemen amateurs were more prominent in both museums and science, and there was more overlap; but although for example A. R. Wallace and T. H. Huxley were involved with museum projects, curators seem to have been specialising more in museum work.[93] Display techniques were often borrowed from fairs, exhibitions and advertising,[94] although museums also sought to differentiate themselves from such popular forms, and to justify themselves on the basis of their specialist knowledge and educational intent.

Museums can be seen, therefore, to have struggled with a number of variables in attempting to shape the way they communicated with their visitors. Not only did they have wildly differing levels of resources, they also had different aims, which can be traced back to the curators, donors, and councils in question. Thus in Liverpool, the museum had well-developed visitor routes, realistic and scientifically authoritative displays, and an overall scheme of evolutionary progress from the formation of the earth to bygone Liverpool. These can be linked to the professionalisation of the museum, and its links with the new university; to the importance of the West African trade for the elite merchant group there, who were influential in both the supply of objects to the museum and on the council committee running the museum; and to what may be described as a municipal socialism or welfare approach to the increasingly enfranchised and labour-conscious 'masses' on the part of Liverpool Council.[95] The museum's messages focus on its own authority and knowledgability; on the advanced and superior nature of western civilisation, and on the concomitant inferiority of Africa, with Britain in a protective, guiding role; and on providing access to knowledge in a popularly entertaining way, with plenty of spectacle.

In Preston the space and displays were monumental, decontextualised, and following a combination of aesthetic and historic criteria. The full aesthetic experience contained within the museum was not available to everyone in Preston; it was designed to be a closed, exclusive experience, open only to those who already had the knowledge, and developed artistic sensibilities, to appreciate it: the professional and manufacturing elite. The display space of the Harris Museum, although technically open to all, communicated social groupings and divisions through its uncontextualised, massive series of statues; its huge central well of space; and the elite was constantly present in the shape of acknowledgements of donors, and busts and portraits of local notables.[96] In Birmingham, by contrast, there was a much clearer educational rationale, and a much-quoted link between the museum and the working people of the city. In places such as Sheffield, Leicester and Hull, the space and display are more a result of the slow changeover from a voluntary society museum to a municipal museum with a professional curator; attempts to produce a more modern, useful, universally accessible institution are incomplete.

Museums' different strategies for, and differing success in, shaping the experiences of their visitors suggests both the strengths and weaknesses of municipal museums at this time. They were very local institutions, established in an environment which was not fully convinced of their right to public support; their purpose was unclear; and they were subject to various bids for control. On the other hand, this meant they could respond to local needs, industries, social structures and elite groups. If popular education was not a priority of elite, council or curator, then popular education would not figure largely in the museum. Municipal museums can not be regarded monolithically, as tools in the reshaping of the working class, because many of them continued to serve the niche interest of the amateur scientist, or turned to increasing the prestige and authority of the elite instead.

Notes

[1]   See S. Giedion, *Space, Time, and Architecture: The Growth of a New Tradition*, (Oxford 1967); Samuel J. M. M. Alberti, 'Field, Lab and Museum: The Practice and Place of Life Science in Yorkshire, 1870-1904', (Unpublished PhD thesis, University of Sheffield 2000), p. 84; Carla Yanni, *Nature's Museums: Victorian Science and the Architecture of Display*, (London 1999), pp. 9, 160.

[2]   Tony Bennett, *The Birth of the Museum*, (London 1995), pp. 22-3.

[3]   *Ibid.*, p. 6.

[4]   *Ibid.*, p. 101.

[5]   *Ibid.*, see especially chapters 1 and 7; although Yanni points out that this was essential for the maximum utilisation of top lighting: Yanni, *Nature's Museums*, p. 9. Foucauldian ideas are also developed in Eilean Hooper-Greenhill, *Museums and the Shaping of Knowledge*, (London 1992).

[6]   Bennett, *Birth of the Museum*, p. 52.

[7]   Thomas A. Markus, *Buildings and Power: Freedom and Control in the Origin of Modern Building Types*, (London 1993), especially chapter 7.

[8]   Sophie Forgan, '"But Indifferently Lodged...": Perception and Place in Building for Science in Victorian London', in Crosbie Smith and Jon Agar (eds) *Making Space for Science: Territorial Themes in the Shaping of Knowledge*, (London 1998), p. 198.

[9]   K. Hill, 'Municipal museums in the north-west, 1850-1914' (unpublished PhD thesis, Lancaster University 1996), p. 129.

[10]   Bennett, *Birth of the Museum*, p. 182.

[11]   Yanni, *Nature's Museums*, pp. 46-61.

[12]   Brears and Davies, *Treasures for the People, The Story of Museums and Galleries in Yorkshire and Humberside*, (Yorkshire and Humberside Museums Council 1989), pp. 36-7.

[13]   Markus, *Buildings*, p.14. See also Hillier and Hanson, *The Social Logic of Space*, (Cambridge 1984), chapter 4.

[14]   Markus, *Buildings*, pp. 16-19.

[15]   Hill, 'Municipal museums', pp. 115-6.

[16]   *Ibid.*, pp. 119-123.

[17]   *Ibid.*, p. 238.

[18]   S. Davies, *By the Gains of Industry, Birmingham Museums and Art Gallery 1885-1985*, (Birmingham 1985), pp. 15-22.

[19]   Markus, *Buildings*, p. 208.

[20] Davies, *By the Gains*, p. 42.

[21] J. Taylor (ed), *Illustrated Guide to Sheffield*, (Sheffield 1879), p. 130; E. Howarth, *Visitors' Guide to the Sheffield Public Museum, Weston Park*, (Sheffield 1883).

[22] Howarth, *Visitors' Guide*.

[23] M. Tooby, *'In Perpetuity and Without Charge'; The Mappin Art Gallery 1887-1987*, (Sheffield 1987), p. 6.

[24] Kate Hill, '"Roughs of both sexes": the working class in Victorian museums and art galleries', in Gunn and Morris (eds), *Identities in Space: Contested Terrains in the Western City since 1850*, (Aldershot 2001).

[25] *Sheffield and Rotherham Independent*, 5 August 1887.

[26] *White's History, Gazeteer, and Directory of the Counties of Leicester and Rutland*, (Sheffield 1877), p. 309; F. B. Lott, *The Centenary Book of the Leicester Literary and Philosophical Society*, (Leicester 1935), p. 31.

[27] Hillier and Hanson, *Social Logic*, pp. 195-6.

[28] For example, on Whit Monday 1882, there were two extra police officers on duty in Sheffield Museum: Sheffield Museum Daily Report, 29 May 1882. For a treatment of art museums which gives equal attention to matters such as regulations, as to space and buildings, see Daniel J. Sherman, *Worthy Monuments: Art Museums and the Politics of Culture in Nineteenth-Century France*, (Cambridge, Massachussetts 1989).

[29] Sherman, *Worthy Monuments*, p. 177. Sherman also refers to the importance of grand staircases and plenty of busts and statues in the buildings.

[30] For so-called 'economist' lobbies in mid-nineteenth century councils, see E. P. Hennock, *Fit and Proper Persons: Ideal and Reality in Nineteenth-Century Urban Government*, (London 1973), pp. 31-33, and Davies, *By the Gains of Industry*, p. 10; see also the report of a meeting of ratepayers in the *Preston Chronicle*, 11 March 1854, which resolved 'that any undertaking at the present juncture, calling for increased taxation, will be unwise on the part of the corporate body, and unjust and oppressive to the ratepayers.' It was not long after this that the first attempt to adopt the Free Public Libraries and Museums Act in Preston failed.

[31] *Report of the 57th Meeting of the British Association for the Advancement of Science, 1887* (London 1888), pp. 119-121; Kenneth Hudson, *A Social History of Museums*, (New Jersey 1975), pp. 70-1, 78-79; Alberti, 'Field, Lab and Museum', p. 84.

[32] Hooper-Greenhill, *Museums*, pp. 185-188.

[33] Bennett, *Birth of the Museum*, chapter 7.

[34] Forgan, ' "But Indifferently Lodged..."', p. 201.

[35] Sophie Forgan, 'Bricks and Bones: Architecture and Science in Victorian Britain', in P. Galison and E. Thompson (eds) *The Architecture of Science*, (Cambridge, Massachussetts 1999), pp. 194-200. See also Pitt-Rivers' Rotunda, in W. R. Chapman, 'Arranging Ethnology: AHLF Pitt-Rivers and the Typological Tradition', in Stocking (ed) *Objects and Others: Essays on Museums and Material Culture*, (Madison 1985), pp. 39-41.

[36] The disapproving tone with which a *Preston Guardian* report spoke of 'popular attractions' in the 'Chamber of Horrors' of Preston's museum (in fact human skulls and dinosaur footprints); and hoped the curator could 'see his way ... to make it a little less like Mme Tussaud's exhibition', indicates the kind of thing which was seen as sensational; however, there was not necessarily much clarity from commentators on this point. *Preston Guardian*, 14 November 1896.

[37] Yanni, *Nature's Museums*, p. 3.

[38] Alberti, 'Field, Lab and Museum', p. 89.

[39] Rev. H. H. Higgins, 'Synopsis of An Arrangement of Invertebrate Animals in the Free Public Museum of Liverpool with Introduction', *Proceedings of the Literary and Philosophical Society of Liverpool* 28 (Appendix), (1873), p. iv.

[40] *Ibid.*, p. iv.

[41] *Ibid.*, p. vii.

[42] *Ibid.*, p. ix.

[43] *Ibid.*, p. xi.

[44] See for example W.H. Flower, *Essays on Museums*, (London 1898), p. 52.

[45] Higgins, 'Synopsis', p. xiii.

[46] *Ibid.*, p. x.

[47] AR Liverpool 1888 and 1903.

[48] Donna Haraway, 'Teddy Bear Patriarchy: Taxidermy in the Garden of Eden, New York City, 1908-1936', *Social Text* 11 (1984), p. 24; Jordanova, 'Objects of Knowledge – A Historical Perspective on Museums', in Vergo (ed) *The New Museology*, (London 1989), p. 32.

[49] Jordanova, 'Objects of Knowledge', p. 35; Haraway, 'Teddy Bear Patriarchy', p. 34.

[50] Richard Altick, *The Shows of London*, (Cambridge, Massachussetts 1978), p. 237.

[51] Yanni, *Nature's Museums*, p. 3.

[52] AR Liverpool 1914.

[53] John M. MacKenzie, *The Empire of Nature: Hunting, Conservation and British Imperialism*, (Manchester 1988), p.36.

[54] M. Worboys, 'The Imperial Institute: the state and the development of the natural resources of the Colonial Empire 1887-1923' in John M. MacKenzie (ed) *Imperialism and the Natural World*, (Manchester 1990), p. 164.

[55] Cynthia Browne, *Cherished Possessions: A History of the New Walk Museum and Leicester Museums Service*, (Leicester 2002), pp. 8-9.

[56] *Annual Report of the Free Public Libraries and Museum Committee* (Sheffield 1904), cited in Alberti, 'Field, Lab and Museum', p. 89.

[57] *Ibid.*, p. 84.

[58] *Ibid.*, p. 90.

[59] *Ibid.*, p. 91.

[60] Annie E. Coombes, *Reinventing Africa: Museums, Material Culture and Popular Imagination*, (New Haven 1994), p. 154; P. Greenhalgh, 'Education, Entertainment and Politics: Lessons from the Great International Exhibitions' in Vergo (ed), *The New Museology*, (London 1989), p. 83.

[61] A. Hewitson ('Atticus'), *History of Preston*, (Preston 1883), p. 312.

[62] *Ibid.*, p. 312.

[63] FPLC Minutes, 24 May 1894.

[64] A. R. Wallace, 'Museums for the People', *Macmillan's Magazine*, (1869), pp. 246-248.

[65] *Preston Guardian* 14 November 1896.

[66] FPLC Minutes, 17 July 1894.

[67] See chapter five for a discussion of trophies.

[68] See chapter five.

[69] By the late nineteenth century, the Pitt-Rivers collection and its typological arrangement had become the dominant paradigm, but for museums trying to display ethnographic material before this, there was little guidance. See Chapman, 'Arranging Ethnology'; David van Keuren, 'Museums and Ideology: Augustus Pitt-Rivers, anthropological museums and social change in later Victorian Britain', *Victorian Studies* 28 (1984); Ghislaine Lawrence, 'Wellcome's Museum for the Science of History', in Ken Arnold and Danielle Olsen (eds) *Medicine Man: The Forgotten Museum of Henry Wellcome*, (London 2003).

[70]   A.C. West, 'Notes on the history of the Ethnography Department' (unpublished paper in NML Archives) (1981) p. 3.

[71]   Minutes, Liverpool, 30 July 1884.

[72]   West, 'Notes', p. 4.

[73]   Coombes, *Reinventing Africa*, p. 7.

[74]   *General Guide to the Collections contained in the Free Public Museums (William Brown Street) Liverpool* (1906) p. 15.

[75]   Coombes, *Reinventing Africa*, p. 122.

[76]   *Ibid.*, p. 136.

[77]   *General Guide* (1906) p.15.

[78]   Coombes, *Reinventing Africa*, p. 142.

[79]   *Ibid.*, p. 55.

[80]   *General Guide* (1906) p. 11.

[81]   *Ibid*, p.17.

[82]   *Ibid.*, p. 17. See Alan J. Kidd ' 'Local History' and the Culture of the Middle Classes in North-West England, c.1840-1900', *Transactions of the Historic Society of Lancashire and Cheshire*, 147, (1997), pp. 115-138, for discussion of how local history was concerned with 'the recovery of a local past from the neglect of a rapidly changing present'.

[83]   Coombes, *Reinventing Africa*, pp. 37-9, 61.

[84]   Janet Minihan, *The Nationalisation of Culture: The Development of State Subsidies to the Arts in Great Britain*, (London 1977), p. 136.

[85]   Whitworth Wallis, 'The Museum and Art Gallery', in J. H. Muirhead (ed) *Birmingham Institutions*, (Birmingham 1911), p. 491; Minihan, *Nationalisation*, p. 135.

[86]   Wallis, 'The Museum and Art Gallery', pp. 486-488.

[87]   That these principles were important at the South Kensington Museum is shown by I. Wolfenden, 'The Applied Arts in the Museum Context' in S.Pearce (ed) *Museum Studies in Material Culture*, (London 1989), and L. Purbrick, 'South Kensington Museum: The Building of the House of Henry Cole' in M. Pointon (ed) *Art Apart*, (Manchester 1994).

[88]   *Preston Corporation Art Gallery Illustrated Catalogue 1907*.

[89]   FPLC Minutes, 15 October 1894.

[90]   M. Hall, *On Display: A Design Grammar for Museum Exhibitions*, (London 1986), p. 29.

[91]   Bennett, *Birth of the Museum.*, p. 52; Giedion, *Space, Time and Architecture*, pp. 234, 246.

[92]   See chapter four.

[93]   Wallace, 'Museums for the People'; Stearn, *The Natural History Museum at South Kensington*, (London 1981), p. 67.

[94]   For the display techniques of London fairs, exhibitions, and sideshows, see Altick, *The Shows of London*; for advertising and exhibition techniques see T. Richards, *The Commodity Culture of Victorian England: Advertising and Spectacle 1851-1914*, (London 1990).

[95]   See chapter three.

[96]   FPLC Minutes, 18 February 1907.

CHAPTER SEVEN

Consuming the Museum:
Museum Visitors

The visitors are the great unknowns of Victorian museums. Despite the great weight of speculation, assumptions and pedagogy targeted at them by museum staff, there is very little indeed to tell us how they experienced the space, objects and ideas contained within the institutions. And yet this is central to our understanding of Victorian municipal museums. In order to function as the significant shapers of society alleged by recent studies, they would have to have been consumed in the way intended by a substantial proportion of people. With evidence so thin on the ground, at best it can only be said to be unproven; and there is some indication that at times museums may have been consumed in a way that fundamentally subverted the intentions behind them.

Examining visitors' use of museum and art gallery space is also important because of the light it may shed on the construction of class identities through cultural consumption in the late Victorian period. By the 1880s places such as the public street saw social roles becoming fluid; appearances were deceptive, and class identities were increasingly hard to maintain.[1] There were ways in which middle-class identities could be protected in public spaces, but this period also sees the creation of semi-public spaces where middle class identity could more easily be defined and protected; places such as department stores and concert halls.[2] There was also some development of middle-class roles, particularly among women, who increasingly took on public work in charity, for example; but they still needed to occupy a privileged position in public space in order to do so.[3] If we turn to working-class and lower middle-class identity in public and semi-public spaces, an increasing range of roles, behaviour, appearance is apparent, and, especially among the young, a sense of creating new social identities. In general, there is a more autonomous, commercial culture evident in the working class from around the 1880s.[4]

It is of course the case that identities are constructed partly through a process of exclusion, and when different class groups met in public spaces, middle-class identities were particularly dependent upon the perception of certain roles and attitudes among the working class, such as deference and ignorance. If these were not present, the middle class's own identity as superior, cultural and social guides to the working class was threatened. Museums and art galleries can therefore be seen as relatively neutral, universally accessible spaces which could be configured so as to try and reshape working-class identities and remake the way they consumed culture. At the same time museums and galleries could be part of a project to define and maintain middle-class identities through elite consumption. In fact, it is my argument that this is the only aspect that succeeded; working-class visitors continued to defy prescribed roles, and deserted museums when they became too coercive; leaving middle-class visitors exclusive possession.

The problem of evidence about the views of museum visitors themselves has been noted before. Kenneth Hudson's 1975 book, *A Social History of Museums*, is subtitled 'What the Visitors Thought', but it fairly swiftly runs into the problem of finding out precisely what it was that they thought. After noting that the first visitor survey ever undertaken in a museum was not until 1897, he says

> One searches for comments wherever they are to be found, realising that only the exceptional person is ever likely to write down his feelings and find a published outlet for them and that the great majority of men, women, boys and girls who have ever entered a museum and art gallery have been interested or bored, stupefied or invigorated, without anybody but themselves or their friends knowing about it.[5]

Although he does uncover some useful information about visitors' views, it is noticeable that there is a constant tendency, in considering the interaction between museum and visitor, to switch to the intentions and views of the museum, which are of course much easier to establish.

What follows, then, will be an attempt to establish some picture of visitors to municipal museums during the second half of the nineteenth century. We do know quite a lot about numbers, and something about the social characteristics of different groups who used the museum. We can piece together a few ideas about how museums were used, from the comments, heavily value-laden though they were, of people who observed museum visitors. And in a few cases we have the direct testimony of museum visitors themselves.

Municipal museums, accountable to their rate payers, kept records of visitor numbers, and these figures are very impressive. Visitor figures were such that a fairly large proportion of the working class must have visited such an institution at least once. Some museums and art galleries clocked up huge numbers of visitors; between 1888 and 1905, the Public Museum and Mappin Art Gallery in Sheffield consistently had over 200,000 visitors annually, and the highest daily figure, usually on Easter Monday or possibly August Bank Holiday, was over 7,000 between 1887 and 1893.[6] Birmingham Art Gallery claimed an astounding 18,000 visitors a week in 1888, while rate-supported museums and galleries in Bolton, Bradford, Derby, Liverpool, Nottingham, Salford and Dundee had 4,000 visitors a week or more.[7] Moreover, attendance tended to be higher at those times when the working class were free to go: evenings, Sundays and Mondays. This does not in itself prove that it was the working class who were going, of course; Kevin Moore's work on Mechanics' Institutes exhibitions in the first half of the nineteenth century indicates that the middle class might be happy to attend cultural events at times specifically set aside for the working class, for a variety of reasons, not least financial.[8] Nevertheless, there is enough evidence to suggest that at least some of the visitors who came to museums and art galleries such as that in Sheffield were working-class: while commentators interpreted the behaviour of visitors in stereotyped terms, their analysis of social status was detailed and certainly more reliable than the bland assurances of social unity given by curators and managers. For example, Francis Place argued that three-quarters of visitors to art galleries were working people. Elsewhere, labourers were identified by their fustian jackets.[9] The popularity of Mondays is also suggestive; while many of the middle class were restricted to Saturday afternoons, Sundays, and evenings just as much as the working class were, the practice of not working on 'St Monday' was a working-class custom, if most common among domestic and skilled workers.[10] Moreover, Thomas Wright, the chronicler of and commentator on the skilled working class, refers several times to visits to an art gallery or Hampton Court as typical activities for St Monday.[11] There can be little doubt that, particularly in the first years after the opening of a museum or art gallery, members of the working class were among its visitors in significant numbers, even if there were also plenty of middle-class visitors.

Numbers of visitors are such, then, that a variety of social groups must have been represented. How to think about these social groups, though, is less clear. We can distinguish the different audiences museums themselves thought they were catering to. They frequently spoke in terms of an expert and a general audience, who might be admitted at different times, with one day a week set aside for 'students', or scientific societies using the museum in the evening for soirees. There might also be different collections and displays for these groups, with drawers or storage areas containing extensive collections of, for example, bird skins, deemed too dull for general display. The museum officially defined such special visitors in terms of knowledge and purpose, 'those who are able to read and appreciate' research collections,[12] rather than social status, but there was certainly a high degree of correlation between experts and high-status visitors. The useful thing about this group is that they were aware of and in agreement with their designation; unlike, for example, when visitors were described as 'intelligent...working-class', but we have no idea how accurate such a label might be. How did the 'expert' or 'student', who had privileged access to the museum, use it?

Although students were considered to be an important constituency for municipal museums, which maintained the approach of the scientific societies in their collections and concern that specialised research still be a function of the institution, it seems that they did not always use such museums in the numbers anticipated. While in Sheffield, Howarth recorded that 'the interest taken in the collections by Students has also steadily increased...Eighteen students have availed themselves in the past year of the privilege of studying in the Museum on Fridays, when it is closed to the public',[13] the 1887 Report of the British Association for the Advancement of Science stated that 'about fifty' museums reported frequent use by 'local naturalists, archaeologists, and medical and art students,' but did not indicate which fifty museums these were. Moreover, it went on to say that an equal number said very little such use was made of them. In terms of the facilities for study, 'many museums report that they would welcome students and give them every assistance, but that none apply.' About twenty had rooms set aside for students, while about thirty had tables, but not entire rooms. In only a few cases were these facilities used to a considerable extent.[14] It has been argued that the 'students' envisaged were distinguished solely by an educated background and could thus be anyone of a suitable background who chose to apply. However, museums also thought of themselves as offering a specialist reference service to autodidacts in natural history and craftsmen seeking examples of their trade to emulate, though the response from this group could be equally underwhelming. In Birmingham, Wallis maintained that

> It is to be regretted, I think, that our art students and young workpeople do not make more use of our industrial collections, in the way that students do of the similar collections in London, Berlin and Paris....Our manufacturers might also take greater advantage of these collections.[15]

This may explain why there are no signs of tension between the student visitors and ordinary visitors; no disagreements over the respective periods of admittance for the two categories. An art student in France, on the other hand, clearly thought the museum in Dijon did not do enough for students who were self-evidently the most important type of visitor.[16]

The scientific and social elite also visited the museum in the course of soirées and conversaziones. It has recently been argued that these events show how active the consumption of science by this audience could be. They took place in a variety of public and semi-public places, but predominantly civic spaces, and museums were popular as scientific societies' collections were often held there. In addition, societies sometimes borrowed museum objects for their soirées, although by 1900 Liverpool Museum was refusing such a request from the Lord Mayor.[17] The audience would be reasonably exclusive, middle and upper class, and included both men and women. The main activity was viewing exhibits, the museums' own along with any displayed for the event by amateur collectors. There might be talks given on particular objects, or a more formal lecture, or even a demonstration of some apparatus or experiment. The prevailing tone was sociable; alcohol might be served, there might be a musical performance, and the volume of small talk and chatter was frequently said to be deafening. The other notable element is how involved the audience could be; microscopes might be available for general use, and of course the whole point of the evening was for everyone to discuss with each other the exhibits. The conversazione held to mark the opening of the Harris Museum and Art Gallery in Preston in 1893 included 'Microscopical Entertainment' and electrical experiments as well as music; at least thirteen individuals and two companies loaned microscopes to the event.[18] Thus the middle-class elite had opportunities to consume the museum, and the knowledge it contained, in a markedly different way from the general public. There were also other events: in Liverpool, where the museum had a particularly close relationship with the Chamber of Commerce by the turn of the nineteenth century, their annual meeting was held there in 1907, and the British Medical Association held its annual meeting in the Harris Museum in 1913.[19] The conversazione has been seen as constituting part of a growing upper middle-class civic culture which marked that group as culturally sophisticated, and this seems a valid conclusion.[20] However, such use of museums did not go unchallenged by the excluded; in Leicester in 1909 one member of the public wrote that they

> would like to know why the Art Gallery is used for receptions, tea meetings, and other festive private gatherings. I live opposite, and see the building a blaze of light night after night, although the doors are closed and the general public excluded...Do the entertainers pay for the light consumed, or is it a charge on the rates?[21]

In considering what may be termed general or popular use of the museum, we really start to run into difficulties. It is very hard to piece together an overall picture, but some clues can be gathered from public comments and disagreements over museums, usually undertaken in the pages of the local newspaper. As Daniel Sherman argues in looking at French provincial art galleries, public contestation of the way such institutions work reveals what audiences' values are embodied in it, who, among the public, feels ownership of it.[22] An example of this may be the question of Sunday opening. For most museums and galleries the question of Sunday opening was a vexed one which increasingly came to dominate public discussion of the institutions. At the time of the British Association for the Advancement of Science's Report on provincial museums in 1887, only two museums specifically stated that they were open on Sunday afternoons; these were Birmingham Museum and the Ancoats Art Museum in Manchester. As this may indicate, Sunday opening was felt to be very much a boon for the working man, and rational recreationalists had long held that Sabbatarianism merely delivered the working classes into the clutches of the public house; but the other, equally strongly held view, was that opening museums and art galleries on Sunday, particularly publicly owned ones, was a dangerous precedent as well as being inherently sinful. However, a frequently underexamined aspect of this debate is the extent to which Sunday opening increasingly became a focus of *public* concern. The Harris Museum and Art Gallery in Preston may be a good example here. In 1902 the Free Public Library Committee received a Resolution from the Operative Cotton Spinners' Society, asking for the opening of the institution on Sundays,

> inasmuchas only on that day have the majority of workers of this town an opportunity of visiting such an institution;...such opening would be of advantage to the whole of the municipality.

In the next two months the FPLC received a number of other resolutions from various organisations in Preston: the Trades Council, the ILP, the Electrical Trades Union and the Furnishing Trades Association were in favour of Sunday opening, while the YMCA, the Church of England Sunday School Association, the Sunday School Union, and the Grimshaw Street Men's Bible Class were against. This is a predictable enough division of organisations, but it is not clear that either side represented any particular social group within Preston. The FPLC resolved not to open on Sundays; however, the matter was reopened within the Council as a whole. Though still defeated, it was more popular with the whole council than it was with the FPLC. Two years later the question was revisited after a resolution from the ILP phrased in somewhat stronger language: 'This Public Meeting of Ratepayers is of the opinion that the Art Gallery, Museum and Reading Rooms ought to be open to the Public on Sundays.' Thereafter, the FPLC resolved to open from 3 to 5 pm on Sundays, despite protests from the Loyal Orange Institute and the St Mark's Young Men's Bible Class.[23]

Similar debates took place elsewhere, particularly in newspapers; the editor of Leicester Daily Mercury wrote in favour of Sunday opening in 1874, and received at least one response protesting that the holiness of the Sabbath must be respected (the museum introduced Sunday opening in 1891).[24] It is clear, then, that a reasonably wide section of the public not only visited the museum, but expressed views on its operation as a publicly funded institution. It was not felt to be appropriate for small privileged groups to use it in too overtly possessive a way, or to impose controversial changes such as Sunday opening; but if this came from a public meeting of ratepayers, that very Victorian guarantee of legitimacy, changes were possible.

A number of fears were expressed about the way the working class used museums and art galleries. Pessimists feared that working-class visitors wandered around them without any way of understanding the exhibits, learning, or in any way being able to benefit. To a certain extent, though, as we have seen, some municipal museums made enormous efforts to make their exhibits accessible and educational on a popular level, even if others remained distinctly dry and indigestible. The pessimists had worse fears though, and could be vociferous; in 1887, a letter to the *Sheffield Independent* read:

> To the editor:- I was astonished to learn that the Mappin Gallery was the scene of an invasion of Sheffield roughs of both sexes last Sunday afternoon. ... I am told that some hundreds of the worst played at gymnastics over the seats, and afterwards, with girls at their sides, made a promenade of the galleries to the annoyance of all who were anxious to see the paintings. ... The worst behaved of the roughs are youths and girls from 15 to 18 or 19 years of age. They do not look at the pictures, excepting a few remarkable ones, on which their comments are such as, if repeated, would pollute your columns.[25]

Although a note from the editor maintained that 'our correspondent has received a somewhat exaggerated account of what took place', this started off a series of letters, most of which agreed with the original correspondent on the nature and gravity of the problem. One referred to 'roughs out of the crofts', who pass 'audible remarks of the lowest description', and another argued that the gallery had become 'a remarkably free and easy Sunday afternoon promenade.'[26] Nevertheless it was maintained by another that 'the behaviour of this large quantity of people was most admirable, and the interest in the pictures of a very strongly marked character.'[27]

This correspondence indicates some of the difficulties and issues involved in examining the working class's use of and attitudes towards museums and art galleries. Descriptions such as these, from middle-class visitors, clearly view workers through the categories of respectable and rough, yet we know that such labels do not necessarily reflect the lived patterns of working-class life. Progressive museum staff and founders worked on the expectation that exposure to such cultural institutions would improve the working class, and make them more rational and civilised. Yet evidence of the kind quoted above suggests that visitors could resist and even subvert the technologies of the museum and gallery.

The middle-class image of these visitors is structured round a set of dichotomies: rough and respectable, family groups and young single people, manual labour and service. Peter Bailey has outlined the middle-class perception of 'two discrete and exclusive constituencies in working-class life', and how this shaped the provision of 'rational recreation' activities, such as Henry Solly's founding of the working men's club movement as an opportunity for the respectable to enjoy their leisure away from the rough.[28] Commentators on museums and art galleries also made this distinction, contrasting the roughs who did not look at the exhibits, but promenaded and used coarse language, with a more respectable type of working-class visitor, whose characteristic reaction was awe and wonder, untutored but willing to learn. When the Tate Gallery opened, it was alleged that 'the majority of the visitors came from the immediate [working-class] neighbourhood. ... [T]he crowd, nothing loth, entered yesterday into possession of their new palace of art, ... and ...tried to understand the pictures, in which lay a new world of romance and mystery, ... mingled with the world they know better; on the one hand the allegories of Watts, on the other the realism of Frith.'[29] Greenwood's idea of the respectable worker's reaction to an art gallery is summed up in the following passage:

> I have more than once seen a wife with a pale, careworn face cling
> more closely to the arm of her husband as some picture of child life
> was being looked at, or something else suggestive to them, perhaps,
> of little fingers lying cold in mother earth.[30]

In general, as this suggests, it was supposed that the respectable museum or gallery visitor came in a family group, while the roughs were more likely to be young and single. Thomas Wright's excursionists to Hampton Court and an unnamed gallery were overwhelmingly sedate couples, with young single men more likely to choose a sporting activity for St Monday.[31] The family group was felt to guarantee a certain degree of propriety, and to discourage rough behaviour.[32] Those who wrote to the newspapers complaining about conduct in the Mappin Art Gallery in Sheffield were particularly displeased that there was no effort made to encourage family groups and discourage unaccompanied teenagers. The regulations stated that no children under the age of eight were to be admitted at all, and yet over the age of fourteen there were no restrictions at all. This was felt to result in respectable families being turned away, while groups of youths aged between fourteen and twenty filled the place and led to the disturbances that were complained about.[33]

There was also a certain degree of correlation assumed between manual work and roughness, and more service-oriented occupations and respectability. A correspondent of the *Sheffield Independent* who wrote to defend the behaviour he found there argued that visitors were 'small tradesmen and their wives, clerks and the more intelligent of the working men and youths,' and referred to 'a young person having the style of what we call a "shopgirl"', who was very impressed by the realism of one picture.[34] There is, then, a slight tendency to downplay class categories in favour of the rough/respectable division; the upper section of the working class and the lower middle class are run together as defined by a common respectability that divides them from the rough remainder of the working class. However, commentators consistently stress *either* the rough *or* the respectable in their description of working-class behaviour in museums and art galleries; in other words, they express either optimism or pessimism about the principle of universal access to such cultural institutions. As one Sheffield pessimist said, 'I confess that I never did much like the notion of having the Gallery opened on Sunday.'[35]

The previous chapter has examined the space in which consumption of the museum took place. It is clear that the marble, the quiet, the space, all seemed to designate the gallery a 'place of escape from the cares of the outside world';[36] it was supposed to form a contrast with, for example, the street, a place where decorum was absent, roles were confused, and cultural markers could not be relied upon. In this sense it can be compared with the interior of department stores, except that where department stores could usually rely on keeping its clientele relatively exclusive, the gallery had to manage an encounter between a wide range of social groups.[37] Magazine illustrations of galleries tended to picture them with a small scattering of visitors, well below capacity, so as to stress their spaciousness.[38] These are spaces in which Foucauldian self-regulation might well work; visitors are isolated and emphasised by the space all around them.

However, we know that at times art galleries were nothing like this, but positively crowded. One Sunday soon after the opening of the Mappin, there was said to be a queue of about one hundred people to get in.[39] This, then, worked against self-policing, as noise levels inevitably rose, and individuals were less conspicuous.

Magazine illustrations also foreground certain kinds of behaviour and deportment, those which would not interfere with the space and quiet of the gallery. Contemplating the pictures was a serious affair, undertaken in ones and twos, without much sign of conversation. This is in line with a moral and spiritual view of art appreciation. However, these idealised gallery spaces were also seen as places for socialising; there are plenty of small groups of well-dressed people engaged in polite conversation. An air of calm decorum prevails, and both genders engage in pleasant social intercourse. Thus it is a matter of demonstrating a certain, learned attitude towards art, and of following the rules of polite sociability. The working class were thought to be largely incapable of following this model, as is indicated by, on the one hand, a different set of expectations, and on the other, the provision of separate institutions in some cases.[40] Thus, working-class visitors are praised for good humour, curiosity, orderliness and appreciation of narrative and domestic art rather than anything more difficult.[41] Different standards of aesthetic appreciation and attitude, as well as social intercourse, were thought to mark the morally refined middle-class visitors, and the cheerful, robust working-class one. It was generally felt that the working class could respond to 'vulgar' paintings but could not (yet) appreciate the finest art; opinion differed as to whether they could learn to.[42] This, then was the way in which museum and gallery managers wished to stage the encounter between class groups in their space, by allotting distinct roles and behaviour to each which would maintain a social division, confirm the subordination of the working class and the authority of the middle, while also confirming social harmony. Museum managers did in fact take measures to try and ensure that the social encounter worked on these terms, measures which can clearly be seen in Foucauldian terms, though they are perhaps less subtle than those identified by Bennett.[43] Thus visitors had to enter the Mappin Art Gallery through a single file turnstile, which evidently caused queues on busy days. The interior of the gallery was closely monitored by attendants and a policeman, and on one occasion two attendants are described as closing a door to redirect visitors' flow round the gallery in a rational movement, rather than 'every possible way' round it. The policeman exhorted visitors at the Mappin's most popular painting, Crofts' 'Wellington's March from Quatre Bras', not to touch, and to move to the left.[44] Elsewhere, the use of police was common; at a popular national museum, South Kensington, annual expenditure on the police rose to £6,800 in 1864.[45]

However, it does seem that these measures failed to produce, or at least consistently to produce, the right kind of working-class visitor, who could confirm middle-class identities; rather working-class visitors could be extremely disruptive. In order to understand this, we need to look at the kind of spaces and behaviour that working-class culture was producing. Peter Bailey's 1978 article, '"Will the real Bill Banks please stand up?" Towards a role analysis of mid-Victorian working-class respectability', offers some ways of interpreting this question. He gives the example of 'Bill Banks' Day Out', by Thomas Wright, as offering a contradiction of the exclusivity of the categories of rough and respectable imagined by middle-class observers. Bill Banks and his wife save for their day out, they visit Hampton Court and are informed about it; but equally, they eat and drink to excess, indulge in 'irrational' recreation like the music hall, and spend money frivolously and lavishly. Bailey interprets Bill Banks as representing an 'easy association of rational recreation and traditional play patterns', the absorption of new practices and ideas of respectability without the displacement of old values, particularly values of sociability, informality and conviviality.[46] Thomas Wright's other writing paints a similar picture, with observers of St Monday indulging in ostentation, plentiful eating and drinking, as well as dancing, betting, and thoroughly rational amusements.[47]

There is some wider evidence to support particularly the argument that the working class added new forms of recreation to their repertoire rather than substituting them, and that they did not distinguish between rational and irrational activities in the way the middle class tended to. Moreover, they used both public spaces like the street, and, increasingly, commercial ones like the music hall. Bailey's evaluation of the space of the music hall forms an interesting parallel to that of the gallery: neither fully public nor private, crowded, yet producing as well a certain 'self-consciousness of conduct and appearance'.[48] Significantly, promenades persisted in some halls into the twentieth century, despite attempts to eradicate them.[49] In this setting, it is argued, visitors indulged in competitive display, flirtation and courtship, in the process producing a social drama of roles and identities. It seems entirely possible that this is the best way of understanding the activities of some working-class visitors in museums and art galleries.

This emerges quite clearly from what we know of working-class behaviour in galleries. The most common report tends to be of their promenading, lounging around, chatting to each other, and not taking any notice of the pictures. It was said of the National Gallery, 'Many persons use it as a place to eat luncheons in, and for refreshments … many persons who come, do not come to see pictures'.[50] Working-class youths are described as laughing 'in a lewd manner' at paintings with nude figures in them, and as not recognising the difference 'between a sublime work of the highest spirituality and the base materialism of an obscene print'; as well as showing a preference for and genuine response to sentimental subject matter in pictures. One of the most interesting comments by a middle-class newspaper correspondent in Sheffield was that he had overheard one 'fellow say to his fair companion, "Tha knows, lass, its ahrs. It don't belong to them b---- swells!"'[51]

The characteristics of working-class attitudes towards museums and art galleries can therefore be suggested. They tended not to recognise such institutions as being different, quasi-spiritual spaces.[52] In contrast to the middle-class view of the special nature of the museum or gallery space, deserving of a particular type of behaviour, appropriate dress, and so on, the working class tended not to distinguish such space from the rest of the city, carrying over activities, such as eating and socialising, that were practised in other spaces. This is reinforced by the experience of other rational recreation initiatives such as parks; 'working-class behaviour outside the parks was quickly replicated inside,' as park users were happy to move from park to pub.[53]

Secondly, modes of appreciating and consuming art were taken from other working-class cultural forms. The lewd innuendo as well as the sentimentally sad are known to have been relished in music hall, popular drama and popular literature.[54] References to the reception of nude paintings and statues are few, and rather coy, but it does seem that some visitors did not display a correctly aesthetic appreciation. Some newspaper correspondents seem to have felt this, and Sherman suggests that it was also the case in France. In Preston, a lifesize reproduction of Michelangelo's *David* was moved from its prominent position on the ground floor, to the furthest room on the top floor, after it was alleged that quite large groups of working-class women and girls used to gather in front of it, laughing and pointing.[55] The working class were not unfamiliar with visual art, as dioramas and panoramas had spread from London to become part of the attractions of the largest cities by the second half of the nineteenth century, as well as cheap prints for the home.[56] Visual art, like music and drama, was to be consumed as part of a group, as an essentially sociable activity, where appreciation occurs through the exchange of views on a picture. Moreover, the gathering of a crowd in a semi-public place actually became an integral part of the cultural experience, in the way Bailey has described for the music hall.[57] The space of the gallery, then, rather than disciplining, could encourage self-display. On the other hand, the middle class were publicly committed to the romantic consumption of art as an individual activity, where communion with the sublime takes place through the painting.[58] This in fact is where its very benefit was felt to lie, in the possibility of uplifting and purifying the individual human spirit. Thus, use of the gallery space, and attitudes towards art, were important markers of class difference.

Thirdly, the working class rejected attempts to position them as recipients of culture, stressing rather their communal ownership of such municipal institutions. Again, this has parallels in working-class attitudes to parks. In Manchester, when keepers at Philips Park attempted to remonstrate with misbehaving young men, they were on occasion presented with copies of the inaugural placard which stated that the park 'was Purchased by the People, was made for the People, and is given to the People for their protection.'[59] All of these characteristics of working-class attitudes to museums and art galleries made it less likely that the technologies of building and display would be able to transform them either outwardly or inwardly, as commentators have suggested.

The problem was that such working-class consumption of the museum interfered with elite use. Although surrounded by a rhetoric of universal access, and even referred to as the universities of the working class, galleries were increasingly middle-class spaces, for the practice of self-definition. Individual, spiritual communion with art was essential, but increasingly a rather comfortable wander around a museum or gallery provided sociable leisure, in a suitably self-improving context, where propriety and order were guaranteed.[60] As we have seen, soirées provided just this mix of serious and sociable, but at a time that protected the elite from contact with working-class visitors. In many ways an analogy can be drawn with developments in other forms of middle-class leisure, such as the Halle orchestra concerts studied by Simon Gunn. Here, in an increasingly exclusive upper middle class group, the function of display, of placing oneself and others within a hierarchy, in a ritualised way, became very important. However, equally notable was the way in which consuming music was redefined, primarily through the encouragement of silence during the performance and restrained applause afterwards. In this way, as with painting, music was redrawn as a 'sublime' individual experience, which required a certain reverential attitude for its appreciation.[61] Both the development of the sociable aspects of middle-class leisure, and of the almost sacred nature of art, made it much less likely that the middle classes would tolerate the more aberrant kinds of working-class behaviour in museums and galleries. As far as the management of the museums was concerned, it was particularly the latter issue, the way in which the working class disrupted the reverential, individual process of art appreciation, that caused a problem. It could be said that their attempt to manage the space so as to allow a variety of social groups to benefit from the culture on show had failed.

A majority of those who wrote to the Sheffield newspapers in 1887 were horrified by the behaviour they had witnessed or heard about, and the consensus was clearly that such behaviour made 'proper' use of the museum impossible. In Liverpool, where very similar problems had been experienced during late evening opening on a Monday, such opening was stopped.[62] In Sheffield, this option was not possible, as it was a condition of the Mappin bequest that it be accessible on a Sunday. Both museums subsequently reported improvements in the behaviour of visitors at these particularly popular times, although the improvement seems to have been much swifter at the Mappin than in Liverpool. What does such an improvement represent? Can it be that the working class adapted to middle-class norms of museum visiting? Certainly this was the favoured interpretation of the museums themselves. In Liverpool it was taken to indicate 'an advance and improvement in the popular feeling', while in Sheffield, Sunday visitors were said to 'show a marked improvement in behaviour'.[63] Thereafter, there are no complaints, that I have found, of rowdy youths in museums or galleries. It is likely that to a certain extent behaviour had changed; Tony Bennett argues that by the end of the nineteenth century, 'the social and architectural relations of popular recreation' had shifted in a similar way to those in the museum, so that rowdiness had diminished in many cultural activities, and museums benefited from this rather than bringing it about.[64] However, it may also be the case that rowdiness decreased because rowdy people ceased to go to museums and galleries. The 1880s and 1890s were the high-water point of the popularity of municipal museums and galleries, and thereafter attendance generally declined. In fact, it was common for attendance never to reach the dizzy heights it achieved in the first year or two of opening. In 1893, commenting on the decreased numbers of Sunday visitors to the Mappin Gallery, the curator said:

> This decrease in the Sunday visitors is by no means to be regretted, for there has been no decline whatever in the very large numbers who come here for the express purpose of inspecting and enjoying the contents of the Gallery, but the absentees have been confined to those who did not make this the sole object of their visit, and who probably found it more agreeable to pursue their purpose in the open air ... It is a source of sincere satisfaction to know that the visitors to the Gallery are limited to those who come for the express purpose of enjoying and benefitting by its art treasures.[65]

This, although a nice piece of self-justification, tends to confirm the idea that as visitors fell off, it was the middle-class who remained. In France, conflict and a move towards more exclusivity was more overt; vandalism was a significant problem around 1900, and led to greater security measures and a suspicion of art students. Most surprisingly, entrance fees were introduced in several French museums; as Sherman says, 'Those in charge of museums could hardly have felt much concern if fees caused workers to visit museums even less often than they had before.'[66] In England, the desire to make museums middle-class spaces was much less straightforward; attempts persisted, if somewhat half-heartedly, to keep them inclusive.

By the end of the nineteenth century, there was of course much more for the working class to choose from for weekend or Bank Holiday entertainment. If, as

Martin Hewitt has suggested, private parks with lots of entertainment were preferred to the rather puritan municipal parks, a similar process may well have been taking place for museums and art galleries.[67] As early as the 1920s, it was commonly felt that municipal museums and art galleries were out of touch, neglected and unpopular, and this may well be the culmination of their abandonment by the working class.[68] Surveillance and self-regulation can not work on a popular constituency which is no longer there; the weakness of rational recreation at the end of the nineteenth century was still that it had to attract to improve, and increasingly the working class would not be attracted on those terms.

Another insight into working-class consumption of museums is given by Annie E. Coombes, who examines reactions to the Horniman Museum in south London. This museum started as a private collection, was initially opened to the public on Bank Holidays and by appointment only, but expanded its opening hours in response to demand, and in 1901 became a free public rate-supported museum, owned by London County Council. Coombes shows that it was unusually popular with the working classes, despite being situated in a predominantly middle-class area; groups such as the Lad's Rest (Dulwich), South Place Institute Ramblers' Club, Working Men's Club and Institute (Clerkenwell and Deptford) as well as various board schools and other schools all visited it. While some of these may well have had middle-class control, and indeed could be seen as instruments of rational recreation, others were more autonomous working-class groups. Coombes suggests that the Horniman was more popular with the working class because of its displays. Because of its origins as an idiosyncratic personal collection of curios, it did not have, initially at least, the systematic classification and scientific narrative, especially of evolution, that was to be found in other museum displays of ethnography. Instead, the collection was displayed in such a way as to emphasize spectacle, trophies, and an emotional reaction to exhibits; prominent in an 1890 Guide were a Spanish 'Torture Chair', mummy hands, and in one room, 'Human skeleton and Gods'.[69] While other museums, and the Horniman later, attempted to compete with exhibitions and fairs by differentiating themselves on the grounds of their more academic and educational stance, this differentiation is less visible at the Horniman in the 1890s. However, looking at newspaper reports of the museum, Coombes argues that middle-class visitors consumed the displays in terms of an evolutionary and classificatory paradigm even before this was in place; 'the middle-class viewer was too thoroughly steeped in evolutionary doctrines in relation to the material to avoid their association with any interpretation of the displays.'[70] It is entirely possible, of course, that working-class visitors did so too, but if Coombes' argument is, as it appears to be, that the Horniman was unusual both in its unscientific and sensational display, and in its high proportion of working-class visitors, this is suggestive. It is reminiscent of the dilemma faced by curators of natural history displays, who, as the previous chapter showed, tried to strike a balance between the thoroughly scientific and the bold, striking and even sensational.

What does this indicate about the consumption of museums and art galleries in the second half of the nineteenth century? A large proportion of the urban population may have visited municipal museums during the period, but they did so on different terms, with different aims, and with different approaches to 'reading' the exhibits. While this chapter has paid a good deal of attention to the class groupings within the museum space, clearly these were not the only groupings or identities understood by contemporaries. One important distinction is between 'scientific' and 'popular' audiences, as described by Coombes, where 'popular' 'is not... a short-hand term for working-class culture', but has more of a sense of exchange between classes.[71] There are, though, differences between her idea of a scientific audience, based on an academic community asserting the authority of their disciplines; and a provincial scientific community which in most cases was still heavily amateur and unspecialised. Of course, class identities are not stable, and could be seen as particularly shifting during this period, as consumption in a variety of fields becomes more widespread and complex. This justifies the emphasis on the investigation of class identities and modes of consumption within this chapter. Tony Bennett has said that the museum instilled 'new codes of public behaviour which drove a wedge between the respectable and the rowdy',[72] and this statement needs at the very least to be qualified. Certainly this was an aim of municipal museums and galleries, but the rowdy did enter them, along with the respectable, in several cases. The problem with this analysis is that it perpetuates the dualities in the middle-class perception of the working class, which do not, it seems, actually reflect their use of such institutions. If we focus instead on working-class strategies and modes of consumption, a different picture emerges. The space of the music hall or the park or the pub or the museum was a space for sociability, a place that they had a right to enter, and where certain norms of cultural appreciation were followed. Working-class identity was increasingly made up of a variety of possible roles, and cultural space was valued for its ability to provide a setting for the enactment of these roles. Elite groups attempted to reinforce the idea of the museum as a sacred space, a space for education, contemplation, and individual communion with art, with forceful or more subtle means, and attempted to limit the understandings of working class identity possible in that space; sometimes they had to restrict access to it in order to do so. However, in the light of municipal museums' decline after the First World War, it may be the case that sections of the working class actively rejected municipal museums and galleries, and turned to entertainment more accommodating to their modes of consumption. The line between exclusion and rejection is a fine one, and clearly rejection can be a form of self-exclusion, but it is important to note that just because the working class were in what has always been regarded as a middle-class space, they did not become blank canvases upon which the middle class could paint. Indeed they used that configuration of space for display and the creation of new roles, rather than being regulated by it, and as policing of the gallery increased they rejected it.

Notes

[1]   J. Walkowitz, *City of Dreadful Delight: Narratives of Sexual Danger in Late-Victorian London*, (London 1994), chapter 2; see also Andy Croll, 'Street disorder, surveillance and

shame: regulating behaviour in the public spaces of the late Victorian British town', *Social History* 24, 3, (1999), who looks at a very different urban environment, that of Merthyr Tydfil, but finds anxiety to be the predominant middle-class attitude towards certain public streets.

[2] Walkowitz, *City*, p. 48; Erika Rappaport, '"The Halls of Temptation": Gender, Politics and the Construction of the Department Store in Late Victorian London', *Journal of British Studies* 35, 1, (1996), pp. 73-4; S. Gunn, 'The middle class, modernity and the provincial city: Manchester c.1840-80' in Alan Kidd and David Nicholls (eds) *Gender, Civic Culture and Consumerism, Middle-Class Identity in Britain 1800-1940*, (Manchester 1999), examines both bourgeois anxieties about Manchester's public spaces and their strategies for dealing with it.

[3] It is clear from Walkowitz's work that a strong sense of superiority, and indeed of actual power and influence, allowed charity workers to go about their business. Walkowitz, *City*, pp. 53-8.

[4] J. M. Golby and A. W. Purdue, *The Civilisation of the Crowd: Popular Culture in England 1750-1900*, (London 1984), p. 190: 'It was, overwhelmingly, to the highly market-conscious commercial leisure industry that the more affluent working class of the late nineteenth century looked for diversion and self-fulfilment in their leisure time'. See also Gareth Stedman Jones, *Languages of Class: Studies in English working class history 1832-1982*, (Cambridge 1983), pp. 203-210, and Peter Bailey, '"Will the Real Bill Banks Please Stand Up?" Towards a role analysis of mid-Victorian working-class respectability', *Journal of Social History* 12, (1978).

[5] Kenneth Hudson, *A Social History of Museums; What the Visitors Thought*, (New Jersey 1975), p. 7.

[6] Sheffield Public Museums Annual Reports, 1885-1905

[7] Thomas Greenwood, *Museums and Art Galleries*, (London 1888), pp. 370-1.

[8] K. Moore, '"Feasts of Reason?" Exhibitions at the Liverpool Mechanics' Institution in the 1840s', in G. Kavanagh (ed) *Museum Languages*, (London 1991).

[9] Tony Bennett, *Culture, A Reformer's Science*, (London 1998), p. 113.

[10] E.P. Thompson, *Customs in Common*, (Harmondsworth 1991), p. 375, suggests that St Monday was most common among 'small-scale, domestic and outwork industries', but it seems to have been particularly widespread in Sheffield. The report of a US Consul in Sheffield was included in A. Young, *Labour in Europe and America*, (Philadelphia 1875), p. 408: 'In the great steel manufactories of Sheffield employing each several thousands of men scarcely any work is done on Monday, and very little on Tuesday. I am informed that this is true of a large portion of the labouring population of this town.'

[11] Thomas Wright ['A Journeyman Engineer'], *Some Habits and Customs of the Working Classes*, (New York 1967 [1867]), p. 118; Peter Bailey, '"Will the Real Bill Banks Please Stand Up?"', p. 341. The inference about Monday visitors being working-class was also made at the time. Bennett, *Culture*, p. 113.

[12] Samuel J. M. M. Alberti, 'Field, Lab and Museum: The Practice and Place of Life Science in Yorkshire, 1870-1904' (unpublished PhD thesis, University of Sheffield 2000), p. 93.

[13] Alberti, 'Field', p. 94.

[14] *Report of the 57th Meeting of the British Association for the Advancement of Science (1887)*, (London 1888), p. 125.

[15] Whitworth Wallis 'The Museum and Art Gallery', in J. H. Muirhead (ed) *Birmingham Institutions*, (Birmingham 1911), p. 496.

[16] Daniel J. Sherman, 'The Bourgeoisie, Cultural Appropriation, and the Art Museum in Nineteenth-Century France', *Radical History Review* 38 (1987), p. 52.

[17] Minutes, Liverpool, 23 September 1869; 29 January 1900.

[18] FPLC Minutes, 20 October, 17 November 1893.

[19]   Minutes, Liverpool, 14 June 1907; FPLC Minutes, 16 June 1913.

[20]   This whole discussion of conversaziones draws heavily on Samuel J. M. M. Alberti 'Conversaziones and the experience of science in Victorian England', *Journal of Victorian Culture*, 8.2 (2003).

[21]   Cynthia Brown, *Cherished Possessions, A History of New Walk Museum and Leicester City Museums Service*, (Leicester 2002), p. 12.

[22]   Sherman, 'The Bourgeoisie', p. 52.

[23]   FPLC Minutes, 18 July, 28 July 1904.

[24]   Brown, *Cherished Possessions*, p. 8.

[25]   *Sheffield Independent*, 11 August 1887.

[26]   *Sheffield Independent*, 13 August 1887; *Sheffield Telegraph*, 13 August 1887.

[27]   *Sheffield Independent*, 5 October 1887. Very similar reports came from provincial museums in France, where youths in Marseilles museum hung around chatting, as well as flirting and giggling with girls; Daniel Sherman, *Worthy Monuments: Art Museums and the Politics of Culture in Nineteenth-Century France*, (Cambridge, Massachussetts 1989), p. 223.

[28]   Bailey, '"Will the Real Bill Banks Please Stand Up?"', p. 338.

[29]   The Daily Graphic, quoted in B. Taylor, 'From Penitentiary to 'Temple of Art': Early metaphors of improvement at the Millbank Tate', in M Pointon (ed), *Art Apart: Art Institutions and Ideology across England and North America*, (Manchester 1994), p. 22.

[30]   Greenwood, *Museums*, p. 174.

[31]   Wright, *Some Habits and Customs*, pp. 116, 119.

[32]   Bennett, *Birth of the Museum*, p. 32, indicates the civilising influence wives were believed to exert over male, working-class museum visitors.

[33]   *Sheffield Telegraph*, 13 August 1887. Sherman pays quite a lot of attention to the regulations in place in provincial French museums, and it seems there was a similar concern to keep small children out, while paying little attention to teenagers, who did cause problems; Sherman, *Worthy Monuments*, p. 219.

[34]   *Sheffield Independent*, 5 October 1887.

[35]   *Sheffield Telegraph*, 13 August 1887.

[36]   Taylor, 'From Penitentiary to Temple of Art', p. 16.

[37]   Although for an instance of less exclusive use of department stores – the sales – see Christopher Hosgood, 'Mrs Pooter's Purchase: lower-middle-class consumerism and the sales, 1870-1914', in Kidd and Nicholls (eds) *Gender, Civic Culture and Consumerism*, (1999).

[38]   See for example the illustration of the Tate Gallery, taken from the *Penny Illustrated Magazine*, in Taylor, 'From Penitentiary to Temple of Art', p. 21.

[39]   *Sheffield Evening Star*, 2 August 1887.

[40]   Institutions such as the Manchester Art Museum and the Whitechapel Art Gallery were set up primarily for the working classes, though the hope was that the middle classes would mingle with the humbler visitors so as to set an example both socially and in art appreciation. It is clear that these institutions were closely linked; the men behind them, respectively T. C. Horsfall and Canon Barnett, were friends, and both drew on the ideas of Ruskin. Interestingly, the Manchester Art Museum differed from institutions such as the Tate or the Mappin in creating a homely rather than imposing interior, and taking a very utilitarian approach to art. M. Harrison, 'Art and Philanthropy: T. C. Horsfall and the Manchester Art Museum', in A. J. Kidd and K. W. Roberts (eds) *City, Class and Culture: Studies of cultural production and social policy in Victorian Manchester*, (Manchester 1985); Seth Koven, 'The Whitechapel Picture Exhibitions and the Politics of Seeing' in D. Sherman and I. Rogoff (eds) *Museum Culture: Histories, Discourses, Spectacles*, (London 1994).

[41]   For example, a description of visitors at the Mappin: 'The crowd ... was curious, and

impressed by the clever painting of a gunshot wound – they were not mischievous'. *Sheffield Evening Star*, 2 August 1887.

[42] Bennett, *Culture*, p. 114.

[43] Bennett, in *The Birth of the Museum*, sees discipline and interpretation of displays as being exerted primarily through the organisation of space. See for example his concept of 'backwalking', propounded in chapter 7, and the section on space and self-regulation, pp. 48-58.

[44] *Sheffield Evening Star*, 2 August 1887.

[45] Barbara J. Black, *On Exhibit: Victorians and Their Museums*, (Charlottesville and London 2000), p. 104.

[46] Bailey, '"Will the Real Bill Banks Please Stand Up?"', p. 342.

[47] See particularly 'Saint Monday - its worship and worshippers' in Wright, *Some Habits and Customs*.

[48] P. Bailey, 'Custom, capital and culture in the Victorian music hall', in R. D. Storch (ed), *Popular Culture and Custom in Nineteenth-Century England*, (London 1982), p. 199.

[49] P. Bailey, 'Introduction', in Bailey (ed) *Music Hall: The Business of Pleasure*, (Milton Keynes 1986), p. xvii.

[50] Select Committee on the National Gallery, 1853, quoted in C. Trodd, 'Culture, Class and City: The National Gallery, London, and the spaces of education, 1822-57', in M. Pointon (ed) *Art Apart*, (Manchester 1994), p. 44.

[51] *Sheffield Telegraph*, 16 August 1887; *Sheffield Independent*, 5 October 1887.

[52] Trodd, 'Culture, Class and City', p. 45.

[53] Martin Hewitt, *The Emergence of Stability in the Industrial City: Manchester, 1832-67*, (Aldershot 1996), p. 163.

[54] Romance and sexual innuendo in popular literature throughout the century, stemming from the broadside tradition, are described in Golby and Purdue, *The Civilisation of the Crowd*, pp. 127-129; the risque and the sentimental in music hall performances are demonstrated in J. S. Bratton, 'Jenny Hill: Sex and Sexism in Victorian Music Hall', in J. S. Bratton (ed) *Music Hall: Performance and Style*, (Milton Keynes 1986), pp. 92-110.

[55] Sherman, *Worthy Monuments*, p. 221; personal communication from Social History curator, Harris Museum and Art Gallery.

[56] For panoramas in Manchester, see Hewitt, *The Emergence of Stability*, p. 164.

[57] Peter Bailey, 'Introduction', p. xvii.

[58] The Curator of Birmingham Museum and Art Gallery referred to Ruskin in an article on his institution: 'All museums ought to be places of noble instruction, where, free from the distractions of the outside world, one can devote a portion of secluded and reverent life to the attainment of divine wisdom'. Whitworth Wallis, 'The Museum and Art Gallery', in J. H. Muirhead (ed), *Birmingham Institutions*, (Birmingham 1911). See also Trodd, 'Culture, class and city', p. 44: 'To see art is, for Hazlitt, to be absorbed by the vision it creates; it is to enter a space of pure vision which is beyond the body. However, at the same time, he presents aesthetic pleasure as a process which establishes and secures individual identity'.

[59] Hewitt, *The Emergence of Stability*, p. 163.

[60] Taylor examines the way the new Tate Gallery on Millbank was increasingly viewed in the context of middle-class leisure, grouped with Henley Regatta and Sandown Races, depicted as containing well-dressed visitors in a setting whose order was guaranteed by attendants and policemen. Taylor, 'From Penitentiary to 'Temple of Art'', p. 24.

[61] Simon Gunn, 'The Sublime and the Vulgar: the Hallé concerts and the constitution of 'high culture' in Manchester c.1850-1880', *Journal of Victorian Culture* 2, 2 (1997).

[62] AR Liverpool, 1889, refers to earlier attempts to open the museum on Monday evenings, but that it had to be abandoned.

[63]   AR Liverpool, 1889; Report to the Trustees of the Mappin Art Gallery, July 1887-January 1888.

[64]   Bennett, *Birth of the Museum*, p. 58.

[65]   Report to the Trustees of the Mappin Art Gallery, January 1893-July 1893.

[66]   Sherman, *Worthy Monuments*, p. 235.

[67]   Hewitt, *The Emergence of Stability*, pp. 163-4.

[68]   Criticism was expressed particularly in Sir Henry Miers' Report for the Carnegie United Kingdom Trust in 1928, which alleged, 'most peoples in this country do not really care for museums or believe in them;... how dull many of them have become and how low the worst of them have sunk.' Quoted in Geoffrey D. Lewis, 'Museums in Britain: 1920 to the present day', in John M. A. Thompson (ed) *Manual of Curatorship*, (London 1984), p. 39.

[69]   Annie E. Coombes, *Reinventing Africa: Museums, Material Culture and Popular Imagination in Late Victorian and Edwardian England*, (New Haven and London 1994), pp. 113-7.

[70]   Coombes, *Reinventing Africa*, p. 116.

[71]   Coombes, *Reinventing Africa*, p. 3.

[72]   Bennett, *Birth of the Museum*, p. 102.

CHAPTER EIGHT

Conclusion

This book has argued that municipal museums were important arenas or tools for the formation of social identities and hierarchies, although there was no predetermined group or identity that they were designed to promote, and they responded most clearly to local factors. Of course, the museum's relationship with the social fabric of the town was both under- and overlaid with national and individual factors. Though several commentators have noted the local autonomy and variation in nineteenth-century towns,[1] by the end of the period particularly standardisation and centralisation were becoming increasingly apparent, both in museum practice and in local government.[2] Nevertheless, this does not alter the fact that the museum was an important means by which, in each town, social groupings and hierarchies were asserted and communicated. This was done partly through claims of ownership and control of the museum. In theory every citizen had a claim of ownership, but in practice some had much more control than others. Councillors, staff, and large donors all asserted such ownership, and established it more firmly by their uses of the building itself, with social events for both councils and scientific societies, and a generous sprinkling of busts, portraits and memorial plaques to each other.[3] The converse of this was that everyone else had less claim on the museum, and was allowed into the museum conditionally, as long as they behaved properly.[4] In fact, behavioural and recreational reform of the working class was a major aim of the municipal museum. It was attempted primarily through the use of space to create awe, and through dispersal of crowds and increased visibility, to encourage self-policing. It was also attempted through the use of attendants and even policemen, and by making such concessions as evening opening and lecture series dependent on good behaviour from the public.[5]

However, concerns about behaviour were less frequently expressed towards the end of the period.[6] This would seem to be the outcome of a number of developments. Firstly, by this time it was clear that, contrary to expectations, working-class visitors could be relied on, usually, to behave in an appropriate way; there was self-congratulatory comment on their earnest but ill-informed attempts at appreciation.[7] Bad behaviour was seen as the preserve of youths.[8] Secondly, by the end of the century, the working class were becoming a more important and organised force politically; on occasion, they made public assertions of their rights as ratepayers to some measure of control of the museum.[9] Thirdly, and most interestingly, it seems that efforts were now concentrated on another project, defining middle-class identities and differentiating them from other groups. In other words, although control of the working class, and the provision of rational recreation for them, was attempted in and through municipal museums, it was not the central project of the institution. This is not really surprising, considering the fairly lukewarm attitude of most middle-class people to the concept of rational recreation, involving as it did mingling with the working class at play.[10] Efforts to differentiate social groups through the museum were as prominent as efforts to bring them together, and they existed in some tension with each other, especially in the rhetoric surrounding the museums.

Social differentiation was achieved mainly through use of the museums as a communication medium; and this can be further subdivided. Firstly objects worked to create, in Bourdieu's term, distinction.[11] They could embody a social and cultural value that could only be appropriated by the elite with specific skills of aesthetic appreciation, or cultural capital.[12] The museum and the valued object both worked to increase each other's cultural and symbolic value; the museum held treasured objects and therefore was valuable, and the object was in an important museum and therefore must be significant. And this cultural value could accrue to those with the taste to appreciate it. This process is most clearly found in Preston; a very specific type of object with massive cultural value in terms of aesthetic, historical, and civilised qualities, is defined as the main category of museum object. However, competence in appreciating the statues is a particularly rare skill, made artificially more so by the deliberate decontextualisation in their presentation. This makes them ideal for the display of cultural capital by the elite. However, here again it should be realised that a public museum must offer, if unwillingly, opportunities for all to acquire cultural capital, and, as shown earlier, there is indeed some intention to spread culture to the masses. Thus, as Paul DiMaggio says,

> the tension between monopolisation and hegemony, between exclusivity and legitimation, was a constant counterpoint to the efforts ... of ... urban elites.[13]

This is where the tension between donors and controllers of the museum can be understood; for different social groups have cultural competences in different kinds of objects and different kinds of knowledge, and each stand to gain legitimation if 'their' objects are enshrined in the museum. Those with economic, social, and political power have the most ability to place the objects they want in the museum, but do not have total control.

In addition, social hierarchies could be reinforced or created through a subtler process of communication, where displays themselves tell a story that is authenticated as 'true'. Here, arbitrary distinctions and hierarchies can be naturalised and made to seem part of objective reality.[14] This is particularly so for the natural sciences, and those disciplines which at the time followed a scientific paradigm, such as ethnography.[15] This technique is most clearly seen in Liverpool, where by the turn of the century the entire museum formed one integrated system of hierarchies, covering the natural and man-made world, infinitely classifiable into sub-hierarchies.

This use of display is sophisticated and hard to challenge, at least in terms of getting the displays changed. There are no instances of any social group other than the elite challenging a museum display and getting it altered. However, it requires the investment of a significant amount of resources, in both time and money, to build up the discursive authority that Liverpool Museum created. Furthermore, there is no way of telling how far it is working; that is to say, being accepted and internalised by visitors. Its strength is that it overcomes the problems of conflicting exclusivity and hegemony; it actively encourages non-elite visitors, and communicates with them, whilst still preventing any blurring of social divisions and hierarchies.

This book has aimed to make a case for municipal museums as distinct from other forms of museum, though no less revealing and worthy of study. The various chapters have shown how municipal museums had quite distinct processes of birth; were the product of a different social constituency; had their own criteria for and patterns of acquisitions of objects; deployed the space and objects within the museum in certain ways; and had their own patterns of interaction with their visitors. This is not, most certainly, to say that all municipal museums followed an identical blueprint; but equally, they can not be lumped together with national museums as part of an identical phenomenon. Studies based largely on national museums have stressed the modernity, efficiency and progressiveness of museums; they have seen them as part of a new mode of power which harnessed culture to the task of governing, producing a seamless, creative and dispersed power suited to the government of, and indeed implicated in the creation of, a modern atomised population. This view of museums does find some echoes in municipal museums, which employed rhetoric stressing democracy, utility and progress. Thomas Greenwood certainly characterised municipal museums this way; even more so than national museums, as they were accessible to a greater number of people in aggregate.[16] Such museums were demonstrably more accessible and accountable than their predecessors, had a more educational stance, and encouraged a different type of behaviour than many other leisure pursuits. Yet the similarities with predecessors and competitors are also striking: the persistence of the voluntary scientific society's influence and the difficulty in building a professional identity for curators; the tendency to defer to and glorify donors; the continuing provision for and privileged access for 'expert' visitors; the use of either sensational methods of display, or, more often, those based solely on scientific or aesthetic rationales with no help with interpretation for the ordinary visitor. All these points suggest the municipal museum was densely related to previous and contemporary forms of leisure, not all of which were as progressive and modern as the new national museums. In addition, the rhetoric surrounding municipal museums was not matched in the institutions themselves because of resource issues. The museums, then as now, never had enough money, and rarely were able to implement displays, layouts, accession policies or staffing in the way they might have wished, because of this. It is notable that several of the examples that are sometimes given of modern museums are of schemes that were never built, such as Pitt-Rivers' Rotunda.[17]

If municipal museums were not as modern, progressive and efficient as often argued, then they could not be serving the purposes that many have found in nineteenth-century museums. These ideas range from improving the behaviour of the working classes, educating and civilising them; transforming the subjectivity of the modern citizen; to symbolically supporting a system of objects which underpins a capitalist economy. Such projects would need a coherence and unity of approach which was simply not present in municipal museums.[18] The differences between them are striking. Liverpool Museum, which has since become a national group of museums, was large, well-resourced, with an unusually large and specialised staff, and succeeded in establishing itself as an important source of autonomous authority. Museums such as those of Hull, Leicester and Preston may have been more typical of museums from the second half of the nineteenth century in having fewer resources and staff, and being less able to separate themselves from direct council control, and the influence of donors and the amateur scientific community. Museums which became municipal even later seem to have been smaller still. Scunthorpe Museum, opened in 1911, consisted of one room.[19] Yet beyond the straightforward questions of size and wealth, there were fundamental differences about what a municipal museums should be and do. Should they offer a specialist service of scientific reference? Should they be a 'working-class university' offering comprehensive and easily accessible education? Should they be principally about reforming behaviour, 'civilising' and offering polite leisure? Should they glorify the town, and of course its leaders, proclaiming its culture and civic identity? Should they be an economic resource, either directly aiding workers, improving standards of taste in consumption, or acting as a kind of legitimating advertisement for certain trades and industries? All of these views could be found in various proportions among proponents of municipal museums; equally, though, opponents of museums argued that either these aims were unnecessary, or would not best be served by municipal museums.

The variety of views meant that museums might well be found in manufacturing towns; and in towns with perceived problems with class relations, and with the working-class population. However they were just as likely to be found in towns with a tradition of voluntary science societies; with a new or changed middle class; or with a fast-developing local government and civil society. This is, of course, quite all-encompassing; but it may explain why municipal museums were disproportionately found in the Midlands and North, while by no means being absent from the rest of England.

Municipal museums, then, could never function in a unified and coherent way to implement any particular agenda; they were not a single project for a single end. Rather, they were a reasonably neutral institution whose effect was not predetermined, but depended very much on local agendas and configurations of power and culture. What, then, do they have to tell us? To see the significance of municipal museums we have to look again at the social constituencies they served, and the cultural and social environment in which they grew.

The middle class in the nineteenth century, particularly in the second half of that century, was not only growing, it was changing quite rapidly in terms of the sub-groups within it and their relative status. New groups were emerging, older groups were developing. This meant that to a certain extent, there was competition within the middle class for status and authority. In addition, the middle class was continuing to change, and also to consolidate, its role within an expanded local government, and was moving towards new leisure patterns which foregrounded consumption and identity. All these factors can be seen in municipal museums. Among the distinct middle-class groups involved in museums in some way, although not exhaustive and probably overlapping, we can distinguish a Sabbatarian group, local amateur science communities, the growing professional voice of the curators, 'Economist' and rate payer lobbies, the 'merchant princes' of Liverpool and other council elites, commercial interests, academics, general visitors looking for polite recreation, and social reformers. Nearly all of these groups had their own views on local museums, and in many ways the museums can be seen as the outcome of the competition between the groups to define them. There was no one straightforward 'winner'; rather a series of negotiations and challenges, so that while rate-payer lobbies might not be able to prevent the setting up of a museum, they might be able to keep it chronically short of funds. In addition, local factors could be very important in structuring and determining the course of such struggles; thus in Preston, with commercial and academic interests effectively absent, little success in developing independent curatorial authority, and an amateur science community which either disengaged from or was pushed out of the new museum, it worked very much to embody civic pride, and to glorify and legitimate the civic elite. In Leicester, by contrast, the main dynamic seems to have been between the amateur science community and the professional curator, with curatorial authority growing slowly over time. Why precisely these differences occurred can not always be fully accounted for; it is not just a question of the socio-economic make-up of the town, as the case of Leicester shows. The pattern of previously existing cultural institutions and activities was also important; what forms of cultural capital were already circulating in different towns, what potential new forms were available, and who was in the best position to appropriate this cultural capital?

These middle-class groups were asserting their own version of the museum in an urban environment that was itself in flux, socially and politically, but above all culturally. Within local government, historical narratives and manipulation of a wide variety of symbolic resources were being used both to assert and to contest the legitimacy of new governing groups. Other aspects of the public sphere were similarly increasingly part of an organisation of meaning, where openness and democracy were proclaimed but framed within a set of distinctions that privileged the elite. In the everyday social interactions of the town, moreover, changes may have been even more marked. Towns were increasingly places for consumption and leisure, where identities were constructed with new social and cultural tools. Bailey has recently referred to the 'transactional processes of subjects in space and the dynamic possibilities of agency'; this highlights the maybe unpredictable, creative, even chaotic nature of the late nineteenth-century urban environment. Bailey singles out new spaces for leisure and consumption as being 'particularly lively':

parks, department stores, music halls, though he sees museums as somewhat more regulated institutions. These were, he argues, 'as much ... laboratories as reformatories of manners.'[20]

As a social terrain, then, the Victorian town might be said to embody two competing tendencies: a first towards differentiation between groups, both inter- and intra-class, and towards the stabilisation and codification of status and legitimacy; and the second, towards mobility, fluidity and instability, where signifying systems were undermined and exploited rather than representing any consensus, and group classifications and boundaries were always in a process of change. It was not simply that the middle class wanted to enforce categories and hierarchies, and the working class wanted to contest them; many of the middle class could benefit from mobility, which was essential to the validation of new professional identities, or new categories of valued objects, or new ways of using leisure, for example. All of Victorian urban society was implicated in this tension; and it is this, I would argue, that explains the centrality of municipal museums to attempts to regulate the social and cultural fabric. Compared to their antecedents in small society museums, and to their immediate competitors such as commercial museums and exhibitions, municipal museums were more able to create and police distinctions, to fix cultural categories and hierarchies; to stabilise the urban environment. However, they also offered possibilities, as open, theoretically democratic institutions which were visited by a mass urban population, for acting as laboratories, not just of behaviour, but of identity, authority, and cultural capital, in a way that no other institution or organisation could manage: neither new town halls, civic rituals and elite forms of culture, nor more demotic or commercial spaces such as shops, pubs or dioramas.

As Bailey points out, museums were different, less consumerist than other forms that were emerging at a similar period.[21] It is probably also the case that the meaning and idea of a municipal museum became more fixed over time, and they came to be much more alike. This meant that over time they ceased to be so popular and central; in particular they become less accommodating to those seeking a 'laboratory of manners', or a space for unpredictable social encounters, new modes of behaviour and cultural consumption, from any social class. Most noticeably, the working class visited less, as commercialised leisure really expanded. By 1914, municipal museums were functioning much more to produce and validate differences and hierarchies, according to incontestable knowledge and cultural norms, than had been the case in the previous fifty years. They had been 'won' by professional curators and by civic elites; but they were arguably less dynamic places than they had been, certainly less popular; a lot less was at stake and there was less to attract a popular audience, although they were certainly now safer places for middle-class visitors and their sensibilities.

The museum reveals the mutual constitution of the social and the cultural, which must be seen, in Daniel Miller's formulation, as being a perpetual process of becoming which is never completed.[22] Objects and cultural formations themselves give rise to social distinctions and hierarchies, which then feed back in to the system of objects. Thus social and cultural formations are constantly changing. This is clearly borne out by the investigation of municipal museums. Dominant social groups create and control the museums, as a set of culturally valued objects, and as producers of 'true', authenticated knowledge. In both these aspects the museums recreate and reinforce social divisions and hierarchies. Thus far, though, this describes an interlocked, circular, non-developmental process. It must be modified to allow for more complexity. The constitution of museums as public institutions allowed other social groups into the loop; social developments such as urban democratisation may be linked to a lessening of exclusivity in the museums, and at the same time the increasing access to cultural capital the museum offered allowed people to increase their social standing. These very threats to elite dominance were met with more sophisticated, less visible and personal, means of creating and deploying knowledge to shape social formations.

The museum provided a space for such differences to be asserted and negotiated, a space that was dominated by the middle class. On the other hand, among certain groups, it allowed alliances to be formed, overcoming differences; for example, the alliance between colonial, academic, and commercial groups in Liverpool around 1900.

Museums, as they had developed by the end of the period, offered an inclusive, rather than exclusive, version of middle-classness. The original scientific society museums were much more exclusive, consisting only of the scientific community, and demanding considerable amounts of knowledge and time from members. The municipal museums by the end of the century catered for a popular audience in Coombes' sense; whilst by no means unvisited by the working class, especially working-class schoolchildren, the bulk of visitors came from a broadly based middle class.[23] The museum offered them a chance of a suitably rational recreation, one that enhanced their intellectual or cultural capital and their middle-class status, while demanding relatively little.[24] Thus it was part of the solution to the 'problem' of middle-class leisure that Bailey identified.[25] Institutions such as museums allowed a 'lowest common denominator' of middle-class roles and behaviour patterns to be established, at least at a provincial level.[26] This has been, in part, a study of the creation of professional authority and autonomy by museum curators. However, in a wider sense it is also about the stabilisation of middle-class identities by the beginning of the twentieth century around new hierarchies of cultural capital.

The municipal museums that came into existence in England particularly in the second half of the nineteenth century were a response to the new urban environment in so far as they offered a means by which new social identities and hierarchies could be constructed, contested and legitimated. However, they were not an automatic response to that environment, nor can they be seen as a unified part of modernism and progressive government. They were essentially local, and responded to local factors, social, but also importantly cultural. This may well be why the nineteenth century was their heyday; as centralisation progressed in the twentieth century, so they declined from their central position in the fabric and emotional landscape of the town.

Notes

[1]   John Garrard 'Urban Elites, 1850-1914: The Rule and Decline of a New Squirearchy?' *Albion* 27, 3, (1995), p. 589; J. Smith   'Labour Tradition in Glasgow and Liverpool', *History Workshop Journal* 17, (1984), p. 49.

[2]   G. Lewis, *For Instruction and Recreation: A Centenary History of the Museums Association,* (London 1989), chapter 2. See for local/national government, D. Fraser, *Power and Authority in the Victorian City,* (Oxford 1979), pp. 152-164.

[3]   In 1869 alone a statue of Joseph Mayer and a bust of William Rathbone were installed in Liverpool Museum; and in 1907 Sir W.E.M. Tomlinson, MP for Preston, presented a picture of himself to the Harris Museum. Minutes of the Museums Sub-Committee, Liverpool, 7 January 1869; Minutes of the Free Public Library Committee, Preston, 18 February 1907.

[4]   Daniel Sherman has examined the way French museums symbolically excluded the working class at this time. D. Sherman, 'The Bourgeoisie, Cultural Appropriation, and the Art Museum in Nineteenth-Century France', *Radical History Review* 38, (1987).

[5]   In 1870 a notice was hung in Liverpool Museum stating that if any more bad behaviour occurred, late opening on Monday evenings would cease. Minutes of the Museums Sub-Committee, Liverpool, 8 December 1870. Cf. D. Sherman, *op. cit.,* p. 52.

[6]   See chapter four.

[7]   Tony Bennett, *Culture: A Reformer's Science,* (London 1998), p. 114.

[8]   C. Trodd, 'Culture, Class, City: the National Gallery, London, and the Spaces of Education 1822-1857', in M. Pointon, (ed.) *Art Apart,* (Manchester 1994), pp. 44-46; M. Harrison, 'Art & Philanthropy: T.C. Horsfall and the Manchester Art Museum' in Kidd & Roberts, (ed.) *City, Class and Culture,* (Manchester 1985), p. 134.

[9]   M. Savage, *The Dynamics of Working-Class Politics: The Labour Movement in Preston 1880-1940,* (Cambridge 1987).

[10]   Peter Bailey, *Leisure and Class in Victorian England: rational recreation and the contest for control 1830-1885,* (London 1978), p. 45.

[11]   Pierre Bourdieu, *Distinction: A Social Critique of the Judgement of Taste,* tr. R. Nice, (London 1984), p. 228.

[12]   'Cultural capital' is defined by Paul DiMaggio as "knowledge and familiarity with styles and genres that are socially valued and that confer prestige upon those who have mastered them". P. DiMaggio 'Cultural Entrepreneurship in nineteenth-century Boston: the creation of an organizational base for high culture in America', *Media, Culture and Society* 4, (1982), p. 35.

[13]   *Ibid.,* p. 48.

[14]   Donna Haraway 'Teddy Bear Patriarchy: Taxidermy in the Garden of Eden, New York City 1908-1936', *Social Text* 11, (1984-5) p. 25.

[15]   Annie E. Coombes, *Reinventing Africa,* (New Haven 1994), p. 44.

[16]   Thomas Greenwood, *Museums and Art Galleries,* (London 1888), p. 229.

[17]   W. R. Chapman, 'Arranging Ethnology: AHLF Pitt-Rivers and the Typological Tradition', in Stocking (ed) *Objects and Others: Essays on Museums and Material Culture,* (Madison 1985), pp. 19-41.

[18]   Carla Yanni, *Nature's Museums: Victorian Science and the Architecture of Display,* (London 1999), p. 8.

[19]   Other examples include the libraries with small museums in them, such as Doncaster's, opened in 1898, and Brighouse's, also from 1898. Brears and Davies, *Treasures for the People, The Story of Museums and Galleries in Yorkshire and Humberside,* (1989), pp. 34-7.

[20] Peter Bailey, 'Adventures in Space: Victorian railway erotics, or taking alienation for a ride', *Journal of Victorian Culture* 9.1, (2004), p. 3.

[21] See note 16 above.

[22] D. Miller, *Material Culture and Mass Consumption*, (Oxford 1987), p. 11.

[23] Coombes, *Reinventing Africa*, p. 3.

[24] Cf. Alberti, 'Conversaziones and the experience of science in Victorian England', *Journal of Victorian Culture*, 8, 2, (2003).

[25] Peter Bailey, '"A mingled mass of perfectly legitimate pleasures": The Victorian middle class and the problem of leisure', *Victorian Studies* 21, (1977).

[26] Cf. the role of concerts in Manchester; Simon Gunn, 'The Sublime and the Vulgar: The Halle Concerts and the Constitution of High Culture in Manchester, c.1850-1890', *Journal of Victorian Culture* 2, 2.

Bibliography

Archive Material

National Museums Liverpool Archives:
    Minutes of the Museums Sub-Committee 1868-1920
    Annual Reports from the Museum 1857-1920
    Liverpool Gallery of Inventions and Science – 3rd Annual Report of the Committee 1863
    Mayer Museum: Curator's Report 1883
    A. C. West, Notes on the history of the Ethnography Department, 1981
    Lord Derby Collection: Knowsley Museum Record Book and letter from Earl of Derby to Liverpool Corporation, 1851
    Ridyard File

Liverpool Record Office
    Liverpool Council Proceedings 1848-1914
    Obituary cuttings, ref. Eq330 and Eq429

Lancashire Record Office:
    Preston Council Minute Book
    Minutes of the Free Public Library and Museum Committee 1878-1920
    Departmental Reports from the Museum

Weston Park Museum, Sheffield:
    Sheffield Museum Annual Reports 1885-1914
    Sheffield Museum Daily Reports 1881-1887
    Reports to the Trustees of the Mappin Art Gallery, 1887-1893

Sheffield Archives:
    Architect's drawing - Edward M. Gibbs, Sketch for Museum in Weston Park prepared for Cllr Bragge (1874)
    Architect's drawing – Edwatd M. Gibbs, Sheffield Public Museum: Cases (1875)

Sheffield Local Studies Library:
    Sheffield Council Minutes 1874-1877
    Report on the Suggested Extension of Sheffield Public Museum in Connection with the Mappin Art Gallery, (Sheffield 1900)

Leicester City Museums:
  Leicester Town Museum, First Report of the Museum Committee to the Town
  Council, 1873
  Handbook to the Leicester Museum, 1868

Birmingham Local History Library:
  Birmingham Council Proceedings 1852-1884

Parliamentary Papers

Act Establishing A Public Library, Museum and Art Gallery at Liverpool (15th
    Vic.)
British Museum (Natural History) Parliamentary Papers 1852-1864
Hansard's Parliamentary Debates, (3rd series) 78, 1845
First Report of the Commissioners of Inquiy into the State of Large Towns and
    Populous Districts, 1844
Second Report of the Commissioners for inquiring into the State of Large Towns
    and Populous Districts, 1845
Population Census of England & Wales, summary tables for Lancashire, 1801,
    1811, 1821, 1831, 1841, 1851, 1861, 1871, 1881, 1891, 1901, 1911
Religious Census 1851
Report from the Select Committee on Arts and Manufactures, 1835, 1836
Report from the Select Committee on National Monuments and Works of Art, 1841
Report from the Select Committee on Fine Arts, 1841

Published Sources: before 1930

Acland, Henry & John Ruskin, *The Oxford Museum*, George Allen, London, 1893.
Aikin, J., *A Description of the Country From 30 to 40 Miles Round Manchester*,
    David & Charles reprint, Newton Abbot 1968 [1795].
Baines, Thomas, *History of the Commerce and Town of Liverpool*, Longman,
    London, 1852.
Baines, Thomas, *Liverpool in 1859*, Longman, London, 1859.
Barret's Directory of Preston and District 1926/7.
British Association for the Advancement of Science, *A Handbook for Birmingham*,
    1913.
Bulletin of the Liverpool Museums 1898, 1900.
Bunce, J.T., *History of the Corporation of Birmingham*, Cornish Brothers,
    Birmingham, 1885.
Catalogue of the Preston Exhibition, T. Snape & Co., Preston, 1875.
*Ceremonies connected with the Opening of the building for a Free Public Library
    and Museum presented by William Brown Esq. to the town of Liverpool*, 1861.

Chamberlain, A. Bensley, 'The Corporation Museum and Art Gallery' in *A Handbook for Birmingham*, British Association for the Advancement of Science, 1913.

Clemesha, H. W., *A History of Preston in Amounderness*, Manchester University Press, Manchester, 1912.

Companion to the Liverpool Museum... of William Bullock, 1808.

Descriptive Guide to the Liverpool Free Public Museum, including the Derby Collection of Natural History and the Mayer Collection of Antiquities and Art, Liverpool, 1869.

Dickens, Charles, *Hard Times*, Penguin, Harmondsworth, 1994 [1854].

Directory of Lancashire, (1834), Pigot.

Directory of Preston and District (1851, 1870, 1914), Mannex, Beverley.

Directory and Gazeteer of Preston (1857), Gillbanks, Preston.

Fishwick, Henry, *The History of the Parish of Preston in Amounderness in the County of Lancaster*, Elliot Stock, London, 1900.

Flower, W.H., *Essays on Museums*, Macmillan, London, 1898.

General Guide to the Collections contained in the Free Public Museums (William Brown Street) Liverpool, (1906).

Goodair, John – 'A Preston Manufacturer', *Strikes Prevented*, London & Manchester, 1854.

Greenwood, Thomas, *Museums and Art Galleries*, Simpkin, Marshall & Co., London, 1888.

Hardwick, C., *History of the Borough of Preston*, Worthington & Co., Preston, 1857.

Hazlitt, William, *Criticisms on Art, and Sketches of the Picture Galleries of England*, Templeman, London, 1856.

Herdman, W.A., 'An Ideal Natural History Museum' in *Proceedings of the Literary and Philosophical Society of Liverpool* vol. 41, 1887.

Hewitson, A. ('Atticus'), *History of Preston*, Preston, 1883.

Hewitson, A. ('Atticus'), *Preston Town Council, or Portraits of Local Legislators*, Preston, 1870.

Hibbert, James, (ed), *Notes on Free Public Libraries and Museums*, Preston, 1881.

Hibbert, James, *A Report to Accompany the Design for the Harris Free Public Library and Museum*, Preston, 1882.

Hibbert, James, *Catalogue of the Pictures and Drawings of the Newsham Bequest*, Preston, 1884.

Higgins, H.H., 'Synopsis of an Arrangement of Invertebrate Animals in the Free Public Museum of Liverpool with Introduction' in *Proceedings of the Literary and Philosophical Society of Liverpool* vol. 28 (Appendix), 1873.

Higgins, H. H., 'Museums of Natural History' in *Proceedings of the Literary and Philosophical Society of Liverpool* vol. 38, 1884.

Hill, J. & W. Midgeley, *The History of the Royal Birmingham Society of Artists*, Cornish Brothers, Birmingham, 1926.

Holden, J., *A Short History of Todmorden*, Manchester University Press, Manchester, 1912.

Howarth, E., *Visitors' Guide to the Sheffield Public Museum, Weston Park*, Sheffield, 1883.

Hume, Rev. A., *Character of the Liverpool Town Museum, with Suggestions for its Interior Arrangement*, reprinted from the *Daily Post*, Liverpool, 1859.

'Lord Derby's Museum – Reminiscences by Mr T. J. Moore', *Liverpool Review* 5 November 1892.

Marks, E. N., *The Guild Guide to Preston*, John Heywood, Manchester, 1882.

Mosley, Charles, 'Inn-Parlour Museums', *Museums Journal* 27, 1927.

Muirhead, J. H., *Birmingham Institutions*, Cornish Brothers, Birmingham, 1911.

Orchard, B. G., *Liverpool's Legion of Honour*, Birkenhead, 1893.

Owen, Richard, *On the Extent and Aims of a National Museum of Natural History*, Saunders, Otley & Co., London, 1862.

Picton, J. A., *Liverpool Improvements and How to Accomplish Them*, E. Howell, Liverpool, 1853.

Picton, J. A., *Notes on the Foundation of a Free Public Library and Museum*, Liverpool, 1857.

Pike, W.T. (ed), *Dictionary of Edwardian Biography: Liverpool*, Edinburgh 1987 [1911].

Preston Chronicle & Lancashire Advertiser, March 1854.

Preston Corporation Art Gallery Illustrated Catalogue (1907), Preston.

Preston Guardian, 1875, 1892, 1896.

Proceedings of the Literary and Philosophical Society of Liverpool no.16 (1861-2), Appendix.

Read, Sir Hercules, 'Museums in the Present and Future', *Antiquaries Journal* vol.1, 1921.

'Report on the Provincial Museums of the United Kingdom' in *Report of the 57th Meeting of the British Association for the Advancement of Science* (1888), John Murray, London.

Ruskin, John, *Unto This Last; The Political Economy of Art; Essays on Political Economy*, J.M. Dent & Sons, London, 1968 [1862].

'Sheffield Museum and the Bateman Collection', *Sheffield Telegraph* 18 December 1891.

Sheffield and Rotherham Independent 1887.

Sheffield Evening Star 1887.

Sheffield Telegraph 1887.

Shimmin, Hugh, *Liverpool Life, Its Pleasures, Practices and Pastimes*, Egerton Smith, London, 1857.

Shimmin, Hugh, *Pen and Ink Sketches of Liverpool Town Councillors*, Liverpool, 1866.

Tangye, Richard, *One and All: An Autobiography*, S.W. Partridge, London, 1889.

Taylor, J. (ed), *Illustrated Guide to Sheffield*, Sheffield, 1879.

'The Egyptian Museum, No. 8 Colquitt Street, Liverpool', *Liverpool Mercury* 1 May 1852.

Wallace, A.R., 'Museums for the People' in *Macmillan's Magazine*, 1869.

Wallis, Whitworth, 'The Museum and Art Gallery' in Muirhead (ed) *Birmingham Insitutions*, Cornish Brothers, Birmingham, 1911.

White's History, Gazeteer, and Directory of the Counties of Leicester and Rutland, (1877), Sheffield.

Wright, Thomas, *Some Habits and Customs of the Working Classes, by a Journeyman Engineer*, Augustus M. Kelley reprint, New York, 1967 [1867].

Published Sources: after 1930

'Africana from the Liverpool Museum', *Liverpool and Africa Exhibition Guide*, Liverpool University, Liverpool, 1974.

Alberti, Samuel J. M. M., 'Field, Lab and Museum: The Practice and Place of Life Science in Yorkshire, 1870-1904' (unpublished PhD. thesis, Sheffield University), 2000.

Alberti, Samuel J. M. M., 'Placing nature: natural history collections and their owners in nineteenth-century provincial England', *British Journal for the History of Science* 35, 2002.

Alberti, Samuel J. M. M., 'Conversaziones and the Experience of Science in Victorian England', *Journal of Victorian Culture* 8.2, 2003.

Alexander, E., 'William Bullock: Little-remembered Museologist and Showman', *Curator* 28, 2, 1985.

Allen, David, *The Naturalist in Britain: A Social History*, Princeton University Press, Princeton, New Jersey, 1976.

Altick, Richard, *Victorian People and Ideas*, J.M. Dent & Sons, London, 1973.

Altick, Richard, *The Shows of London*, Bellknap Press, Cambridge, Massachussetts, 1978.

Arnold, Ken and Danielle Olsen (eds), *Medicine Man: the Forgotten Museum of Henry Welcome*, British Museum Press, London, 2003.

Baggaley, J.W., 'Some notable museums VI: Weston Park Museum and Mappin Art Gallery, Sheffield', *North-Western Naturalist*, 8, 1933, pp. 90-95.

Bailey, Peter, '"A mingled mass of perfectly legitimate pleasures": the Victorian middle class and the problem of leisure', *Victorian Studies* 21, 1977.

Bailey, Peter, *Leisure and Class in Victorian England: Rational Recreation and the Contest for Control 1830-1885*, Routledge and Kegan Paul, London, 1978.

Bailey, Peter, '"Will the real Bill Banks please stand up?" Towards a role analysis of mid-Victorian working-class respectability', *Journal of Social History* 12, 1978, pp. 336-353.

Bailey, Peter, 'Custom, Capital and Culture in the Victorian Music Hall' in R. D. Storch (ed) *Popular Culture and Custom in Nineteenth-Century England*, Croom Helm, London, 1982.

Bailey, Peter (ed), *Music Hall: The Business of Pleasure*, Open University Press, Milton Keynes, 1986.

Bailey, Peter, *Popular Culture and Performance in the Victorian City*, Cambridge University Press, Cambridge, 1998.

Bailey, Peter, 'Adventures in Space: Victorian railway erotics, or taking alienation for a ride', *Journal of Victorian Culture* 9, 1, 2004.

Barrell, John (ed), *Painting and the Politics of Culture: New Essays on British Art 1700-1850*, Oxford University Press, Oxford, 1992.

Belk, R. and M. Wallendorf, 'Of mice and men: gender identity in collecting' in Pearce (ed), *Interpreting Objects and Collections*, Routledge, London, 1994.

Bennett, Tony, 'Useful Culture', *Cultural Studies* 6, 3, 1992.

Bennett, Tony, *The Birth of the Museum*, Routledge, London, 1995.

Bennett, Tony, *Culture, A Reformer's Science*, Sage, London, 1998.

Best, Geoffrey, *Mid-Victorian Britain 1851-1870*, Fontana, London, 1979.

Bishop, Michael J., 'New Biographical Data on Henry Clifton Sorby', *Earth Sciences History* 3, 1984, pp. 69-81.

Black, Barbara J., *On Exhibit: Victorians and Their Museums*, University Press of Virginia, Charlottesville and London, 2000.

Borsay, Peter, *The English Urban Renaissance: Culture and Society in the Provincial Town 1660-1770*, Clarendon, Oxford, 1989.

Bourdieu, Pierre, *Distinction: A Social Critique of the Judgement of Taste*, trans. R. Nice, Routledge and Kegan Paul, London, 1984.

Bowler, P., *The Invention of Progress*, Blackwell, Oxford, 1989.

Bratton, J. S., 'Jenny Hill: Sex and Sexism in Victorian Music Hall' in Bratton (ed), *Music Hall: Performance and Style*, Open University Press, Milton Keynes, 1986.

Bratton, J. S. (ed), *Music Hall: Performance and Style*, Open University Press, Milton Keynes, 1986.

Brears, P. & S. Davies, *Treasures for the People, The Story of Museums and Galleries in Yorkshire and Humberside*, Yorkshire and Humberside Museums Council, 1989.

Briggs, Asa, *Victorian Cities*, Penguin, Harmondsworth, 1968.

Brown, Cynthia, *Cherished Possessions: A History of New Walk Museum and Leicester City Museums Service*, Leicester City Council, Leicester, 2002.

Bullen, S., 'The Cultural Life of Preston, 1742-1842', (unpublished M.A. dissertation, Leicester University), 1970.

Callen, Anthea, *Angel in the Studio: Women in the Arts and Crafts Movement 1870-1914*, Astragal Books, London, 1979.

Cannadine, David, 'Victorian Cities: How Different?' *Social History*, 4, 1977.

Cannadine, David, 'From "Feudal" Lords to Figureheads', *Urban History Yearbook*, 1978.

Cannadine, David, *Lords and Landlords: The Aristocracy and the Towns 1774-1967*, Leicester University Press, Leicester, 1980.

Cannadine, David, 'Residential Differentiation in Nineteenth-century Towns: from shapes on the ground to shapes in society' in Johnson & Pooley (eds) *The Structure of Nineteenth- Century Cities*, Croom Helm, London, 1982.

Cannadine, David, 'The Transformation of Civic Ritual in Modern Britain: The Colchester Oyster Feast', *Past and Present* 94, 1982.

Chapman, W. R., 'Arranging Ethnology: AHLF Pitt-Rivers and the Typological Tradition' in Stocking (ed) *Objects and Others: Essays on Museums and Material Culture*, University of Wisconsin Press, Madison, 1985.

Clifford, J., 'On Collecting Art and Culture' in Simon During (ed) *The Cultural Studies Reader*, Routledge, London, 1993.

Clifford, J., 'Collecting Ourselves', in Pearce (ed), *Interpreting Objects and Collections*, Routledge, London, 1994.

Coleman, B.I. (ed), *The Idea of the City in Nineteenth-Century Britain*, Routledge & Kegan Paul, London, 1973.

Convey, John, *The Harris Free Public Library and Museum, Preston, 1893-1993*, Lancashire County Books, Preston, 1993.

Coombes, Annie E., *Reinventing Africa, Museums, Material Culture, and Popular Imagination*, Yale University Press, New Haven, 1994.

Copley, S., 'The Fine Arts in Eighteenth-Century Polite Culture' in Barrell (ed) *Painting and the Politics of Culture*, Oxford University Press, Oxford, 1992.

Croll, Andy, 'Street disorder, surveillance and shame: regulating behaviour in the public spaces of the late Victorian British town', *Social History* 24, 3, 1999.

Crossick, Geoffrey, *The Lower Middle Class in Britain 1870-1914*, Croom Helm, London, 1977.

Crossick, Geoffrey, *An Artisan Elite in Victorian Society*, Croom Helm, London, 1978.

Crossick, Geoffrey, 'Urban Society and the Petty Bourgeoisie in Nineteenth-Century Britain' in Fraser and Sutcliffe (eds), *The Pursuit of Urban History*, Edward Arnold, London, 1983.

Cunningham, Hugh, *Leisure in the Industrial Revolution, c. 1780-1880*, Croom Helm, London, 1980.

Daunton, M.J., *Coal Metropolis: Cardiff 1870-1914*, Leicester University Press, 1977.

Davidoff, L. & C. Hall, *Family Fortunes: Men and Women of the English Middle Class 1780-1850*, Routledge, London, 1992.

Davies, P.N., 'The African Steamship Company' in Harris (ed), *Liverpool and Merseyside: Essays in the Social and Economic History of the Port and its Hinterland*, Frank Cass, London, 1969.

Davies, Stuart, 'Birmingham Museums and Art Gallery', Birmingham Museum and Art Gallery Sheet 9, 1981.

Davies, Stuart, *By the Gains of Industry: Birmingham Museums and Art Gallery 1885-1985*, Birmingham Museums and Art Gallery, 1985.

Davies, Stuart, 'The making of a municipal museum: Huddersfield and the naturalists', in E.A.H. Haigh (ed), *Huddersfield, A Most Handsome Town*, Kirklees Cultural Services, Huddersfield, 1992.

Davison, A.I., 'Archaeology, Genealogy, Ethics' in Hoy (ed), *Foucault: A Critical Reader*, Blackwell, Oxford, 1986.

Dennis, R., *English Industrial Cities of the Nineteenth Century*, Cambridge University Press, Cambridge, 1984.

Denvir, Bernard, *The Early Nineteenth Century: Art, Design and Society 1789-1852*, Longman, London, 1984.

DiMaggio, Paul, 'Cultural Entrepreneurship in Nineteenth-Century Boston: The Creation of an Organisational Base for High Culture in America', *Media, Culture and Society* 4, 1982.

DiMaggio, Paul, 'Cultural Entrepreneurship in Nineteenth-Century Boston, part II: the classification and framing of American art', *Media, Culture and Society* 4, 1982.

DiMaggio, Paul, 'Classification in Art', *American Sociological Review* 52, 1987.

Dirks, N., G. Eley and S. Ortner (eds), *Culture/Power/History: A Reader in Contemporary Social Theory*, Princeton University Press, Princeton, New Jersey, 1994.

Duncan, Carol, *Civilising Rituals, Inside Public Art Museums*, Routledge, London, 1995.

Duncan, Carol, and A. Wallach, 'The Universal Survey Museum', *Art History* 3.4, 1980.

During, Simon (ed), *The Cultural Studies Reader*, Routledge, London, 1994.

Durrans, Brian, 'The Future of the Other', in Lumley (ed), *The Museum Time Machine*, Routledge, London, 1988.

Dutton & King, 'The Limits of Paternalism: the cotton tyrants of North Lancashire, 1836-54', *Social History* 7, 1, 1982.

Dyos, H. J. (ed), *The Study of Urban History*, Edward Arnold, London, 1983.

Dyos, H. J. & Michael Wolff (eds), *The Victorian City, Images and Realities*, Vol.1, Routledge and Kegan Paul, London, 1973.

Eley, Geoff, 'Nations, Publics and Political Cultures: Placing Habermas in the Nineteenth Century' in Dirks, Eley and Ortner (eds) *Culture/Power/History: A Reader in Contemporary Social Theory*, Princeton University Press, Princeton, New Jersey, 1994.

Ford, W. K., 'Notes on the Collections in the Department of Invertebrate Zoology at the Liverpool Museums', *North-Western Naturalist*, 1954.

Ford, W. K., 'Notes on the Earlier History of the City of Liverpool Public Museums' *Liverpool Bulletin* 5, 1955.

Forgan, Sophie, ' "But Indifferently Lodged...": Perception and Place in Building for Science in Victorian London', in C. Smith & J. Agar (eds), *Making Space for Science*, Macmillan, London, 1998.

Forgan, Sophie, 'Bricks and Bones: Architecture and Science in Victorian Britain', in Galison & Thompson (eds), *The Architecture of Science*, MIT Press, Cambridge, Massachussetts, 1999.

Foster, John, 'Nineteenth-Century Towns - A Class Dimension' in H.J. Dyos (ed), *The Study of Urban History*, Edward Arnold, London, 1983.

Foucault, M., *Archaeology of Knowledge*, Tavistock Publications, London, 1972.

Foucault, M., *Discipline and Punish*, Allen Lane, London, 1977.

Fraser, Derek, *Urban Politics in Victorian England: The structure of politics in Victorian cities*, Leicester University Press, Leicester, 1976.

Fraser, Derek, *Power and Authority in the Victorian City*, Blackwell, Oxford, 1979.

Fraser, Derek & A. Sutcliffe (eds), *The Pursuit of Urban History*, Edward Arnold, London, 1983.

Fyfe, G. and J. Law (eds), *Picturing Power: Visual Depictions and Social Relations*, Routledge, London, 1988.

Gadian, D.S., 'Class Consciousness in Oldham and other North-West Industrial Towns 1830-50' in Morris and Rodger (eds), *The Victorian City, A Reader in British Urban History 1820-1914*, Longman, London, 1993.

Galison, P. & E. Thompson (eds), *The Architecture of Science*, MIT Press, Cambridge, Massachussetts, 1999.

Garrard, John, *Leadership and Power in Victorian Industrial Towns 1830-1880*, Manchester University Press, Manchester, 1983.

Garrard, John, 'Urban Elites 1850-1914: the rule and decline of a new squirearchy?', *Albion* 27, 3, 1995.

Giedion, S., *Space, Time and Architecture: The Growth of a New Tradition*, Oxford University Press, Oxford, 1967.

Girouard, Mark, *Alfred Waterhouse and the Natural History Museum*, Yale University Press, New Haven, 1981.

Golby, J. M. and A. W. Purdue, *The Civilisation of the Crowd: Popular Culture in England 1750-1900*, Batsford Academic, London, 1984.

Goldsmith, Mike and John Garrard, 'Urban governance: some reflections' in Trainor and Morris (eds) *Urban Governance: Britain and Beyond since 1750*, Ashgate, Aldershot, 2000.

Greenhalgh, Paul, 'Education, Entertainment & Politics: Lessons from the Great International Exhibitions' in Vergo (ed), *The New Museology*, Reaktion Books, London, 1989.

Gunn, Simon, 'The Sublime and the Vulgar: The Halle Concerts and the Constitution of High Culture in Manchester c.1850-1880', *Journal of Victorian Culture* 2, 2, 1997.

Gunn, Simon, 'The Middle Class, Modernity and the Provincial City: Manchester c. 1840-1880' in A. Kidd and D. Nicholls (eds) *Gender, Civic Culture and Consumerism, Middle-Class Identity in Britain 1800-1940*, Manchester University Press, Manchester, 1999.

Gunn, Simon, *The Public Culture of the Victorian Middle Class, Ritual and Authority and the English Industrial City, 1840-1914*, Manchester University Press, Manchester, 2000.

Gunn, Simon, 'Ritual and Civic Culture in the English Industrial City, c. 1835-1914', in Morris and Trainor (eds) *Urban Governance: Britain and Beyond Since 1750*, Ashgate, Aldershot, 2000.

Haigh, E. A. Hilary, *Huddersfield, A Most Handsome Town: Aspects of the History and Culture of a West Yorkshire Town*, Kirklees Cultural Services, Huddersfield, 1992.

Hall, Margaret, *On Display: A Design Grammar for Museum Exhibitions*, Lund Humphries, London, 1986.

Haraway, Donna, 'Teddy Bear Patriarchy: Taxidermy in the Garden of Eden, New York City, 1908-1936', *Social Text*, 11, 1984-5.

Harris, J.R. (ed), *Liverpool and Merseyside: Essays in the Economic and Social History of the Port and its Hinterland*, Frank Cass, London, 1969.

Harrison, M., 'Art and Philanthropy: T. C. Horsfall and the Manchester Art Museum' in Kidd and Roberts (eds) *City, Class and Culture*, Manchester University Press, Manchester, 1985.

Hartnell, R., 'Art and civic culture in Birmingham in the late nineteenth century', *Urban History* 22, 2, 1995.

Helfand, Michael, 'T.H. Huxley's "Evolution and Ethics": the Politics of Evolution and the Evolution of Politics', *Victorian Studies* 20, 1977.

Hennock, E.P., *Fit and Proper Persons: Ideal and Reality in Nineteenth-Century Urban Government*, Edward Arnold, London, 1973.

Hennock, E.P., 'The Social Composition of Borough Councils in Two Large Cities 1835-1914' in H.J. Dyos (ed), *The Study of Urban History*, Edward Arnold, London, 1983.

Hewitt, Martin, *The Emergence of Stability in the Industrial City: Manchester 1832-1867*, Scolar Press, Aldershot, 1996.

Hill, Kate, 'Municipal Museums in the North-West, 1850-1914: Social Reproduction and Cultural Activity in Liverpool and Preston' (unpublished PhD. thesis, Lancaster University), 1996.

Hill, Kate, '"Thoroughly Embued with the Spirit of Ancient Greece": Symbolism and Space in Victorian Civic Culture' in Kidd and Nicholls (eds) *Gender, Civic Culture and Consumerism: Middle-Class Identity in Britain 1800-1940*, Manchester University Press, Manchester, 1999.

Hill, Kate, '"Roughs of Both Sexes": The Working Class in Victorian Museums and Art Galleries', in Gunn and Morris (eds) *Identities in Space: Contested Terrains in the Western City since 1850*, Ashgate, Aldershot, 2001.

Hill, Kate, 'The middle classes in Victorian Lincoln', in Andrew Walker (ed) *Aspects of Lincoln*, Wharncliffe Books, Barnsley, 2001.

Hillier, Bill & Julienne Hanson, *The Social Logic of Space*, Cambridge University Press, Cambridge, 1984.

Hooper-Greenhill, Eilean, *Museums and the Shaping of Knowledge*, Routledge, London, 1992.

Hooper-Greenhill, Eilean (ed), *Museum, Media, Message*, Routledge, London, 1995.

Hooper-Greenhill, Eilean, *Museums and the Interpretation of Visual Knowledge*, Routledge, London, 2000.

Hosgood, Christopher, 'Mrs Pooter's Purchase: Lower Middle-Class Consumerism and the Sales, 1870-1914' in Kidd and Nicholls (eds) *Gender, Civic Culture and Consumerism*, Manchester University Press, Manchester, 1999.

Howe, Anthony, *The Cotton Masters 1830-1860*, Clarendon, Oxford, 1984.

Hoy, David Couzens (ed), *Foucault: A Critical Reader*, Blackwell, Oxford, 1986.

Hudson, Kenneth, *A Social History of Museums: What the Visitors Thought*, Humanities Press, New Jersey, 1975.

Impey, O. & A. MacGregor (eds), *The Origins of Museums*, Clarendon, Oxford, 1985.

Johnson, J. H. & C. G. Pooley (eds), *The Structure of Nineteenth-Century Cities*, Croom Helm, London, 1982.

Jordanova, L., 'Objects of Knowledge - A Historical Perspective on Museums' in Vergo (ed) *The New Museology*, Reaktion Books, London, 1989.

Joyce, Patrick, *Work, Society and Politics, The Culture of the Factory in Later Victorian England*, Methuen, London, 1980.

Kavanagh, G., *History Curatorship*, Leicester University Press, Leicester, 1990.

Kavanagh, G. (ed), *Museum Languages*, Leicester University Press, Leicester, 1991.

Kellett, J.R., 'Municipal Socialism, Enterprise and Trading in the Victorian City', *Urban History Yearbook*, 1978.

Kelly, T., *For the Advancement of Learning: the University of Liverpool 1881-1981*, Liverpool University Press, Liverpool, 1981.

Kidd, Alan J., '"Local History" and the Culture of the Middle Classes in North-West England, c. 1840-1900', *Transactions of the Historic Society of Lancashire and Cheshire* 147, 1997.

Kidd, Alan J. & David Nicholls (eds), *Gender, Civic Culture and Consumerism: Middle-Class Identity in Britain 1800-1940*, Manchester University Press, Manchester, 1999.

Kidd, Alan J. & David Nicholls, 'Introduction' in Kidd and Nicholls (eds) *Gender, Civic Culture and Consumerism*, Manchester University Press, Manchester, 1999.

Kidd, Alan J. & K. W. Roberts (eds), *City, Class and Culture: Studies of Social Policy and Cultural Production in Victorian Manchester*, Manchester University Press, Manchester, 1985.

Kirk, N., *The Growth of Working-Class Reformism in Mid-Victorian England*, Croom Helm, London, 1985.

Koven, Seth, 'The Whitechapel Picture Exhibition and the Politics of Seeing' in Sherman and Rogoff (eds) *Museum Culture: Histories, Discourses, Spectacles*, Routledge, London, 1994.

Kusamitsu, T., 'Great Exhibitions before 1851', *History Workshop Journal* 9, 1980.

Lane, Tony, *Liverpool: Gateway of Empire*, Lawrence and Wishart, London, 1987.

Lawrence, Ghislaine, 'Wellcome's Museum for the Science of History', in K. Arnold and D. Olsen (eds) *Medicine Man: The Forgotten Museum of Henry Wellcome*, British Museum Press, London, 2003.

Lewis, Geoffrey D., 'Collections, collectors and museums in Britain to 1920' in John Thompson (ed) *The Manual of Curatorship*, Butterworth, Oxford, 1984.

Lewis, Geoffrey D., 'Museums in Britain: 1920 to the Present Day' in John Thompson (ed) *The Manual of Curatorship*, Butterworth, Oxford, 1984.

Lewis, Geoffrey D., *For Instruction and Recreation: A Centenary History of the Museums Association*, Quiller Press, London, 1989.

Liverpool Libraries, Museums and Arts Committee Bulletin: volumes 1 & 2, 1951; vol. 2, 1952-3; 1955.

Loftus, Donna, 'Industrial conciliation, class co-operation and the urban landscape in mid-Victorian England' in Morris and Trainor (eds) *Urban Governance: Britain and Beyond since 1750*, Ashgate, Aldershot, 2000.

Lott, F. B., *The Centenary Book of the Leicester Literary and Philosophical Society*, W. Thornley and Son, Leicester, 1935.

MacDonald, S. & R. Silverstone, 'Rewriting the Museum's Fictions: taxonomies, stories and readers', *Cultural Studies* 4, 2, 1990.

MacKenzie, John M., *The Empire of Nature: Hunting, Conservation and British Imperialism*, Manchester University Press, Manchester, 1988.

MacKenzie, John M. (ed), *Imperialism and Popular Culture*, Manchester University Press, Manchester, 1989.

MacLeod, Diane Sachko, *Art and the Victorian Middle Class: Money and the Making of Cultural Identity*, Cambridge University Press, Cambridge, 1996.

Markus, Thomas A., *Buildings and Power: Freedom and Control in the Origin of Modern Building Types*, Routledge, London, 1993.

Maver, Irene, 'The role and influence of Glasgow's municipal managers, 1890s-1930s', in Trainor and Morris (eds) *Urban Governance: Britain and Beyond since 1750*, Ashgate, Aldershot, 2000.

Meller, H. E., *Leisure and the Changing City 1870-1914*, Routledge and Kegan Paul, London, 1976.

Miller, Daniel, *Material Culture and Mass Consumption*, Blackwell, Oxford, 1987.

Miller, Edward, *That Noble Cabinet: A History of the British Museum*, Andre Deutsch, London, 1973.

Mills, Dennis, & Michael Edgar, 'Social history in Lincoln's Victorian residential streets', *Local Population Studies Society Newsletter* 27, September 2000.

Millward, Robert, 'Urban government, finance and public health in Victorian Britain', in Trainor and Morris (eds) *Urban Governance: Britain and Beyond since 1750*, Ashgate, Aldershot, 2000.

Minihan, Janet, *The Nationalisation of Culture: The Development of State Subsidies to the Arts in Great Britain*, Hamish Hamilton, London, 1977.

Moore, Kevin, '"Feasts of Reason?" Exhibitions at the Liverpool Mechanics Institution in the 1840s' in Kavanagh (ed) *Museum Languages*, Leicester University Press, Leicester, 1991.

Morris, R. J., 'Voluntary Societies and British Urban Elites 1750-1850: An Analysis', *Historical Journal* 26, 1, 1983.

Morris, R. J., 'The Middle Class and British Towns and Cities of the Industrial Revolution, 1780-1870', in D. Fraser and A. Sutcliffe (eds) *The Pursuit of Urban History*, Edward Arnold, London, 1983.

Morris, R. J., *Class, Sect, and Party, The Making of the British Middle Class: Leeds 1820-1850*, Manchester University Press, Manchester, 1990.

Morris, R. J., 'Clubs, societies and associations', in F. M. L. Thompson (ed) *The Cambridge Social History of Britain 1750-1950*, vol. 3, Cambridge University Press, Cambridge, 1990.

Morris, R. J., 'Civil Society and the Nature of Urbanism: Britain 1750-1850', *Urban History* 25, 3, 1998.

Morris, R. J., 'Governance: Two Centuries of Urban Growth' in Morris and Trainor (eds) *Urban Governance: Britain and Beyond Since 1750*, Ashgate, Aldershot, 2000.

Morris, R. J. & Richard Rodger (eds), *The Victorian City: A Reader in British Urban History 1820-1914*, Longman, London, 1993.

Morris, R. J. & R. Trainor (eds), *Urban Governance: Britain and Beyond Since 1750*, Ashgate, Aldershot, 2000.

Nenadic, Stana, 'Businessmen, the urban middle classes, and the "dominance" of manufacturers in nineteenth-century Britain', *Economic History Review* 44, 1, 1991.

O'Gorman, Francis, 'Victorian Natural History and the Discourses of Nature in Charles Kingsley's *Glaucus*', *Worldviews: Environment, Culture, Religion* 2, 1998.

Ormerod, H., *The Liverpool Royal Institution, a Record and a Retrospect*, Liverpool University Press, Liverpool, 1953.

Ovenell, R. J., *The Ashmolean Museum 1683-1894*, Clarendon Press, Oxford, 1986.

Paviere, S., *Harris Museum and Art Gallery: Summary Guide*, Preston, 1932.

Pearce, Susan, 'Objects as Signs and Symbols', *Museums Journal* 85, 1986.

Pearce, Susan (ed), *Museum Studies in Material Culture*, Leicester University Press, London, 1989.

Pearce, Susan, *Museums, Objects and Collections: A Cultural Study*, Leicester University Press, London, 1992.

Pearce, Susan (ed), *Interpreting Objects and Collections*, Routledge, London, 1994.

Pearce, Susan, *On Collecting: An Investigation into Collecting in the European Tradition*, Routledge, London, 1995.

Pearce, Susan, 'Collecting as Medium and Message' in E. Hooper-Greenhill (ed) *Museum, Media, Message*, Routledge, London, 1995.

Perkin, Harold, *The Origins of Modern English Society, 1780-1880*, Routledge & Kegan Paul, London, 1969.

Pike, D. (ed), *Australian Dictionary of Biography*, Melbourne University Press, Melbourne, 1972.

Pointon, Marcia (ed), *Art Apart: Museums in North America and Britain since 1800*, Manchester University Press, Manchester, 1994.

Pooley, C. G., 'Choice and Constraint in the Nineteenth-Century City: a Basis for Residential Differentiation' in Johnson & Pooley (eds), *The Structure of Nineteenth-Century Cities*, Croom Helm, London, 1982.

Prior, Nick, *Museums and Modernity, Art Galleries and the Making of Modern Culture*, Berg, Oxford, 2002.

Purbrick, Louise, 'South Kensington Museum: the building of the house of Henry Cole' in Pointon (ed) *Art Apart*, Manchester University Press, Manchester, 1994.

Rabinow, P. (ed), *The Foucault Reader*, Pantheon Books, New York, 1984.

Rappaport, Erika, '"The Halls of Temptation": Gender, Politics and the Construction of the Department Store in Late Victorian London', *Journal of British Studies* 35, 1, 1996.

Richards, T., *The Commodity Culture of Victorian England: Advertising and Spectacle 1851-1914*, Verso, London, 1990.

Robson, R. (ed), *Ideas and Institutions of Victorian Britain, Essays in honour of George Kitson Clark*, G Bell & Sons, London, 1967.

Rubinstein, W. D., 'The Victorian Middle Classes: Wealth, Occupation, and Geography', *Economic History Review* 30, 1977.

Russell, Alice, 'Local Elites and the Working-Class Response in the North-West, 1870-1895: Paternalism and Deference Reconsidered', *Northern History*, 23, 1987.

Rydell, Robert W., *World of Fairs: The Century of Progress Expositions*, University of Chicago Press, Chicago, 1993.

Saumarez-Smith, C., 'Museums, Artefacts and Meanings' in Vergo (ed), *The New Museology*, Reaktion Books, London, 1989.

Savage, M., *The Dynamics of Working-Class Politics: The Labour Movement in Preston, 1880-1940*, Cambridge University Press, Cambridge, 1987.

Schadla-Hall, Tim, *Tom Sheppard, Hull's Great Collector*, Highgate Publications, Beverley, 1989.

Secord, Anne, 'Science in the Pub: Artisan Botanists in Early Nineteenth-Century Lancashire', *History of Science* 32, 1994.

Seed, John, '"Commerce and the Liberal Arts": the political economy of art in Manchester 1775-1860' in Wolff and Seed (eds) *The Culture of Capital: Art, Power and the Nineteenth-Century Middle Class*, Manchester University Press, Manchester, 1988.

Sheets-Pyenson, S., *Cathedrals of Science: The development of colonial Natural History museums during the late nineteenth century*, McGill-Queen's University Press, Kingston and Montreal, 1988.

Sherman, Daniel J., 'The Bourgeoisie, Cultural Appropriation and the Art Museum in Nineteenth-Century France', *Radical History Review* 38, 1987.

Sherman, Daniel J., *Worthy Monuments: Art Museums and the Politics of Culture in Nineteenth-Century France*, Harvard University Press, Cambridge, Massachussetts, 1989.

Sherman, Daniel J. & Irit Rogoff (eds), *Museum Culture: Histories, Discourses, Spectacles*, Routledge, London, 1994.

Shinner, Peter J., 'The Exercise of Power in Nineteenth-Century Britain: The Case of Grimsby' (unpublished PhD thesis, University of Lincolnshire and Humberside), 2001.

Smith, Crosbie & Jon Agar (eds), *Making Space for Science: Territorial Themes in the Shaping of Knowledge*, Macmillan, London, 1998.

Smith, Dennis, *Conflict and Compromise: Class Formation in English Society 1830-1914*, Routledge & Kegan Paul, London, 1982.

Smith, Joan, 'Labour Tradition in Glasgow and Liverpool', *History Workshop Journal* 17, 1987.

Spring, David, 'English Landowners and Nineteenth-Century Industrialism' in Ward, J. T. & R. G. Wilson (eds), *Land and Industry*, David & Charles, Newton Abbot, 1971.

Stearn, W. T., *The Natural History Museum at South Kensington*, Heinemann, London, 1981.

Stewart, Susan, *On Longing: Narratives of the Miniature, the Gigantic, the Souvenir, the Collection*, Duke University Press, Durham, 1993.

Stocking, G., *Objects and Others: Essays on Museums and Material Culture*, University of Wisconsin Press, Madison, 1985.

Storch, R. D. (ed), *Popular Culture and Custom in Nineteenth-Century England*, Croom Helm, London, 1982.

Sutcliffe, Anthony, 'The Growth of Public Intervention in the British Urban Environment during the Nineteenth Century: A Structural Approach' in Johnson & Pooley (eds), *The Structure of Nineteenth-Century Cities*, Croom Helm, London, 1982.

Taborsky, E., 'The Sociostructural Role of the Museum' in *International Journal of Museum Management and Curatorship*, 1, 1982.

Taylor, Brendan, 'From Penitentiary to "Temple of Art": Early Metaphors of Improvement at the Millbank Tate' in Pointon (ed) *Art Apart*, Manchester University Press, Manchester, 1984.

Teather, J Lynne, 'Museology and its Traditions: the British Experience 1845-1945', (unpublished DPhil thesis, Leicester University), 1983.

Thackray, A., 'Natural knowledge in cultural context: the Manchester model', *American History Review* 79, 1974.

Thompson, E. P., *The Making of the English Working Class*, Penguin, Harmondsworth, 1991 [1963].

Thompson, E. P., *Customs in Common*, Penguin, Harmondsworth, 1991.

Thompson, F. M. L., *The Rise of Respectable Society*, Fontana, 1988.

Thompson, F. M. L., 'Town and City' in Thompson, F.M.L. (ed), *Cambridge Social History of Britain 1750-1950*, Vol. 1, Cambridge University Press, Cambridge, 1990.

Thompson, F. M. L. (ed), *The Cambridge Social History of Britain 1750-1950*, vol. 3, Cambridge University Press, Cambridge, 1990.

Tooby, Michael, *'In Perpetuity and Without Charge': The Mappin Art Gallery 1887-1987*, Sheffield Arts Department, Sheffield, 1987.

Trainor, R. H., 'Urban elites in Victorian Britain', *Urban History Yearbook*, 1985.

Trainor, R. H., *Black Country Elites:The Exercise of Power in an Industrialised Area 1830-1900*, Clarendon Press, Oxford, 1993.

Trainor, R. H., 'The "decline" of British urban governance since 1850: a reassessment' in Trainor and Morris (eds) *Urban Governance: Britain and Beyond since 1750*, Ashgate, Aldershot, 2000.

Trodd, Colin, 'Culture, Class and City: the National Gallery, London, and the spaces of education 1822-1857' in Pointon (ed) *Art Apart: Art Insitutions and Ideology across England and North America*, Manchester University Press, Manchester, 1994.

Turner, F. M., *The Greek Heritage in Victorian Britain*, Yale University Press, New Haven, 1981.

van Keuren, David K., 'Museums and Ideology: Augustus Pitt-Rivers, anthropological museums and social change in later Victorian Britain', *Victorian Studies* 28, 1984.

Vergo, Peter, 'The Reticent Object', in Vergo (ed), *The New Museology*, Reaktion Books, London, 1989.

Vernon, James, *Politics and the People: A Study in English Political Culture, c. 1815-1867*, Cambridge University Press, Cambridge, 1993.

Vickery, A.J., 'Town Histories and Victorian Plaudits: some examples from Preston', *Urban History Yearbook, 1988.*

Walker, Andrew (ed), *Aspects of Lincoln*, Wharncliffe Books, Barnsley, 2001.

Walkowitz, Judith, *City of Dreadful Delight: Narratives of Sexual Danger in Late Victorian London*, Virago, London, 1992.

Waller, P. J., *Democracy and Sectarianism: A Political And Social History of Liverpool 1868-1939*, Liverpool University Press, Liverpool, 1981.

Waller, P. J., *Town, City and Nation: England 1850-1914*, Oxford University Press, Oxford, 1983.

Walton, John K., *Lancashire: A Social History 1558-1939*, Manchester University Press, Manchester, 1987.

Walton, John K., 'The North West' in F.M.L. Thompson (ed), *Cambridge Social History of Britain 1750-1950*, Vol. 1., Cambridge University Press, Cambridge, 1990.

Walton, J. & A. Wilcox (ed), *Low Life and Moral Improvement in Mid-Victorian England: Liverpool through the Journalism of Hugh Shimmin*, Leicester University Press, Leicester, 1991.

Whittle, M., 'Philanthropy in Preston: The Changing Face of Charity in a Nineteenth-Century Provincial Town', (unpublished PhD thesis, University of Lancaster), 1990.

Williams, Raymond, *Culture and Society 1780-1950*, Chatto and Windus, London, 1958.

Wolfenden, I., 'The Applied Arts in the Museum Context' in Pearce (ed) *Museum Studies in Material Culture*, Leicester University Press, London, 1989.

Wolff, Janet & John Seed, *The Culture of Capital: Art, Power and the Nineteenth-Century Middle Class*, Manchester University Press, Manchester, 1988.

Worboys, Michael, 'The Imperial Insitute: The state and the development of the natural resources of the Colonial Empire, 1887-1923' in MacKenzie (ed) *Imperialism and the Natural World*, Manchester University Press, Manchester, 1990.

Yanni, Carla, *Nature's Museums, Victorian Science and the Architecture of Display*, Athlone Press, London, 1999.

Index